FAMILY LAW
AN
INTERDISCIPLINARY
PERSPECTIVE

HOWARD H. IRVING, D.S.W.

Professor, University of Toronto

Editor

THE CARSWELL COMPANY LIMITED

Toronto, Canada

1981

Canadian Cataloguing in Publication Data

Main entry under title:
Family law, an interdisciplinary perspective
(Carswell's family law series)

ISBN 0-459-33380-1 bd.   ISBN 0-459-33390-9 pa.

1. Divorce — Addresses, essays, lectures. 2. Domestic relations —
Addresses, essays, lectures. 3. Child welfare — Addresses, essays,
lectures. I. Irving, Howard H., 1936-

HQ814.F35   306.8'9   C80-094857-2

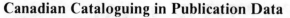

Carswell's Family Law Series

ANDREWS: *Family Law in the Family Courts*

McCAUGHAN: *The Legal Status of Married Women in Canada*

BAXTER & EBERTS: *The Child and the Courts*

IRVING: *Family Law: an Interdisciplinary Perspective*

To the memory of the late
Frederick G. Gans, Q.C., a lawyer
who had a deep appreciation for the art
of negotiation in the resolution of family
law disputes.

FOREWORD

Lawyers and those in the "helping professions" both try to help. The lawyer deals with the problems in terms of rights and obligations, and among the lawyers I know best, these are rights and obligations between spouses dealing mostly with custody of and access to children, division of property, financial provision for the dependant spouse and the children, and, eventually, dissolution of the marriage by divorce. The lawyer spends most of his time in the office advising and taking instructions from his client and negotiating terms of settlement with the lawyer for the other spouse; but always in an atmosphere of intimidation created by the knowledge that the alternative to agreement is a court proceeding. Intimidating, because court proceedings are accusatory tending to exaggerate out of proper balance the negative side of each party's behaviour — the very side each wants to forget — and intimidating also, because of the great expenditures of time and money that are anticipated. Some lawyers, whether by reason of the cases they allow themselves to take, or personal philosophy, or natural aggressiveness, may be more court prone than others; but whoever the lawyer, the client feels the presence of the court because of the constant references made to what a judge would do. This is the traditional context with the lawyer advising, as best he can in a system bound by precedent, as to what the rights and obligations of the parties amount to. However, in as much as no two cases are ever exactly the same and predictions about what a court would do in a particular case based on what has gone before vary greatly, the client is justified in thinking that his or her rights and obligations are far from certain.

The lawyer acts "for" his client to define the client's rights and obligations at law, and to deal with them "on behalf of" the client. This way of proceeding may give the client a feeling of non-involvement on the sidelines almost as a spectator. And in acting "for" and "on behalf of" the client, the lawyer is generally expected to seek maximum rights and minimum obligations. This means that frequently one side argues for a high result, for example, and the other for a low — each seeing in the pattern of past court decisions a "fit" or a justification of his position. Good settlement discussions lead to a compromise arrived at by closing in from the high-low limits of the range which is established, with neither side feeling he or she is giving up more than the other. The potential for misunderstanding and a sense of a lack of justice is, nevertheless, great.

It necessarily follows from the uncertainty in the system that each party should be separately represented by his or her own lawyer. To have only one lawyer acting for both sides introduces a conflict of interest, or what may be just as bad, the appearance of one. A lawyer can not act for two parties unless their interests in the outcome are the same. Where the interests of one party are in obtaining maximum benefits and those of the other in contracting minimum liabilities, there can be no such identity of interests. The settlement agreement or court judgment is a compromise of those interests, but must first proceed from each party knowing his or her best position and having the right to put it forward as persuasively as possible.

Those in the helping professions function in a much different milieu. If a social worker were to think in terms of representation at all, he would more likely see his client as the family rather than the individual spouse, parent or child. He does not act "for" or "on behalf of" any single family member, and certainly not against any other. He works to gain the trust and confidence of everyone in the family and sits down with them to solve a common problem for their common benefit. He sees his function as helping each member within the interaction of the family to make his or her own decision, and provides encouragement and emotional support while they — not him — implement these decisions. His role is to bring understanding to the problem and to promote a healthy change in growth from within. He does not work with coercive elements like the lawyer, and has no rigid body of rules which he seeks to apply.

Rights and obligations are external, while personal decisions to enforce rights and define obligations are internal. On the simplest level the lawyer works in the outside world while the social worker functions on the inside. The difference can be illustrated by the kind of related questions the two professionals are trained to deal with.

The lawyer properly deals with questions of the kind, "Am I, as a matter of law, entitled to a divorce?" and "Am I entitled to custody of the children?"; the behavioural scientist with the questions, "Should I seek a divorce?" and "Should I claim custody of the children?"

It is difficult both for the lawyer and the social worker to avoid dealing with questions more properly falling within the sphere of the other. Sometimes this is done unwittingly, and the only real protection for the family is that both the lawyer and the social worker become well informed of the limits of their fields. This necessitates a familiarity on the part of each professional with the principles and methodology of each discipline while retaining an identity and expertise with one — it is impossible to serve in a professional capacity as both an attorney and social worker.

The need for each to have a better appreciation of the other's role has become a matter of great concern to family law practitioners following the sudden dawning upon the community that children are persons and that issues such as their custody (disputes between parents) and protection (disputes with the state) require a re-examination of what is in the best interests of the child. This leads legal practitioners to consider the right of children to be heard in court proceedings; their right to representation; and, generally, to a re-thinking of the criteria for determining their best interests. No truly satisfactory enforcement of the legal rights of children can be accomplished unless all those involved in the decision-making processes possess a great deal of understanding about their needs. This understanding must be furnished by behavioural scientists in the helping professions. Where children are involved, collaboration between the disciplines becomes less of an option and more of a necessity.

The availability of publications such as this is one of the obvious methods by which a mutual understanding of the relevant issues and collaboration in finding workable solutions can be achieved.

James C. MacDonald, Q.C. of the
Ontario Bar, co-author of
Canadian Divorce Law and Practice
and *Law and Practice under the
Family Law Reform Act of Ontario*

PREFACE

Approximately seven years ago, the University of Toronto embarked on its first interdisciplinary course in the field of family law. The faculties of law and social work combined their efforts in a joint enrolment of students in courses of interest to both professions. These interdisciplinary seminars provided the impetus for this book.

It is increasingly self-evident that legislation and practice in family law must result in a convergence through intense collaboration between law and the behavioural sciences. The human ramifications of family law are too complex to be dealt with by a single profession. It has become a truism that cooperative effort between relevant disciplines results in less fragmentation and a more comprehensive and useful service to families. An analysis of different emphases and viewpoints of family law must lead to experimentation and ultimately, to improved methods of dispute processing. This book is an effort to further develop that objective.

Part One consists of four chapters which examine alternative methods for resolving disputes between and among family members as they experience marital breakdown. The authors approach these topics from various legal and non-legal perspectives within a framework of theory, research and practice.

In chapter one (previously published in the Canadian Journal of Family Law, Vol. 1, 1978, p. 39) Irving and Bohm utilize a systems and role model to underscore the value of interdisciplinary collaboration in family dispute resolution. In chapter two Smith builds upon the previous argument and offers non-judicial alternatives to the adversary system in custody and access situations. An empirical study is drawn upon by Irving *et al.* in chapter three to support and point out the efficacy of mediation and conciliation in settling custody and access disputes out of court. The current alternative of joint custody is critically examined in chapter four by Folberg and Graham as they argue for more empirical studies.

Part Two consists of four papers which are devoted to child welfare and how the legal system and helping professions in this most complex and critical area of family law interact. The matters of control and communication between and among the various subsystems often create destructive conflict rather than helpful, co-operative efforts.

Benjamin, in chapter five, examines the organizational problems and how this impacts on the workings of interdisciplinary teams in cases of child abuse. Cruickshank, in chapter six, discusses the advantages and disadvantages in processing child welfare matters through the family court system. Alternatives to the traditional approach are presented. This material is reprinted from *The Child and the Courts* (Carswell, 1978) and was previously published in (1978) 12 U.B.C. Law Rev. 248. This is followed by Frank's paper in chapter seven, which examines the decision-making process through content analysis of the deliberations at a team meeting where there is suspected child abuse. The central issues concerning children in the court system are presented by Catton in chapter eight. The author reviews empirical research relative to these issues offering an analysis and critique of the present system. This paper was originally published in the Canadian Journal of Family Law, Vol. 1, 1978, p. 329.

Compiling an interdisciplinary work such as this is always a collaborative effort. I am indebted, first, to all those contributors who geographically and professionally are representative of family law throughout North America. I am fortunate in having many colleagues and friends who have shared with me their views in trying to help practitioners understand the value of interdisciplinary family law practice.

To give proper recognition to all who had a hand in developing this effort is extremely difficult, since they include the many faculty, students and practitioners who played a part in the development of my own interest and practice. A special debt of gratitude is owed to Professors Bernard Green, Ian Baxter, Albert Rose and Ralph Garber. I am most grateful to a number of others with whom I have worked: Meyer Elkin, Judges Abraham Lieff, Ted Andrews, Marjorie Bowker and lawyer James Mac-Donald, Q.C. as well as others too numerous to mention. Finally, a special thanks to my editor Bill Rankin.

Howard H. Irving

CONTENTS

Part I: Divorce

An Interdisciplinary Approach to Family Dispute Resolution

Howard H. Irving* and Peter E. Bohm**

Divorce litigation is unique among all legal actions in that it is almost invariably accompanied by the most intense and intimate emotions. It is rarely a clear, cut and dried piece of business with a clear beginning and end which can be handled and filed away. It is a painful process for all concerned — not the least of whom is the lawyer. The legal questions of custody, access and maintenance are often not the real issues but rather the means which divorced couples use to continue their involvement with each other. This paper attempts to identify some of the problems and to offer recommendations for improving the interdisciplinary aspects of dispute resolution.

INTRODUCTION

Conflict in social life is an inevitable, ubiquitous and normal occurrence. Its causes can be traced to various forms of goal obstruction between two or more persons.[1] In the arena of domestic conflict, however, a variety of approaches might be invoked towards resolution.

The conceptual knowledge and analytical approach available in the social sciences can provide the family law practitioner with a framework for understanding the complex interactional phenomena[2] which arise in the course of his practice. "In a period of great change of sex roles, there is necessarily considerable tension in the day-to-day interaction of husbands and wives" (Goode, 1966, p. 310). This tension can extend into the spouses' relations with third parties as well.

*   Howard H. Irving, D.S.W., is a Professor at the Faculty of Social Work, University of Toronto, and the Research Director of the Conciliation Project at the Provincial Court Family Division), Toronto, Ontario.

** Peter E. Bohm, M.S.W., is a Doctoral Candidate at the Faculty of Social Work, University of Toronto, and a Research Assistant for the Conciliation Project at the Provincial Court (Family Division), Toronto, Ontario.

The role behaviour of lawyers, of clients who are seeking a legal remedy for their family problem, and of counsellors who may also be involved is all potentially dysfunctional in achieving a resolution to a dispute. This dysfunction can be attributed, in large measure, to conflicting interests *within* the different roles of these three participants.

A familiar example of what can occur is a situation where a client withholds important information from his own lawyer, who does not understand why or how to deal with this circumstance and where the counsellor neither appreciates nor supports the lawyer's need for the suppressed information. The basis for the resulting conflict can here be traced to some major source of stress experienced by each of these three factors:

1. The client's vulnerability originating in the strain of his family breakdown (Glasser, 1975);
2. The lawyer's lack of knowledge or skill in dealing with emotional problems surrounding interpersonal crisis (Irving and Irving, 1974); and
3. The counsellor's inability to comprehend legal issues as they affect the counselling process (Elkin, 1973).

The purpose of this paper is to describe a practical social science model of this conflict. Such a conceptual model can be helpful in appreciating the genesis and possible solutions to some of these kinds of disputes. By using role theory to guide the clinical and legal expert in analysing the interdisciplinary aspects of family dispute resolution, it is hoped that a better understanding of the dynamics of these conflict situations may be facilitated. Firstly, the causes of interpersonal conflict may be made clearer. Secondly, in family law practice, some plausible solutions to these difficulties will become apparent from analysing the model. And lastly, the model may generate some hypotheses for possible research.

ROLE EXPECTATIONS

A brief review of the lawyer's, counsellor's and client's respective role expectations serves as a useful point of departure. In general, because the courts function upon an adversarial basis, a lawyer who undertakes a case involving a family dispute works to obtain the "best" settlement possible in terms of his client's material and parental wishes. In this sense, the lawyer's role may *appear* to be clear. However, as will be illustrated shortly, this is not always the case, since the adversarial approach, unfortunately, de-emphasises concern for the feelings and social functioning of the children (Schlesinger, 1977), as well as of the spouse on the "other side". The lawyer's expectations and subsequent role behaviour may serve to destroy family relationships through assuming an adversarial rather than a conciliatory stance, and by attempting to prove that fault resides with the "other side".[3]

Meanwhile, the counsellor and the client must attempt to resolve not only the conflicts inherent in this interpersonal crisis but also those conflicts which are created by the adversarial litigation process itself.

(a) Lawyer's role in dispute resolution — the advocate

When a lawyer recognizes that he is dealing with emotional as well as strictly legal issues and where he wishes to assist his client to come to grips with these very real problems, he may nevertheless be stymied in attempts to counsel his client, simply because his traditional role and legal training do not prepare him to function in such a manner. "Legal training is calculated to promote close reasoning and argumentation in favour of a partisan interest; in short, to develop the art of advocacy" (Rosenheim, 1953). Even if the lawyer is open to functioning in a new role, his client tends to see him as an advocate and, indeed, seeks someone to champion his cause in an adversarial manner rather than to serve as an impartial counsellor. These expectations will, of course, vary from client to client and from situation to situation — for which reason it is important to learn ways in which to clarify role expectations, regardless of whether the goal is to "win" or to "conciliate". In either case, it is certainly desirable to minimise the damage done in passing by avoiding excessive role conflict (Coogler, 1977).

The canons of professional ethics effectively prohibit a lawyer from active collaboration with the opposing side[4] against the interests of his own client, thereby making it more difficult to effect a real resolution of the dispute between the parties. Moreover, some lawyers perceive reconciliation as a threat to the partisan advocacy which they offer to their clientele. "Reconciliation can be a costly affair for an attorney" (Conway, 1970). In effect, the lawyer may offer to his client a Hobson's choice between a strict legal battle or nothing at all, simply because he cannot ethically be acting for both parties.[5]

(b) Role of the counsellor — the helper

By contrast, counselling requires a non-partisan approach to the total family situation. While giving advice to *his* client is the lawyer's basic technique, the development of communication and interaction skills[6] between *both* parties is the counsellor's forte. The lawyer acts for *his* client; the counsellor tries to help the entire family to act *for themselves*. The lawyer is visibly on one side; the counsellor is usually on no one's side.

The behaviour of each person in a family dispute obviously does not occur in a vacuum. Contrary to the system long established at law, fault for the breakdown, cannot be allocated exclusively to one party (Wheeler, 1974, p. 12). Part of the counsellor's role is to provide an atmosphere in which each member of the family feels free to bring out and openly to examine his pains and disappointments with respect to his own as well as to other family members' failure to fulfil his expectations.

Ideally, the goals of counselling should be:

1. to help the clients to gain sufficient insight into their marital and family problems to come to a realistic understanding of their present situation[7] and of the possibility for change; and
2. to support *both*[8] clients and to assist in activating whatever emotional resources they have towards making decisions and towards accepting the responsibilities which are inevitably involved, either in trying to make their marriage work or in dissolving it in as constructive a manner as possible.

How a family makes use of counselling depends upon the emotional capacity of the members for change, the point in time at which they involve themselves in the process and their motivation (or potential motivation) to work on their existing problems.

A major, but not always successful, aim of counselling is to induce the couple to become rational and responsible enough to cooperate in making mutually acceptable compromises (*i.e.*, conciliation). Voluntary settlements, which are devised by both parties on an emotional as well as on an intellectual level, are not only more humane than those imposed through litigation but are also more practical and less costly, both to the parties themselves and to society.[9] Mutual agreement insures that neither party feels himself to be the "loser" or someone of whom advantage has been taken — thereby reducing the likelihood of any later eruption of revenge or of new and protracted legal battles.[10]

(c) Role of the client — the "helpee"

In too many instances, the client may have no understanding of what is expected of him or her; or that understanding could be so minimal or distorted that communication and problem solving are seriously impaired. This may be further complicated by a divergence of views between the lawyer and the counsellor regarding each other's role in sharing different parts of the same client system[11] with divergent goals and objectives.

ROLE THEORY

Before any discussion of case situations and of the operational applications of specific procedures of conflict resolution, it may be instructive to present a general theoretical perspective.

(a) Role behaviour and status expectations

Role-set theory was first developed by Merton (1957). It is best suited to the definition and analysis of interaction patterns (behaviour exchanges between two or more persons) which are marked by sharply conflicting perceptions, activities, demands and power arrangements. This approach, therefore, is relevant to an examination of family breakdown, since, even under the best of circumstances, the death of a marriage involves crisis, conflict and dispute within a complex system of role functions.

Role behaviours are important because they relate directly to intervention tasks.

The concept of role here refers to the behavioural performance of status expectations.[12] "The middle-range theory of role-set holds that each status or position [which] a person occupies in a society does not simply involve one role, but an array of associated roles, and the various statuses held by the person constitute a status set" (Munson, 1976). It follows from this that a lawyer, a counsellor and a client, while usually occupying distinctly different statuses, are simultaneously likely to *share* a number of roles in common. For example, all three may very probably engage in behaviour which involves the role sets of helper, "helpee" and advocate. This alone enhances the development of conflict and confusion. Further conflict between the members of this triad may result when members are seen as usurping the domain of the others. Figure 1 illustrates these remarks.

In this type of role-set analysis, the personality of the individual assumes less importance. While this may appear to oversimplify the situation, simplicity is precisely its advantage. Much of the variability of personality dynamics (*e.g.*, attitudes, values, beliefs, *etc.*) can temporarily be "set aside". This allows for a clearer view of selected role-related behaviours, which are somewhat more constant and predictable. Viewing the dominant roles (circles with solid lines in Figure 1) within the total status/role-set configuration, one has a framework within which personal behaviour variables may better be understood. Because role behaviours are directly related to specific tasks; particular role-sets can be linked to specific intervention practices. The whole process of negotiation in family dispute resolution is made lucid when each participant knows the circumstances when it is appropriate to enact various role behaviours. Conflict may well result in the absence of this knowledge.

For example, the counsellor may unintentionally set up a conflict condition by assuming an advocate role at an inappropriate point in the negotiations; the lawyer may unwittingly precipitate difficulty by engaging in a helping role at a time or in a manner which contravenes the counsellor's efforts; and the client may not know what anyone expects of him and may, therefore, behave in any number of self-defeating ways.

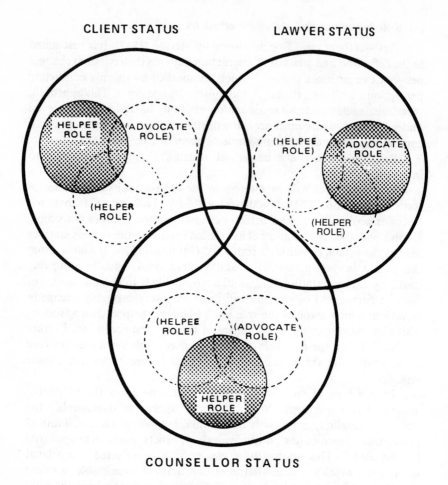

Figure 1: Status/Role-set Configuration

Solid lines around shaded roles indicate the *dominant* role behaviour in a role-set interaction.

Broken lines around roles indicate *potential* roles in an interaction.

A concrete example of this sort of difficulty would be an instance in which a client, say, a married woman, refuses to allow her lawyer to obtain financial information from her husband's employer; her counsellor steps in to point out the husband's right to privacy; and the lawyer advises the wife not to discuss delicate emotional and financial matters with her husband and counsellor if she finds it painful. While these behaviours, *by themselves*, may present little difficulty, yet in combination they could produce a socio-legal nightmare.

For another specific example, take the case of a woman contemplating separation from her alcoholic husband. She consults a lawyer who advises her on aspects of the law pertaining to maintenance and property rights which lead her to believe she would jeopardize her position if she left the home. Following a severe drinking episode, her husband is admitted to hospital and the doctor suggests treatment, giving her hope that the situation will improve. It doesn't. She then seeks help from a counsellor. The counsellor focusses on her tension and the effects on the children of the chaotic home atmosphere, which leads her to believe [that] she should leave her husband. (The lawyer, of course, has advised her that she cannot force her husband out of their jointly-owned home.) To complicate matters further, the husband physically abuses one of the children and the counsellor suggests that the Children's Aid Society should be involved around protection for the children; so our client is now pressured into feeling [that] she had better leave her husband, lest she be considered a neglectful parent. At this point, how on earth can she decide which expert to follow? She would have to know more than any one of the experts to sift out the relative importance of the help [which] she had been given. Where does she go now — back to the lawyer, to the family counsellor, to the doctor, or to the Children's Aid Society? (Knoll, 1969).

(b) Role allocation

In recent literature on conciliation,[13] there appear a few models which attempt to make explicit the role allocation of both the legal and social experts. Henschel and Erickson (1977, p. 4) have developed a model in which dispute mediation is viewed as a "systematic, guided, eclectic and rational process of family decision-making". According to their model, "Any rational decision-making process may be conceptualised as occurring in six fundamental, sequential phases". These phases are:

1. Identification of the problem or problems;
2. Eliciting sufficient factual information essential to the problem's solution;
2. Development and identification of all possible alternative solutions;
4. Evaluation of the probable outcome of each alternative solution;
5. Mutual selection of one of the alternative solutions;
6. Developing an agreement as to the steps which must be taken for complete performance of the selected alternative (Brim, *et al.,* 1962, p. 9).

The Family Mediation Center (1977) of Atlanta, Georgia, has developed quite specific rules for their mediation service based upon this sort of model. The role expectations of the lawyer, the counsellor and the clients are distinctly itemised in clear, understandable language. The role conduct to which all parties in the mediation must adhere is submitted in writing to all parties and mutual agreement thereto is reached before mediation proceedings commence. In a sense, this is similar to arbitration in labour relations disputes; before any arbitrator begins, the opposing parties define and then agree upon his role and his duties.[14]

> The attractions of arbitration as an alternative to the courts should be considered; most fundamentally, the goal of arbitration is not the determination of guilt or innocence, as results from the adversary processes used in the courts. Arbitration may be considered a form of social investigation similar in orientation to adoption proceedings, pre-sentence hearings, or delinquency cases. In none of these contexts — including that of the present model — is Truth being sought; in every case, the object is to find the best possible remedy to a social problem.

> To bring about this result, recourse can be had to all relevant information without adherence to rigorous courtroom standards and formalities. For example, the arbitrator can essentially set his own rules concerning the admissibility of evidence. If he authorizes reports (e.g., from the social worker) and if these are used, the author would presumably be available to the hearing, but the confidentially of sources will be respected. Cross-examination and rebuttal are permitted, the lawyers will probably be present, but the total atmosphere will be less formal and more flexible than in the courtroom.

> ... the flexibility of procedure which is possible [in arbitration] is bound to result in imaginative treatment of the human problems that make up a custody dispute.

> The use of arbitration in this context is also in line with a current tendency of the courts to support the use of arbitration for the resolution of private disputes, as a supplement to traditional court procedures. Among the other advantages of arbitration are its greater speed in resolving disputes (as opposed to the substantial time lags involved in getting a case to court), the probable lesser cost and the reduced likelihood of engendering an atmosphere of conflict, anger and tension. (Irving and Lightman, 1977, p. 17-18).

How this has been applied to resolution of custody disputes is illustrated in the following lawyer's letter of referral, setting out the terms of mediation (MacDonald, 1977).

(c) Case example[15]

May 27th, 197

Mr. Gordon Mead,
Marital and Family Mediator,
102 St. James Avenue South,
TORONTO, Ontario

Dear Mr. Mead:

Re: Ronald G. and Cynthia J. Jackson

Mr. and Mrs. Jackson, by their Counsel, hereby refer to you for mediation questions relating to the custody of their children.

It is understood that you consent to act as mediator and this letter will set out the terms upon which the mediation is to proceed. They are:

1. As mediator, you will attempt to bring about an agreement between the father and the mother as to the determination of the following questions:
    (a) How much time should each child spend with each parent during the forthcoming school summer vacation; and
    (b) Should custody of the children, or any of them, be changed from the mother to the father?

2. In considering these questions, the parents and the mediator shall give primary importance to the needs of the children and how these needs, in the circumstances, can best be met.

3. In working out the custody and access arrangement which best meets the needs of the children, the parent may agree that:
    (a) One or the other of them shall have temporary custody of the children or one or two of them for a trial period; or
    (b) Both of them shall have custody of the children as joint custodians and the children or one or two of them shall live with one or the other parent, or first one parent then the other, during periods that are specified and set out in the agreement; or
    (c) neither of the parents shall have custody of the children, but the periods of time [which] each child is to be with each parent [are] to be specified and set out in the agreement.

    These alternatives are mentioned for the purpose of emphasising that the parties are to make whatever arrangement is in the best interests of the children. Their choice may be one of these alternatives, or any better alternative that might emerge from the mediation meetings.

4. The separation agreement entered into under date of the 23rd day of September, 197 , shall not be binding on the parties in so far as the questions of custody and access are concerned.

5.   The question of the children's maintenance or financial support is excluded from mediation and, if it arises, shall be referred back to Counsel for determination.

6.   In attempting to bring about an agreement, the mediator may meet with and speak to the father, the mother and the child separately or jointly, and may consult such other persons and inspect such reports, records or documents as he deems necessary.

7.   Any agreement reached shall constitute a settlement of the subject matter of the agreement and be produced for the information of the court in the legal proceedings pending between the father and the mother in the Supreme Court of Ontario or in any other relevant proceedings.

8.   In the event that no agreement is reached within the period established for mediation, both parties shall have the right to pursue their legal remedies in the action pending between them in the Supreme Court of Ontario or in such other action or proceeding as they or either of them may be advised to take.

9.   The period of time allowed for the mediation shall be established by the mediator in consultation with both Counsel after the mediator has interviewed both parents, but in no event shall be for more than six weeks from the date of this letter.

10.   Evidence of anything said or of any admission or communication made in the course of the mediation is not admissible in the pending or any other legal proceeding.

11.   The mediator will not be called as a witness by or on behalf of either parent in the pending or any other legal proceeding and the mediator shall not be required or permitted in the pending or any other legal proceeding to give any opinion or to disclose any admission or communication made to him in the course of the mediation.

12.   Except to inform Counsel that:
    (a)   No agreement has been reached; or
    (b)   What the terms of the agreement are,
    there shall be no report made by the mediator of the mediation.

13.   Your fee for the mediation shall be borne by the parents in equal shares and payable on such terms as are determined by you.

The mediation is agreed to by both parents in the confident expectation that, with your assistance, they can determine the questions above in a way that will be more satisfactory than any settlement imposed by a court or other process.

Please feel free to telephone either Counsel at any time for whatever information or assistance [which] they might be in a position to give. Counsel will refrain from initiating any contact with you in order to give you full freedom to act without interference.

We thank you for consenting to this referral and for acting as the mediator.

Yours very truly,

"L.M. Kelly"

....
Solicitor for Ronald G. Jackson

"Mary Rankin"

....
Solicitor for Cynthia J. Jackson

The following annotations elaborate further upon some of the points in the above referral.

Paragraph 1: "... the following questions ...": The first question relates to access as it has come to be considered by lawyers (as opposed to custody). Access, as defined by present-day practice, can be exercised outside the custodial home and is often spelled out in separation agreements and in court orders to include holiday periods of a specific duration (*e.g.*, "the month of July or August each summer"). The second question is directed to a consideration of a possible change in permanent custody from the mother to the father.

Paragraph 2: "... primary importance to the needs of the children": This provision is intended to emphasise to the parties and the mediator that, in settling questions of custody and access, they are governed by the best interests or welfare of the children. In applying this principle, the guidelines discussed by Goldstein, Freud and Solnit in *Beyond the Best Interests of the Child* (1973) would hopefully be accepted. These authors argue that it is misleading to speak of what is "best" for the child, because of the tendency to address the problem in terms of an ideal home and not in terms of what is available. One should not search for the "best" arrangement, but for the one which is, for the child, the least detrimental alternative to safeguarding the child's growth and development. In its report, the Justice Society of England (1975, p. 28) adopted this principle in formulating the general rule that:

> The welfare of any child, [who is] the subject of a custody suit, ... is best served by whatever decision will minimise the risk of his suffering (or suffering further) injury, whether emotional, psychological or physical.

Paragraph 3: "... the parents may agree ... [to] temporary custody, ... [or to] custody ... as joint custodians ... [or to a timetable for the children with custody to neither parent]": This provision is intended to guard against the possibility that the discussion might be trapped into irrelevancies of who should have custody of the children rather than in concentrating on how the parents, in their homes and lives, can best co-operate to contribute to the successful growth and development of their children. A better elaboration of this provision might be something like the following:

> Both parents acknowledge that they require the assistance of an objective third party professional to help them to assess the impact of the separation upon the children, to identify problems raised by the separation, and to attempt to resolve these problems through discussion. They also acknowledge that, in developing solutions to child-parent problems, their own roles as parents must be explored. The parental role, of course, must be seen, not only in terms of the relationship between parent and child, but also in terms of the relationship of the parents to each other. It is expected that, in particular instances, the parents may disagree how to handle a problem centering on the child; accordingly, in the discussion with the mediator, the parents should devise a procedure of consultation with each other or some other means of resolving these conflicts.

> It is also acknowledged that preconceived notions of "custody" and "access" can impede the search for a plan which will enable the parents to provide for the best interests of the children. What is important is the recognition that both parents must be involved in their lives. In attempts to work out a process of collaboration which this entails, the legal labels of "custody" and "access" might be ignored, at least until the conclusion of this referral. In the meantime, consideration might be given to the concept of joint parenting with the children living in the home of one parent as their primary residence, and having frequent contact in the home of their other parent which would be known as their secondary residence.

Paragraph 5: "... the question of ... financial support ... is excluded": This exclusion from the mediation was inserted because it involves legal opinions beyond the training of the mediator. Similar questions relating to entitlement to property (both ownership and possessory rights), to interspousal maintenance and to the grounds for divorce are outside the scope of the referral. These questions should be sent back to the lawyers. It is important that the mediator and the lawyers work within their own limits and avoid overlapping and acting at cross-purposes. Frequent communication between mediator and lawyers is necessary with respect to role definition and to respective responsibilities.

Paragraph 6: "... may consult ... other persons": Under this term, the mediator has the right to interview other persons who have assumed a parenting role or who have had contact with the children, such as grandparents, housekeepers, teachers, and doctors.

Paragraph 6: "... reports, records or documents ...": These references would allow the mediator to examine material such as medical and school reports and other assessments of the family.

Paragraph 10: "communication ... not admissible in ... legal proceedings": This prohibition insures a closed mediation. Communications are to kept confidential and protected from disclosure in any legal proceedings.

Paragraph 9: "The period of time allowed for the mediation ...": The Custody Project of the Clark Institute of Psychiatry in Toronto, which provides mediation as part of its assessment process, advises that it is unusual for the total duration of mediation and assessment to exceed 10 to 15 hours (Form letter, June, 1976). The mediation rules of the Family Mediation Center in Atlanta (1977) require a deposit to cover 10 hours of the mediator's time.

Paragraph 13: "... fee for the mediation ...": This stipulation requires the mediator to be involved to some extent in the arrangement of his fee. Some mediators prefer not to accept this responsibility and instead require payment from the lawyers who, of course, look to their clients. Regardless of how this is done, there should be a definite understanding from the outset about the clients' obligation and an express understanding about who has the responsibility for collection of the fee.

CONCLUSION

The understandings outlined and annotated above, along with procedures adapted from mediation/arbitration experience, serve as tools and methods for reducing role strain, which is inherent in the advisory and counselling processes of dispute resolution. They do this by clearly spelling out the roles and responsibilities of each party.

When confronted with role conflict, the incumbent of a particular status position (lawyer, counsellor or client) may adopt any of a variety of methods of role conflict resolution.[16] For example, the lawyer may lean toward the expectations of his law firm, say, "to win at any cost" (institutional sanctions). This may conflict with his own internal needs. The counsellor may experience a similar role conflict if he works within the court system where participants may have equally divergent expectations of the role which he is to fulfil.

Counselling practices are increasingly recognising the need to clarify roles, as suggested by the adoption of labour dispute techniques above. Generically, these are similar to the clincial concept known as "role induction".[17] This practice is becoming more widely accepted and developed as an aid to initiating a counselling process more efficiently and clearly.

Suffice it to say that role conflict resolution is a topic for study in itself and, while it is of great interest, it is beyond the scope of this paper. The major issue here is how to *prevent* or to *reduce* role conflict before it occurs, through interdisciplinary knowledge and cooperation.

> It is important to open up and expand communication between law and the social sciences, so that each has the knowledge it needs to work productively with the other and [that] neither usurps the other's role. The human ramifications of divorce are too complex to be dealt with by a single profession. Cooperative effort between law and the social sciences would result in less fragmentation and a more comprehensive and meaningful service to the client (Irving and Irving, 1974, p. 265).

REFERENCES

Brim, Orville G. *et al.*: *Personality and Decision Processes — Studies in the Social Psychology of Thinking* (Stanford, Calif.: Stanford University Press, 1962), cited in Bruce W. Callner: "Boundaries of the Divorce Lawyer's Role", Family Law Quarterly, Vol. 10 (1977), p. 389-298 at 390.

Canadian Bar Association Special Committee on Legal Ethics: Code of Professional Conduct — Preliminary Report (Ottawa: Canadian Bar Ass'n, 1973).

Conway, Paul McLane: "To Insure Domestic Tranquilty — Reconciliation Services as an Alternative to the Divorce Attorney", Journal of Family Law, Vol. 9 (1970), p. 408.

Coogler, O.J.: "Changing the Lawyer's Role in Matrimonial Practice", Conciliation Courts Review, Vol. 15(1) (1977), p. 1-8.

Elkin, Meyer: "Conciliation Courts — The Reintegration of Disintegrating Families", Family Coordinator, Vol. 22 (1973), p. 63-72.

Family Mediation Association Inc: *Marital Mediation Rules* (Atlanta, Georga: Family Mediation Ass'n Inc., 3d ed. rev., 1977).

Glasser, Claire L.: "A Case for Counseling in Child Custody Cases", Conciliation Courts Review, Vol. 13(1) (1975), p. 12-13.

Goldstein, Howard: *Social Work Practice — A Unitary Approach* (Columbia, South Carolina: University of South Carolina Press, 1973).

Goldstein, Joseph *et al.*: *Beyond the Best Interests of the Child* (New York: Free Press, 1973).

Goode, William J.: "A Sociological Perspective on Marital Dissolution", in *Sociology of the Family*, Michael Anderson (3d.), (Harmondsworth, England: Penguin Books Ltd., 1971), p. 301-320.

Gross, Neal C. *et al.*: *Explorations in Role Analysis — Studies of the School Superintendency Role* (New York: John Wiley and Sons, 1958).

Haley, Jay: *Problem-Solving Therapy* (San Francisco: Jossey-Bass Publishers, 1976).

Henschel, W.B. and Erickson, S.K.: *Mediation of Family Disputes — A Proposed Model* (Minneapolis, Minnesota: unpublished manuscript, 1977), (personal correspondence).

Irving, Howard H.: "A Social Science Approach to a Problem in Field Instruction — The Analysis of a Three-Part Role-Set", Journal of Education for Social Work, Vol. 5(2) (1969), p. 49-56.

Irving, Howard H. and Gandy, John: "Family Court Conciliation Project — An Experiment in Support Services", Reports of Family Law, Vol. 25 (1977), p. 47-53.

Irving, Howard H. and Irving, Barbara G.: "Conciliation Counselling in Divorce Litigation", Reports of Family Law, Vol. 16 (1974), p. 257-266.

Irving, Howard H. and Lightman, Ernie S.: "Conciliation and Arbitration in Family Disputes", Conciliation Courts Review, Vol. 14(2) (1976), p. 12-21.

Justice (British Section of the International Commission of Jurists): A Report by JUSTICE — Parental Rights & Duties and Custody Suits, Gerald Godfrey, Chairman (London: Stevens & Sons, 1975).

Knoll, Francis A.: What a Lawyer Must Know About A Social Worker (Ottawa: unpublished paper delivered before the Canadian Bar Association, 5 September 1969).

Kressel, Kenneth K. et al: "Mediated Negotiation in Divorce and Labour Disputes — A Comparison", Conciliation Courts Review, Vol. 15(1) (1977), p. 9-12.

Law Society of Upper Canada: Professional Conduct Handbook — Canons of Legal Ethics (Toronto, 1975 rev.).

MacDonald, James C.: "Custody Mediation" (Toronto: unpublished paper presented before the Continuing Education Programme of the Law Society of Upper Canada, 19 November 1977), p. 3-5.

MacDonald, James C.: "Referral Letter Setting out Terms of Custody Mediation", in Custody Mediation — November 19th 1977 (Toronto: Department of Continuing Education, Law Society of Upper Canada, 1977), (limited distribution), p. F-1 and F-2.

Merton, Robert K.: "The Role-Set — Problems in Sociology Theory", British Journal of Sociology, Vol. 8 (1957), p. 106.

Mund, Geraldine: "The Need for Community Arbitration", Arbitration Journal, Vol. 31 (1976), p. 109-115.

Munson, Carlton E.: "Professional Autonomy and Social Work Supervision", Journal of Education for Social Work, Vol. 12(3) (1976), p. 95-102.

Rosenheim, Margaret Keeney: "The Lawyer as a Family Counselor — As the Social Worker Sees Him", University of Kansas City Law Review, Vol. 22 (1953), p. 28.

Rubin, Jeffrey Z. and Brown, Bert R.: The Social Psychology of Bargaining and Negotiation (New York: Academic Press, 1975).

Sarat, Austin: "Alternatives in Dispute Processing — Litigation in Small Claims Court", Law and Society Review, Vol. 10 (1976), p. 339-375.

Schlesinger, Benjamin: "Children and Divorce — A Selected Review", Conciliation Courts Review, Vol. 15(1) (1977), p. 36-40.

Stagner, Ross and Rosen, Hjalmar: *Psychology of Union-Management Relations* (Belmont, Calif.: Wadsworth Pub., 1965).

Watzlawick, Paul *et al.*: *Pragmatics of Human Communication — A Study of Interactional Patterns* (New York: W.W. Norton & Co., 1967).

Wheeler, Michael: *No-Fault Divorce* (Boston: Beacon Press, 1974).

---

1 See Stagner and Rosen, 1965, p. 106. "Conflict occurs as individuals with different interests, goals, problems and perspectives seek to achieve a maximum share of the values which any society provides."
It is "normal" in the sense that it is an expected part of any significant interpersonal relationship. Even though it is normal, however, it is not generally welcomed and resolution is elusive as well as difficult (Sarat, 1976, p. 339).

2 Human behaviour is viewed here as communication which always has an interactional aspect (direct or indirect) for all members of a social group or collectivity (Watzlawick, 1967, p. 62).

3 Wheeler (1974, p. 12) suggests that "the fault system is inconsistent, expensive and hypocritical". As serious as these shortcomings are, the system might be tolerable if it somehow contributed to family stability in our society. But it does no such thing. If anything, it obscures the real issues in marital breakdown and thus makes their solution the more difficult. The fundamental weakness of fault-oriented divorce is that it is predicated upon a false assumption — namely, that marriage breakdown can be attributed solely to the marital misconduct of one spouse.
The premise is in error on two counts: first, a fight ". . . is seldom the fault of one person . . . Second, wrong-doing is not the only thing that can kill marriages. Time changes people . . ."

4 Rule Number 2 (Acting for Both Sides) of the Law Society of Upper Canada (1975, p. 11) provides: "A solicitor must not act for two or more clients where their interests are in conflict."
The Canadian Bar Association (1973, p. 36) proposed the following rule for confidentiality of information: "The lawyer has a duty to hold in strict confidence all information acquired in the course of the professional relationship concerning the business and affairs of his client, and he should not divulge any such information unless he is expressly or impliedly authorized by his client or required by law to do so."
And in respect of impartiality and conflict of interest, the Association (p. 41) proposed: "The lawyer must not advise or represent both sides of a dispute and, save after adequate disclosure to and with the consent of the client or prospective client concened, he should not act or continue to act in a matter when there is or is likely to be a conflicting interest."

5 Conway (1970, p. 416-417) put it this way: ". . . he has a Hobson's choice between trying to save the marriage and losing the legal fees if he is successful, or unsuccessfully attempting to save the marriage and again losing legal fees, because he cannot ethically represent either of the parties.

6 In essence, a primary strategy of counselling is teaching to clients improvements in the accuracy with which they transmit and receive information (verbally and non-verbally) with their spouses (Haley, 1976).
For a more detailed explanation of the counselllor's role, see Irving and Irving (1974).

7 "Situation" refers here to the stability of their relationships, finances, emotional state and personal identity, as these factors interrelate.

8 Unlike the expert witness (*e.g.*, psychiatric expert), a counsellor in his role is hired to negotiate in the best interests of all concerned (*i.e.*, towards an equitable compromise), rather than strictly giving evidence for one side.

9 Systematic research has yet to prove this assertion on a cost-benefit outcome, but court-settled disputes are clearly more expensive (ostensibly) than many cases which are successfully resolved out of court, in whole or in part (Wheeler, 1974). Social psychological research on negotation also supports this proposition. Rubin (1975, p. 263) stated (emphasis added): "The general conclusion of this research is that the *early initiation of cooperative behaviour tends to promote the development of trust and a mutually beneficial, cooperative relationship: early competitive behaviour, on the other hand, tends to induce mutual suspicion and competition.*"
Some of these issues are being researched at the Provincial Court (Family Division) in Toronto (Irving and Gandy, 1977).

10 Research is also being undertaken in the Provincial Court (Family Division) at Toronto by the authors to determine what sorts of case situations are most amenable to agreement through conciliation (Irving and Gandy, 1977).

11 "Client system" here refers to a conceptual view of an individual as being intrinsically and continuously influenced by (and influencing) important persons who are part of his or her past or present environment. Therefore, interaction can never be completely unilateral or cleanly limited to those who are physically present in the immediate situation. Within this perspective, even deceased persons' influences (*e.g.*, expectations, promises, values, habits) continue as part of the client's interaction, attitudes and behaviour.

12 Simply put, certain statuses, such as "parent", carry specific social expectations for enacting particular role behaviours, such as "protector" or "provider". While a given status, such as "counsellor", may involve many role expectations (including ones which are appropriate only under *certain* circumstances), there is often a dominant set of role expectations (*e.g.*, "helper").

13 "Conciliation" counselling encompasses both marriage counselling, with the goal of reconciliation and divorce counselling, with the goal of terminating a marriage in a response manner (Irving and Irving, 1974, p. 257).

14 The application of these principles to private disputes has been spurred by the delays, expenses and impersonal aspects of civil litigation (Mund, 1976, p. 109-115).
Kressel *et al.* (1977, p. 10) reports that: "... in the labour mediator's study, four major factors were identified as inhibiting the parties' ability to negotiate constructively: high levels of internal conflict in one or both parties; scarcity of divisible resources; inexperience of the parties with negotiations and with mediated negotiations in particular; and a wide discrepancy in the parties' relative power. Our analysis indicates that these same parameters complicate the task of the divorce mediator ..."
This supports the need for careful role structuring.

15 The authors wish to acknowledge their gratitude to James C. MacDonald, Q.C., of Toronto for allowing them to reproduce this case example.

16 Gross *et al.* (1958) discuss two aspects of "role" which give rise to conflict and which must be considered in its resolution. These involve:
1. the individual's internal needs, which depend upon the importance which he places on the "legitimacy" dimension of the role expectations; and
2. institutional "sanctions", which dictate what is expected in a legalistic or bureaucratic sense.

17 Basically, "role induction" involves the structuring of first interviews in a manner which manifestly articulates to clients exactly what their part in procedures, experiences and results will be (H. Goldstein, 1973, p. 191-230).

Non-Judicial Resolution of Custody and Visitation Disputes*

Elizabeth J. Smith

This article examines the problems created by adversary judicial resolution of child custody and visitation disputes between parents arising during and after dissolution of their marriage. It reviews current responses to these problems and suggests arbitration and mediation as non-judicial alternatives to the adversary system. It concludes that mediation is the method most appropriate for family dispute resolution and that family law practitioners can play a key role in reducing harm to families by counseling their clients toward such non-adversary resolution of child custody and visitation disputes.

Bob and Helen[1] married when Helen graduated from college and Bob was beginning graduate study in history. Helen worked to support the couple until Bob completed his doctoral dissertation and got a university teaching job. Helen then turned her energy toward maintaining their home and became involved in community activities. The couple had three children, ages 15, 13, and 10, when, after 18 years together, Bob and Helen consulted attorney Marsha about a dissolution[2] of their marriage. During Marsha's first interview with the couple it became clear that property and support matters could be worked out by the couple with general planning and tax advice from Marsha. Marsha's question about custody and visitation plans for the couple's children, however, triggered an emotional discussion between Bob and Helen which threatened to escalate and destroy an otherwise amicable separation.

Randy and Barbara were divorced after a stormy marriage. They had married when Barbara was 19 and Randy was 21. A child, Tony, had been born soon thereafter. Barbara received custody of Tony with reasonable visitation to Randy after an emotional court battle. Two years after the

---

* Initially published in Vol. 12, No. 2, University of California Davis Law Review and included in this publication with the permission of The Regents of the University of California which owns the copyright in this article and to whom any request for the use of this material must be directed.

dissolution, when Tony was five, Randy called attorney Alan, complaining that Barbara was accusing Randy of mistreating Tony during weekly visitation. Angrily telling Alan about Barbara's immoral lifestyle, Randy explained the upsetting effects on Tony of living with his mother. Randy told Alan he wanted to take custody of Tony away from Barbara and asked if Alan would take the case.

These scenerios illustrate two ways in which clients frequently present the highly emotionally-charged issue of child custody to a practicing family lawyer. This article will explore how an attorney facing such situations can play a crucial role in minimizing significant harm to the families involved and reduce the burden of custody and visitation litigation on the courts by promoting non-judicial resolution of such disputes.[3] In Part I this article will examine the problems created by the adversary nature of judicial resolution of custody and visitation disputes and some current responses to those problems. Part II will suggest non-judicial dispute resolution as an alternative to the adversary system, and consider arbitration and mediation as possible methods of non-judicial resolution appropriate to custody and visitation disputes. Part III will discuss the attorney's key role in implementing such non-judicial dispute resolution and will recommend supporting legislative and judicial changes.

I. THE PROBLEM

Adversary courtroom proceedings are generally ineffective for the resolution of family disputes. Judicial decisions focus on legal issues, frequently disregarding families' emotional issues, and thus lead to repeated future litigation. Current responses to this problem emphasize reform within the adversary model and so are similiarly inadequate. Non-adversary approaches, however, offer a more constructive method of family dispute resolution.

(a) Adversary judicial resolution

Judicial resolution of custody and visitation disputes places a costly burden on the courts and leads to serious emotional and financial problems for the families involved. Attorneys' adversary approach and ambiguous legal standards aggravate the harm to families and encourage repeated lengthy litigation of custody and visitation matters.

The burden of contested custody cases on the courts increases as the dissolution rate rises[4] and as more fathers, granted an equal right to custody of their children under current law,[5] request custody at dissolution. Initial custody hearings are often lengthy and significant additional court time is expended by post-dissolution litigation over custody and visitation modification,[6] often motivated by unresolved anger and desire for revenge.[7]

No-fault divorce laws designed to minimize emotional conflicts in the courtroom have limited such manipulation of the legal system by angry spouses in the dissolution context. Evidence of misconduct is inadmissable in a dissolution proceeding unless relevant to the issue of child custody.[8] Thus, couples precluded from airing their grievances in the dissolution hearing often use a custody contest to express their anger and frustration.[9]

The emotional strain of these adversary proceedings has a significant effect on the parents and children involved. The adults are often consumed with anger at each other, fear for themselves, and guilt about their children.[10] These emotional conflicts inhibit them from building a new life for themselves and make it difficult for them to respond to their children's emotional needs during the dissolution process.[11]

The children's trauma in a custody proceeding is perhaps more serious, as it results from a situation over which they have little or no control or understanding. They often feel the brunt of their parents' anger and bitterness as parents consciously or unconsciously use their children as weapons against each other.[12] The children's emotional trauma is intensified by the uncertainty of lengthy legal proceedings which too often result in a custody or visitation plan tailored to the wishes of their competing parents rather than their own needs and desires.[13] A child's fear of separation and need for continuity in relationships is frequently disregarded.[14] Studies of children during the post-divorce period, most notably by Judith S. Wallerstein and Joan B. Kelly of the Children of Divorce Project in Marin County, California, provide indications of the severe emotional cost suffered by many children of divorce. Wallerstein and Kelly report developmental regression, feelings of rejection, helplessness, and anger, during the post-divorce period, as characteristic of the various age groups studied.[15] Other researchers have reported trends toward delinquency among children of divorce.[16]

In addition to these serious emotional effects on family members, the financial burden of a contested custody case is significant for the family often already over-burdened by supporting two households on income previously supporting only one. Expert witness fees for psychiatric examination of family members and court testimony, lengthy depositions, and substantial legal fees due in part to the parties' frequent contact with the attorney for emotional support, make a custody case an expensive proposition.

Attorneys' adversary approach to custody cases intensifies these emotional and financial effects on families and encourages repeated and lengthy litigation. Legal education emphasizes a rational, logical approach to dispute resolution within an adversary context. Such training leads attorneys to adopt the adversary stance in family conflicts and leaves them unprepared for the resulting highly emotional response from their clients.[17]

Their attorneys' adversary approach reinforces the clients' desires to publicly humiliate and punish their spouses and the conflict escalates to the detriment of both the family and the legal system.[18]

Ambiguous legal standards further aggravate the strain on families and the courts. For example, the "best interests of the child"[19] standard on which the courts ostensibly base custody determinations is subject to a multitude of interpretations and is highly vulnerable to judicial bias.[20] Likewise, "reasonable visitation" granted to noncustodial parents presents similar implementation problems and creates significant potential for future dispute.[21] Judicial application of these legislative standards in custody determinations leads to the imposition of cultural norms and values on parenting and lifestyles.[22] Judicial decision-making is necessarily influenced by individual judges' backgrounds, personalities, and prejudices.[23] The burden of these custody and visitation problems on families and the courts has led the legislature and the practicing bar to institute various reforms.

(b) Current responses

Legal representation for the child, court-ordered social investigations, and the use of mental health professionals as experts are among the reforms adopted in many states in respect to problems created by judicial resolution of custody and visitations disputes. As noted above, these provisions involve reform within the adversary system and therefore do not effectively deal with the inherent shortcomings of judicial resolution. In contrast, the establishment of Conciliation Courts in a number of jurisdictions, another recent reform, offers a more constructive non-adversary alternative for the resolution of these family conflicts.

Provisions for appointment of counsel for the child are a result of concern for the child's rights in custody and visitation litigation. When the court finds it in the child's best interest, independent counsel is provided for the child and compensation ordered paid by the parents as the court deems just.[24] Some commentators criticize this procedure for increasing the adversary nature of the proceedings and for emphasizing division between parents and children.[25] Other writers and practitioners, however, feel that the child's attorney can act as a mediator between the parents and thus effectively represent the child's best interests.[26]

Over-burdened courts and judges' limited behavioral science training have led to provisions for court-ordered social investigations in contested custody cases.[27] Carried out by probation officers or domestic relations case investigators, these reports condense accusations made by parties, reports of friends and neighbors, and the investigator's own evaluation of the situation for the judge's consideration. This practice recognizes the importance of a behavioral science perspective to custody determinations and enables the judge to utilize the trained observations of the investigator in awarding custody. The preparation of these reports, however, has a detrimental effect on relations between the parents, their children, relatives, and friends. During the investigation, the parties attempt to bring the investigator to their side by presenting themselves in the best light, and their "opponent" parent in the worst possible light. Friends and relatives are often forced to take sides when interviewed as a reference for one side or the other. This process thus tends to emphasize family weaknesses and exacerbates already serious conflict within the family.[28]

Recognition of the value of a behavioral science perspective in custody and visitation determinations has also led attorneys and judges to make use of mental health professionals as expert witnesses in such cases. Mental health professionals however, are often reluctant to become involved in legal proceedings. When they do become involved, they are often left feeling frustrated with the legal system's insensitivity to the psychological and emotional needs of the child.[29]

The reluctance of mental health professionals to become involved in a custody dispute as a witness for one side against the other stems from a number of factors. These professionals' private practices are disrupted by the uncertainty of trial calendars and frequent continuances.[30] They are frustrated by attorneys and judges who ask for specific answers and predictions about human behavior inappropriate to the imprecision of the sciences of psychology or psychiatry.[31] Finally, mental health professionals are reluctant to participate in court proceedings which frequently result in custody or visitation plans which the professional feels are detrimental to the child or family.[32] Experts who familiarize themselves with the legal process and who are prepared by the attorney calling them to testify, however, more often feel they are able to contribute significantly to the court's decision.[33]

Most mental health professionals involved in custody or visitation disputes would rather play a neutral role than represent one side of the dispute against the other.[34] In 1968, the Los Angeles Superior Court established a panel of psychiatric consultants hired by the Family Law Department to fulfill such a neutral role.[35] These psychiatrists interview all significant family members in a contested custody case, prepare a recommended disposition for the court, and are available for cross-examination by both sides at trial.[36] As experts for the court, mental health professionals are better able to sensitize judges to the psychological context of custody disputes. Moreover, they can help to insure decisions tailored to the psychological and emotional needs of the child.[37]

The most innovative and effective response to the problems of adversary resolution of custody and visitation disputes has been the establishment of Conciliation Courts. The California legislature enacted the first Conciliation Court Law in 1939 providing counseling for families in order to encourage reconciliation and avoid divorce.[38] Los Angeles County was the first to establish a Conciliation Court and thus became a model for the state and nation. By the early 1960's Conciliation Courts had been established in a number of other California counties and other states.[39]

The current California Conciliation Court Law allows considerable flexibility of services directed both toward avoiding dissolution and settling disputes between parents during the dissolution process.[40] Conciliation Court counselors, appointed by the county Superior Court, counsel parties involved in proceedings under the Family Law Act and make recommendations for disposition of those proceedings to the judge.[41] Conciliation Court counselors may invoke the aid of outside mental health professionals[42] and any agreement reached during counseling may be reduced to writing and given the force of court order.[43]

County Conciliation Courts in California and in other states have developed a variety of models from this basic structure. Shasta County, in rural northern California, has two part-time Conciliation Court counselors who interview parents involved in custody and visitation disputes at the courthouse immediately after referral from the court. Although counselors usually recommend a disposition to the judge after that initial interview, they sometimes conduct additional investigation before filing the report.[44] In Sacramento County, which serves a diverse urban population, custody and visitation matters are routinely referred to Family Court Services by domestic relations judges. The family meets with a Court counselor for a single three to four hour session within two weeks of court referral. If the parties fail to come to an agreement within that period, the counselor makes a full custody investigation and subsequent recommendation to the court.[45] In Ann Arbor, Michigan, the Washtenaw County Friend of the Court Program uses family law attorneys as referees in informal custody hearings after which a recommendation is made to the court for final determination.[46] The Milwaukee County Family Court Department of Family Conciliation provides social workers to help families evaluate alternatives and develop a custody plan without going to court.[47]

The Conciliation Court's emphasis on non-adversary resolution of custody and visitation disputes makes it the most positive current response to the problems of adversary judicial resolution. Individual county Superior Court judges, however, control the creation and policies of local Conciliation Courts.[48] This results in considerable variation in procedure and program emphasis among counties depending on the philosophy of the current domestic relations judges. It also creates instability as judges change from year to year.[49] Furthermore, Conciliation Courts depend on county funding. As a result, local political and economic conservatism has limited the establishment of Conciliation Courts in many rural areas, with the majority of such services being developed in urban centers.[50] In short, these problems significantly limit Conciliation Courts' effectiveness in the resolution of family conflicts.

II.   MECHANISMS OF NON-JUDICIAL RESOLUTION

Although the Conciliation Court model provides a constructive alternative to traditional proceedings, its limitations require development of an additional non-adversary approach in order to reduce the burden of custody and visitation litigation on the courts and families.[51] This section considers arbitration and mediation as possible non-judicial approaches appropriate to custody and visitation disputes, with mediation being the most useful of the two proposed methods of dispute resolution.

(a) Arbitration

Courts increasingly use arbitration as an alternative to judicial dispute resolution in order to alleviate over-crowding the court's calendar and the expense of courtroom litigation.[52] Its informality, speed of resolution, and reduced cost make arbitration an attractive alternative for many types of conflicts.[53] The conceptual goal of arbitration, to find the best possible remedy to a problem rather than determine guilt or innocence, makes it especially appropriate for resolving family disputes.[54]

Recognizing the growing importance of non-judicial dispute resolution and the need for such services in family law matters, the American Arbitration Association has established its Family Dispute Services.[55] The Association trains family lawyers, the clergy, social workers and other helping professionals to serve as conciliators, mediators, referees, and arbitrators of family disputes. Arbitration rules include provisions for the arbitrator to obtain interviews with the child, professional opinions relevant to the best interests of the child, and the parties' agreement not to include the arbitrator as a witness in any subsequent related court hearings.[56]

Arbitration clauses in marital property settlement agreements have received a mixed reaction from courts. Arbitration of spousal and child support disputes are generally upheld.[57] Courts, however, have recently overturned earlier decisions enforcing arbitration of custody and visitation issues and have found such agreements between parents impermissable.[58] A New Jersey court explained the general judicial objection to enforcement of these arbitrated agreements as follows:

> Since the State is *parens patriae* to children, and since the support, education and welfare of children is the exclusive concern of the courts so that parties can make no permanent binding contract with respect to those matters, child

custody is not arbitrable ... The conscience of equity will not permit the present needs of children to be limited by the agreement of the parties (footnotes omitted.).[59]

In basing their decisions on this premise, however, the courts fail to recognize parents' basic right to raise their children as they choose, a right freely exercised by intact families, subject only to basic health, safety and educational requirements.[60]

Arbitration is a less expensive, faster, and less conflict-producing method of dispute settlement than courtroom adjudication. Like judicial resolution, however, arbitration imposes on a family an outside decision-maker's notion of their "best interests." This imposition conflicts with some commentators' emphasis on family privacy[61] and self-determination[62] as essential for stable, healthy parent-child relationships.

(b) Mediation

Mediation has the advantages of arbitration and also fosters these values of privacy and self-determination in the resolution of family disputes. Mediation counseling provides a non-adversary setting in which families are encouraged to take responsibility for custody and visitation decisions and for the effective implementation of those decisions. Mediation thus makes resort to future litigation less likely.[63] An experienced mediator, whether attorney or mental health professional, can help the parties to realistically assess the financial and emotional costs of a custody trial. The mediator can also share basic principles of child psychology and family dynamics to aid the parents in understanding their children's and their own reactions to the stress of the dissolution process.[64]

A mediator trained in the behavioral sciences can provide psychological counseling to the parties as well as mediating a resolution of their custody or visitation dispute. During the post-divorce period parents have been found to be relatively open to change in their behavior toward their children and each other as co-parents.[65] Parents' guilt about perceived harm inflicted on the children during the divorce process, and their feeling that the divorce presents an opportunity for building a new life, create this openness. The mediator can use this willingness to change to help parents defuse their anger and resolve underlying emotional issues.[66] Finally, a skilled mediator can guide parents in establishing new patterns of relating to each other which are appropriate for their continuing roles as co-parents.[67]

Mediated custody and visitation agreements are more stable and result in a significant reduction in the burden of costly litigation on families and the courts.[68] Mediation limits future litigation by giving the parties a feeling of cooperative give-and-take,[69] as opposed to judicial decisionmaking which tends to polarize parties, increasing animosity between them and making future disputes likely.[70] Agreements drafted using specific language understood by the parties, rather than ambiguous legal terms such as "reasonable visitation" and "best interests of the child" also serve to reduce later litigation.[71] Finally, parents who develop their own custody and visitation plans apply values appropriate to their family, rather than having a particular judge's biases imposed on them.[72] This involvement and self-determination makes parents feel more responsible for the success of their custody and visitation plans, further limiting resort to the courts if problems arise.[73]

Public agencies and private organizations provide a variety of mediation models appropriate to family disputes. California's broad Conciliation Court Law[74] has allowed a number of California counties to focus on mediation of family disputes in an attempt to reduce the burden of litigation on the courts. The Alameda County Conciliation Court, for example, accepts referrals from attorneys and the court on stipulation by the parties that the mediator may testify in court if requested. The Conciliation Court refers families to mediators from a panel of psychologists, psychiatrists, and social workers who serve the Court on a part-time basis. These mediators work with the parents to resolve underlying emotional conflicts, as well as to develop a workable custody or visitation plan.[75]

The Marin County Conciliation Court counselor requires a stipulation by the parties that the counselor will not be called to testify if the case goes to trial, before beginning intensive mediation counseling in which family members are seen every other day for a two week period. In addition to attorney and court referrals, parents may contact the counselor directly for initial mediation or later modification of custody or visitation arrangements. The counselor encourages parents to take responsibility for decisions affecting themselves and their children in drafting custody and visitation agreements which are then given the force of court order.[76]

In Los Angeles County, domestic relations judges refer all custody and visitation cases to the Conciliation Court for mediation. Families go directly from the domestic relations courtroom to the Conciliation Court where counselors are available to mediate their dispute after receiving a stipulation of confidentiality from the parties and their attorneys. The counselor is available for sessions with parents and children, alone and together, to resolve emotional conflicts and draft an agreement which the parties feel is appropriate for their family situation. The parties give the agreement a six-week trial period after which additional sessions can be held to make needed modifications before the agreement becomes a court order. The counselor encourages families to contact the Court for mediation if future problems arise.[77]

Private organizations also have developed alternative methods of family dispute resolution,[78] as have mental health professionals in public and private agencies.[79] Individual helping professionals in the community can also act as mediators for families either on self-referral by parents seeking counseling, or on referral by attorneys.[80] Psychiatrists, psychologists, and licensed marriage and family counselors in private practice bring valuable therapeutic skills to a mediation situation. Ministers, priests, and rabbis with family counseling training are also potential mediators, particularly if they have an established relationship with the family involved.

The success of many of the mediation programs discussed above suggests that the non-judicial model of custody and visitation dispute resolution has strong potential for reducing the burden of these cases on families and the courts.[81] Arbitration and mediation models are less expensive, faster, and less conflict-producing than adversary judicial resolution. Arbitration, however, does not as effectively eliminate the problems of judicial resolution as does mediation. Though less formal than court hearings, arbitration proceedings still promote a somewhat adversary atmosphere by imposing an outside decision-maker on the family. Mediation, on the other hand, emphasizes parental responsibility for custody decisions, thereby more effectively limiting future litigation.

III. IMPLEMENTATION OF NON-JUDICIAL RESOLUTION

As discussed above, mediation of family disputes provides a constructive alternative to adversary judicial resolution. Implementation of this alternative model however, requires recognition by attorneys and judges of the value of the non-adversary approach and the need for skillful and sensitive counseling in family law settings. Moreover, legislative changes are needed to facilitate this change toward non-judicial resolution of family conflicts.

(a) The attorney's role

As the helping professionals[82] to whom families often first turn for counsel, attorneys are in a key position to facilitate or impede change toward non-adversary family dispute resolution. For many attoneys, however, successful implementation of this alternative method of dispute resolution would involve a shift in role from advocate to counselor.[83] Attorneys are generally most comfortable applying a rational, logical approach to dispute resolution as advocates within an adversary context.[84] This detached professionalism, however, does not work well in the frequently emotion-laden context of family law cases.[85] In these emotional situations attorneys must consider the human problem in order to best resolve the legal problem.[86]

Attorneys practicing family law need to develop the skills and understanding of interpersonal and family dynamics necessary for successful resolution of legal problems within an emotional context.[87] Law school and continuing education courses in counseling, psychology, and human development would all be appropriate.[88] The question of whether untrained attorneys should attempt the counseling role is a purely academic one.[89] The very nature of lawyering requires the role of counselor, must as much as the role of advocate. It is essential that all attorneys, and particularly family practitioners, be prepared to skillfully and sensitively fulfill the counseling role.

The attorney's role as counselor is becoming increasingly important in states with "no-fault" divorce laws. In these states, clients frequently feel that paying two attorneys is unnecessary and would rather make their own decisions about property division, support, and child custody.[90] Attorneys can support these clients' wishes for self-determination and a minimum of animosity by providing tax and drafting advice and serving as neutral mediators between the parties.[91] Such dual representation is permissable where the attorney advises both parties of the potential conflicts between them and obtains their informed consent to the arrangement in writing.[92] If, however, an actual conflict does arise between the parties, the attorney must withdraw and both parties should hire new attorneys.[93]

An attorney in this mediator role can help prevent escalation of potential conflicts between the parties by focusing their attention on drafting an agreement which is tailored to their family's needs and which will minimize potential for future disagreement.[94] The attorney can sensitize the parties to the common emotional and psychological effects of dissolution on parents and children and guide them in beginning to form new roles which will allow them to function as co-parents in relation to their children and each other. If there is a potential custody conflict, the attorney can help the parties to realistically assess the financial and emotional costs of a court contest and hopefully help them to evaluate the best interests of their children to reach an agreement. The attorney might also refer the couple to a psychiatrist or marriage and family counselor if the parties feel that more in-depth counseling would help them resolve their differences.[95]

If an actual custody conflict already exists when clients come to the attorney, dual representation is not possible. Attorneys in this situation should explain the financial and emotional costs of contested custody cases to their clients. They should also help the clients to evaluate the strength of their case, as well as their motives for requesting custody. The attorney might suggest that the client and spouse see a third party mediator in an attempt to resolve their differences without an adversary proceeding. If the spouse is represented, cooperation between the attorneys is necessary to facilitate the parties' acceptance of the value of mediation. If the parties agree to mediation, the attorneys should stipulate to exclude the mediator as a witness if the case goes to trial, and provide for payment of the mediator's fee, if any.

The variety of mediation resources discussed above may or may not be available depending on the size of the city and financial status of the clients. Fortunately, mental health professionals in private practice will generally be available for such referrals even in smaller communities. Their fee may seem high to the client, but the attorney should emphasize the even greater cost of taking the case to trial if mediation fails.[96] In larger cities, public agencies and perhaps even Conciliation Court services may be available as sources of referral for mediation.

In order to make effective referrals, family law attorneys should acquaint themselves thoroughly with the counseling resources available in their community. Mental health professionals' training, methods, fees, and willingness to work with attorneys on such problems are important considerations.[97] Attorneys should familiarize themselves with the basic principles of various counseling theories and approaches in order to establish productive working relationships with these professionals.[98]

If mediation is unsuccessful, the attorneys can recommend arbitration of the custody dispute. An arbitrated settlement would, however, probably be subject to judicial review.[99] If the parties nevertheless agree to arbitration, each party could choose one member of the panel with those two selecting a third.[100] The parties could select arbitrators who they felt shared their values and perspective on parenting and the needs of their children.[101] Alternatively, they could use the American Arbitration Association Family Dispute Services mechanism for selecting arbitrators.[102]

If the parties are unable to agree on a mediated or arbitrated settlement, the case will probably go to trial. The attorneys can attempt to minimize the escalation of hostility between the parties, but the adversary nature of the trial process will make this a difficult task. Some cases will require judicial decision and the attorney's role at this point becomes the more traditional one of advocate for the client.

An attorney's emphasis on non-judicial resolution of custody and visitation disputes as described in this section may not conform with the client's concept of the attorney as a weapon against a former spouse. Attorneys who resist this role may occasionally find the client hiring another attorney who better symbolizes their aggression.[103] The benefits of non-judicial resolution of family disputes, however, will far outweigh this burden on the attorney. In addition to reducing the burden of litigation on the courts, and the financial and emotional costs to families, non-judicial resolution of family disputes is also less stressful and more satisfying for attorneys.[104] Moreover, custody determinations made in nonadversary settings result in more stable family relationships and ultimately in healthier, happier living environments for the parents and children involved.

(b) Recommended legislative and judicial changes

State legislatures and local Superior Court judges can also play significant roles in implementing non-judicial resolution of family disputes. A legislative preference for non-adversary alternatives and family self-determination in custody and visitation matters could be reflected in a number of areas.

The legislature should allocate increased funds for community mental health services to allow more extensive divorce and marriage counseling to be provided.[105] Such counseling would not only help couples decide whether dissolution is really the best alternative for them, but also provide support for their adjustment during and after the dissolution process. Such services would also provide attorneys with sources for referrals in cases where reconciliation between the parties is possible, or where in-depth counseling is needed to help the client build a new life following separation.

The legislature should amend the state rules of professional conduct to specifically provide for attorneys' dual representation of parties in a dissolution action when appropriate, and should develop guidelines for attorneys to protect the interests of both parties in such a dual representation situation.[106]

Legislative amendments should also be made to mandate the Conciliation Court counselors' mediator role and set standards of training and supervision for Court counselors.[107] This legislation should insure access to such services in rural as well as urban areas, to families both during and after the dissolution.[108] Such counseling should be provided to parents on a self-referral basis, as well as court and attorney referral bases.[109]

Finally, the legislature should make arbitration of family disputes an option for families who agree to be bound by the arbitrator's finding.[110] Parents should be able to choose arbitrators by a mutually agreeable method and provide in marital settlement agreements for the arbitration of future disputes.[111]

Superior Court judges should support non-adversary resolution of family disputes by backing the establishment of Conciliation Court mediation services in their county.[112] Judges should routinely refer to mediation cases that come to their courts. Moreover, they should encourage attorneys' efforts toward settlement. At trial, judges need to obtain unbiased evaluations of the family involved from mental health professionals who serve as experts for the court.[113] Finally, domestic relations courts need judges trained in the behavioral sciences who will rise to the challenge of family law cases, rather than view them as an undesirable assignment to be endured.[114]

CONCLUSION

Families who become involved in the adversary process too often emerge fragmented and permanently scarred. Family law practitioners can play a key role in reducing such harm and in promoting family stability by counseling their clients toward non-judicial resolution of family disputes. This article has examined several such non-judicial alternatives and has identified mediation as the one most appropriate to family conflicts. Mediation provides rapid, inexpensive resolution of family disputes, and limits future litigation by emphasizing family autonomy in the decision-making process. As new methods of family dispute resolution are developed, however, it is essential that the individual rights of parents and children, as well as the family's rights of privacy and self-determination, be protected. Only then will the best interests of the family truly be served.

---

1 The names and facts in this scenario as well as those in the one that follow are fictitious, but will no doubt be familiar to anyone who works with families in a helping role.

2 The terminology of California no-fault divorce law will be used throughout this article. The trend toward no-fault divorce has resulted in only three American jurisdictions retaining strict fault requirements. Freed & Foster, "Divorce in the Fifty States: An Outline," 11 Fam. L.Q. 297, 300 (1977).

3 The term "custody dispute" will be used in this article to refer to disagreement between the natural parents as to which will have legal custody of the couple's children following dissolution of the parents' marriage. "Visitation dispute" will be used to refer to a controversy between the parents following dissolution, concerning the non-custodial parent's right to visitation of the children. Either of these disputes may occur at the time of dissolution or some months or years later.

4 Nearly one out of every two marriages in the United States end in divorce, involving one million children each year. Bureau of the Census, Dep't of Commerce, Current Population Report Series P-20 No. 287, Marital Status and Living Arrangements: March 1975, at 2-5 (1975).

5 Cal. Civ. Code § 4509 (West Cum. Supp. 1979). But see, Weitzman & Dixon, Child Custody Awards: Legal Standards and Empirical Patterns, this issue.

6 When children are involved court contests continue for about two years in 52% of the cases. Sugar, "Children of Divorce", 46 Pediatrics 588, 590 (1970).

7 Elkin, "Premarital Counseling for Minors: The Los Angeles Experience", 26 Fam. Coordinator 429, 433 (1977).

8 Cal. Civ. Code § 4509 (West Cum. Supp. 1979).

9 Bodenheimer, "The Rights of Children and the Crisis in Custody Litigation: Modification of Custody In and Out of State", 46 U. Colo. L. Rev. 495, 496 (1975).

10   J. Despert, *Children of Divorce*, 195 (1962).
11   Elkin, Post-Divorce Counseling in a Conciliation Court 10 (unpublished manuscript, portions of which were prepared for presentation by the author at the Third Invitational Conference on Marriage Counselors' Education on Oct. 9, 1976, in San Francisco, California, available from the Conciliation Court of the Superior Court, Los Angeles County, California, 90012).
12   Kelly & Wallerstein, "The Effects of Parental Divorce: Experiences of the Child in Early Latency", 46 Am. J. Orthopsych. 20, 27 (1976).
13   J. Goldstein, A. Freud & A. Solnit, *Beyond the Best Interests of the Child* 54 (1973) [hereinafter cited as Goldstein, Freud, & Solnit].
14   *Id.* at 11.
15   Wallerstein & Kelly, "The Effects of Parental Divorce: Experiences of the Preschool Child," 14 J. Am. Acad. Child Psych. 600 (1975); "The Effects of Parental Divorce: Experiences of the Child in Early Latency," *supra* note 12; "The Effects of Parental Divorce: Experiences of the Child in Later Latency," 46 Am. J. Orthopsych. 256 (1976); "The Effects of Parental Divorce: The Adolescent Experience", in 3 *The Child in His Family: Children at Psychiatric Risk* 479 (E. Anthony & C. Koupernick eds. 1974).
16   *E.g.,* McDermott, "Divorce and Its Psychiatric Sequelae in Children," 23 Archives Gen. Psych. 421, 423 (1970). But *cf.* S. Gettleman & J. Markowitz, *The Courage to Divorce* 79-114 (1974) (discussing the potential for positive healthful changes in parent-child relationships following divorce).
17   Elkins, "A Counseling Model for Lawyering in Divorce Cases," 53 Notre Dame Law. 229, 232 (1977).
18   [L]egal education tends to blunt native ability so far as psychological sensitivity is concerned. Together with this functional "blindness," there is a strong inclination for lawyers to be oblivious to the emotional results of their procedures. They appear to believe that they can conduct a vigorous adversary contest and then have the contestants return to some kind of working rapport. Such contests in child custody cases will most surely produce wounds which do not heal adequately to assure a good subsequent working relationship between the parents.
       Watson, "The Children of Armageddon: Problems of Custody Following Divorce," 21 Syracuse L. Rev. 55, 65 (1969) (footnote omitted).
19   Cal. Civ. Code § 4600(a) (West Cum. Supp. 1979).
20   See *e.g., Painter v. Bannister,* 258 Iowa 1390, 140 N.W. 2d 152, *cert. denied,* 385 U.S. 949 (1966), In *Painter,* a five year old boy lived with his grandparents for a year following his mother's death. Able to make a home for him at the end of that year, the father requested custody. The court compared the grandparent's "stable dependable, conventional, middleclass, middlewest background," 140 N.W. 2d at 154, with the father's "Bohemian approach to finances and life in general," *id.* at 154, including his membership in the A.C.L.U., and granted the grandparents custody. The court commented. "In the Painter (father's) home, Mark would have more freedom of conduct and thought with an opportunity to develop his individual talents. It would be more exciting and challenging in many respects, but romantic, impractical and unstable." *Id.* See also Moskowitz, "Divorce-Custody Dispositions: The Child's Wishes in Perspective, 18 Santa Clara L. Rev. 427, 442-43 (1978).
21   Elkin, *supra* note 11, at 6-7; Johnson, "Visitation: When Access Becomes Excess," Fam. Advocate, Summer 1978, at 14; Savage, "The Impact of Changes on Service," Conciliation Cts. Rev., Dec. 1977, at 12, 14.
22   See Batt, "Child Custody Disputes: A Developmental-Psychological Approach to Proof and Decisionmaking," 12 Willamette L.J. 491 (1976).
23   J. Despert, *supra* note 10, at 195.
24   Cal. Civ. Code § 4604 (West Cum. Supp. 1979).

25   *E.g.,* Sheffner & Suarez, "The Postdivorce Clinic," 132 Am. J. Psych. 442, 443 (1975).

26   See *e.g.,* Note, "Lawyering for the Child: Principles of Representation in Custody and Visitation Disputes Arising from Divorce," 87 Yale L.J. 1126, 1172-77 (1978); Interview with Brinkley A. Long, Director Family Court Services, Superior Court of Sacramento County, California, in Sacramento (Sept. 21, 1978).

27   Cal. Code Civ. Proc. § 263 (West 1954).

28   Gozansky, "Court-Ordered Investigations in Child Custody Cases," 12 Willamette L.J. 511, 523 (1976); Savage, *supra* note 21, at 13.

29   See Littner, "The Doctor's Role in Contested Custody Matters," Conciliation Cts. Rev., Dec. 1971, at 34.

30   *Id.,* at 35-36.

31   *Id.* at 34.

32   *Id.* at 36.

33   R. Sadoff, *Forensic Psychiatry: A Practical Guide for Lawyers and Psychiatrists* 47-58 (1975).

34   J. Despert, *supra* note 10, at 191-92.

35   Chase, "Criteria for Psychiatric Evaluations in Child Custody Contests," Conciliation Cts. Rev., Sept. 1977, at 19.

36   Interview with Gary A. Chase, M.D., Senior Psychiatric Consultant, Los Angeles Superior Court Family Law Department, in Los Angeles (Aug. 23, 1978).

37   *Id.*

38   Blum, "Conciliation Courts: Instruments of Peace," 41 J. St. B. Cal. 33, 33-34 (1966).

39   *Id.* at 35.

40   Cal. Code Civ. Proc. §§ 1730-1772 (West 1972).

41   Cal. Code Civ. Proc. § 1744 (West 1972).

42   Cal. Code Civ. Proc. § 1768 (West 1972).

43   Cal. Code Civ. Proc. § 1769(b) (West Cum. Supp. 1979).

44   Interview with Joan Lewis and Paul A. Burdett, Conciliation Court Counselors, Shasta County Superior Court, at Redding, California (Aug. 14, 1978).

45   Interview with Brinkley A. Long, *supra* note 26.

46   Benedek, Del Campo & Bendek, "Michigan's Friends of the Court: Creative Programs for Children of Divorce," 26 Fam. Coordinator 447 (1977).

47   Hansen & Goldberg, "Casework in a Family Court," 48 Soc. Casework 416 (1967).

48   Cal. Code Civ. Proc. § 1733 (West 1972).

49   Interview with Brinkley A. Long, *supra* note 26.

50   Shipman, "In My Opinion: The Role of Counseling in the Reform of Marriage and Divorce Procedures," 26 Fam. Coordinator 395, 404 (1977).

51   See Ginsburg, "American Bar Association Delegation Visits the People's Republic of China," 64 A.B.A.J. 1516, 1520-23 (1978), for a description of the heavy emphasis on conciliation and mediation of matrimonial disputes, rather than adjudication, in the Chinese legal system.

52   Note, "Compulsory Judicial Arbitration in California: Reducing the Delay and Expense of Resolving Uncomplicated Civil Disputes," 29 Hastings L.J. 475, 483-96 (1978).

53   Lightman & Irving, "Conciliation and Arbitration in Family Disputes," Conciliation Cts. Rev., Dec. 1976, at 12, 17.

54   *Id.*

55   American Arbitration Association, Family Dispute Services (available at American Arbitration Association, 140 W. 51st St., New York, N.Y. 10020); Spencer & Zammit, "Reflections on Arbitration Under the Family Dispute Services," 32 Arb. J. 111 (1977); Spencer & Zammit, "Mediation-Arbitration: A Proposal For Private Resolution of Disputes Between Divorced or Separated Parents," 1976 Duke L. J. 911, 921-24.

56   American Arbitration Association, *supra* note 55, at 14, 16.

57 Annot., 18 A.L.R. 3d 1264, 1266 (1968).

58 Annot., 18 A.L.R. 3d 1272, 5(b) (Supp. Aug. 1978).

59 *Westlake v. Westlake,* 127 N.J. Super. 595, 559, 318 A. 2d 446, 448 (1974) (marital settlement agreement providing for arbitration of any financial claim or dispute held invalid).

60 *Wisconsin v. Yoder,* 406 U.S. 205 (1972) (Amish parents not required to send children to school when in conflict with religious beliefs); *Pierce v. Society of Sisters,* 268 U.S. 510 (1925) (state responsibility to educate citizens yielded to parents' right to provide equivalent private school education for their children); *Meyer v. Nebraska,* 262 U.S. 390 (1923) (upheld parents' right to have children taught German in private school).

61 *E.g.,* Goldstein, Freud & Solnit, *supra* note 13, at 7-8.

62 Elkin, "Editorial: Self-Determination and Family Law," Conciliation Cts. Rev., Sept., 1977, at iii; Wald, "State Intervention on Behalf of Neglected Children: Standards for Removal of Children from their Homes, Monitoring the Status of Children in Foster Care, and Termination of Parental Rights," 28 Stan. L. Rev. 623, 638-39 (1976).

63 Druckman & Rhodes, "Family Impact Analysis: Application to Child Custody Determination," 26 Fam. Coordinator 451, 456-57 (1977); Elkin, *supra* note 62; Spencer & Zammit, "Reflections on Arbitration Under the Family Dispute Services," *supra* note 55, at 121. Concern for families involved in the dissolution process has led Professor Brigitte Bodenheimer to comment,

> The only way I can see to give the child full protection in such situations is to assist the parties to come to grips with their feelings and with the realities of divorce insofar as the children are concerned. This must be done in a different setting, in a non-adversary atmosphere.

See note 9 *supra,* at 506-507.

64 See generally J. Despert, *supra* note 10, at 91-115; Goldstein, Freud & Solnit, *supra* note 13, at 38; Sugar, *supra* note 6.

65 Wallerstein & Kelly, "Divorce Counseling: A Community Service for Families in the Midst of Divorce," 47 Am. J. Orthopsych. 4, 6 (1977).

66 Bienenfeld, "Pay-Offs in Post-Dissolution Visitation Counseling," Conciliation Cts. Rev., Dec. 1974, at 27, 28; E. Fisher, *Divorce: The New Freedom* 72 (1974); Marschall & Gatz, "The Custody Decision Process: Toward New Roles for Parents and the State," 7 N.C. Cent. L. Rev. 50, 63 (1975).

67 Bodenheimer, *supra* note 9, at 507; Marschall & Galt, *supra* note 66; Spencer & Zammit, "Mediation-Arbitration: A Proposal For Private Resolution of Disputes Between Divorced or Separated Parents," 1976 Duke L.J. 911, 930-31.

68 Bodenheimer, *supra* note 9, at 507; Conciliation Courts: Hearings Before California Legislature Senate Committee on Judiciary, 1977-78 Reg. Sess. 7 (1978) (statement of Judge Donald B. King, San Francisco Superior Court reporting that out of approximately 1,300 custody and visitation disputes referred to mediation, fewer than 12 resulted in a request for court hearing.)

69 Bodenheimer, *supra* note 9, at 508; Lightman & Irving, *supra* note 53, at 14.

70 Marschall & Gatz, *supra* note 66, at 64.

71 See text accompanying notes 19-21 *supra;* Bienenfeld, *supra* note 66, at 28; Fuller, "Mediation — Its Forms and Functions," 44 So. Cal. L. Rev. 305, 326 (1971).

72 See text accompanying notes 22-23 *supra;* Savage, *supra* note 21; Spencer & Zammit, *supra* note 67, at 932.

73 Druckman and Rhodes, *supra* note 63, at 456-57.

74 See text accompanying notes 40-43 *supra.*

75 Interview with Elizabeth M. O'Neill, Director, Alameda County Conciliation Court, at Oakland, California (Oct. 16, 1978).

76 Interview with Ann Roth, Counselor, Marin County Conciliation Court, at San Rafael, California (Oct. 16, 1978).

77 Interview with Hugh McIsaac, Director, Family Conciliation Service, Los Angeles Conciliation Court, at Los Angeles (Aug. 23, 1978).

78 For example, the Family Mediation Association based in Winston-Salem, North Carolina, serves couples who want to mediate a marital settlement agreement to be incorporated in a proper uncontested dissolution. A mediator meets with the couple to help them develop a realistic and acceptable agreement covering property, support, and child custody matters. An Advisory Attorney provides legal and tax advice and drafts the final agreement. The Association is a non-profit organization to which participating couples pay a membership donation as well as hourly fees for the mediator and Advisory Attorney. Letter from O.J. Coogler, President, Family Mediation Association, 1725D Franciscan Terrace, Winston-Salem, North Carolina, 27107 (Sept. 15, 1978).

The San Fernando Valley Bar Association (Los Angeles County) has established a Family Law Mediator Program. Volunteer family law attorneys are available at the courthouse during the morning short cause calendar and are on call for afternoon long cause hearings to act as mediators in family law matters. Attorneys obtain mediation on referral from the court clerk and by self-referral to resolve some or all issues without going to trial. Stipulations reached in mediation are referred back to the court where the calendar is interrupted to record the stipulation and conclude the matter. This speed of resolution has brought significant support for the program from the Bench, Bar, and public. Letter from Herman J. Isman, Chairman, Family Law Section, San Fernando Valley Bar Association, Suite 203, Encino Law Center, 15915 Ventura Boulevard, Encino, California, 91436 (Sept. 7, 1978).

See also American Arbitration Association Family Dispute Service discussed in text accompanying notes 55-56 *supra.*

79 For example, the center for Legal Psychiatry (formerly U.C.L.A. Section on Legal Psychiatry) acts as a consultant to the Domestic Relations Department of the Los Angeles Superior Court to provide in-depth post-divorce counseling. An inter-disciplinary staff of psychiatrists, psychologists, and social workers applies a therapeutic model to the resolution of family disputes. The counselors require that the parties and their attorneys stipulate that the counselors will not be called to testify at trial, but are willing to consult with attorneys about cases referred to the Center. Interview with Nancy Weston, U.C.L.A. Section on Legal Psychiatry, in Los Angeles (Aug. 23, 1978); Sheffner & Suarez, *supra* note 25, at 442; Suarez, Weston & Hartstein, "Mental Health Interventions in Divorce Proceedings," 48 Am. J. Orthopsych. 273, 273-74 (1978).

80 Armstrong, "Community Resources in Family Counselling," 19 Juv. Ct. Judges J. 16 (1968).

81 All interviewees cited in notes 26, 75, 76, and 77 *supra,* described significant reduction in repeated custody and visitation litigation from families who had reached a mediated settlement through the interviewees' programs.

82 The term "helping pofessional" is used here to refer to mental health professionals such as psychiatrists, psychologists, marriage and family counselors and social workers, as well as physicians, the clergy, and attorneys. In short, any professional who works with families or individuals in a helping role is included.

83 Mussehl, "From Advocate to Counselor: The Emerging Role of the Family Law Practitioner," 12 Gonz. L. Rev. 443, 445-46 (1977).

84 See text accompanying notes 17-18 *supra.*

85 Elkins, *supra* note 17, at 232.

86 Goodpaster, "The Human Arts of Lawyering: Interviewing and Counseling," 27 J. Legal Educ. 5, 9 (1975).

87   Baernstein, "Functional Relations Between Law and Psychiatry — A Study of Characteristics Inherent in Professional Interaction," 23 J. Legal Educ. 399, 418-19 (1971).

88   Buxton & Dubin, "Teaching Psychiatry to Law Students: Toward a Replicable Model," 13 New Eng. L. Rev. 233 (1977); Steinberg, "The Therapeutic Potential of the Divorce Process," 62 A.B.A.J. 617, 618 (1976).

89   Elkins, *supra* note 17, at 232.

90   Note, "Simultaneous Representation: Transaction Resolution in the Adversary System," 28 Case W. Res. L. Rev. 86, 100-101 (1977). The "do-it-yourself" divorce business, as well as divorce services which fill out and file forms are additional manifestations of this growing trend under no-fault divorce laws. San Francisco Chronicle, Oct. 21, 1978, at 2, col. 1. See also, California Summary Dissolution, Cal. Civ. Code §§ 4550-4556 (West Cum. Supp. 1979).

91   Coogler, "Changing the Lawyer's Role in Matrimonial Practice," Conciliation Cts. Rev., Sept. 1977, at 1; Note, *supra*, note 90, at 105.

92   *Klemm v. Superior Court*, 75 Cal. App. 3d 893, 142 Cal. Rptr. 509 (5th Dist. 1977). The court in *Klemm* upheld a marital settlement agreement. One attorney had represented both husband and wife in an uncontested dissolution with the parties' informed written consent. The court commented, "The conclusion we arrive at is particularly congruent with dissolution proceedings under the Family Law Act of 1970, the purpose of which was to discard the concept of fault in dissolution of marriage actions . . . , to minimize the adversary nature of such proceedings and to eliminate conflicts created only to secure a divorce." (*Id.* at 900, 142 Cal. Rptr. at 513). See California Family Law Act of 1970, Cal. Civ. Code §§ 4000-5138 (West Cum. Supp. 1979); Rules of Professional Conduct of the State Bar of California 5-102(B) (1975); American Bar Association Code of Professional Responsibility EC 5-16, DR5-105(C) (1976); "Reports, Proposals and Rulings, Yes. There Are Ethical Issues, ABA Finds," 3 Fam. L. Rep. 2633 (1977).

93   *Rules of Professional Conduct of the State Bar of California* 2-111(B)(2) (1975); *American Bar Association Code of Professional Responsibility* DR2-110(B((2) (1976).

94   Spencer & Zammit, *supra* note 67, at 931.

95   Conway, "To Insure Domestic Tranquility: Reconciliation Services as an Alternative to the Divorce Attorney," 9 J. Fam. L. 408, 412 (1970).

96   An attorney making such a referral should be sure to have the mediator present a separate bill to the clients to comply with fee splitting prohibitions. *Rules of Professional Conduct of the State Bar of California* 3-102 (1975); *American Bar Association Code of Professional Responsibility* DR3-102 (1976); Annot., 6 A.L.R. 3d 1446 (1966).

97   N. Kohut, *Therapeutic Family Law*, chs. 15-21 (1968).

98   Baernstein, *supra* note 87, at 421.

99   See text accompanying notes 57-59 *supra*.

100   Moskowitz, *supra* note 20, at 446-47.

101   Spencer & Zammit, *supra* note 67, at 934.

102   American Arbitration Association, *supra* note 55.

103   Shipman, *supra* note 50, at 402.

104   Steinberg, *supra* note 88, at 620.

105   The California legislature passed several bills of this type in the 1977-78 regular session including legislation requiring increased funding of children's mental health services (1978 Cal. Stats., 10 West Cal. Legis. Service, p. 4255, ch. 1228, to be codified at Cal. Welf. & Inst. Code § 5704.6) and increased financing of community mental health programs (1978 Cal. Stats., 10 West Cal. Legis. Service, pp. 4256-59, chs. 1229, 1230, to be codified at Cal. Welf & Inst. Code §§ 5715, 5721). The general trend toward limited government spending, however, is already having a negative effect on availability of mental health services in California. San Francisco Chronicle, Nov. 30, 1978, at 8, col. 1.

106 Note, "Simultaneous Representation," *supra* note 90, 104-109.

107 Adequate training and supervision of Conciliation Court counselors is necessary to insure that counselors maintain the mediator role rather than becoming judgmental, arbitrary decision-makers. See Burke, "Need for Standards For Conciliation Courts," Conciliation Cts. Rev., Sept. 1971, at 1, which suggests professionally trained counselors with at least master's degrees in the behavioral sciences, supervised by a person with at least five years of clinical counseling experience. See also Elkin, "Conciliation Court Counselor Needs," Conciliation Cts. Rev., Dec. 1970, at 29, 30-31, and Watson "Modern Family Rescue Team — Judge, Lawyer & Behavioral Scientist," Conciliation Cts. Rev., Sept. 1970, at 1, 6.

108 Cal. Code Civ. Proc. §§ 1744, 1744.1, 1744.2, 1745 (West 1972 & Cum. Supp. 1979) should be amended to include this mediator role.

109 Interview with Ann Roth, *supra,* note 76.

110 Spencer & Zammit, *supra* note 67, at 936-37.

111 *Id.* at 931.

112 Lindsley, "Custody Proceedings, Battlefield or Peace Conference?," Conciliation Cts. Rev., Sept. 1975, at 1.

113 J. Despert, *supra* note 10, at 192-93.

114 Cantor & Ferguson, "From the Judge's View — Family Counseling in the Conciliation Courts: An Alternative to Custody Litigation," Conciliation Cts. Rev., Sept., 1976, at 1.

A Study of Conciliation Counselling in the Family Court of Toronto: Implications for Socio-Legal Practice

Howard H. Irving, Michael Benjamin,
*Peter E. Bohm and Grant Macdonald**

INTRODUCTION

Over the past twenty years, the rates of marital separation and divorce have slowly but inexorably risen in both Canada (Stat. Can., 1978) and the U.S. (Norton & Glick, 1979). One consequence of this change has been an enormous increase in the population of troubled and unhappy people seeking help; another has been increasingly urgent concern over the means by which social service systems may be designed to provide the services required by these clients.

A case in point concerns the Family Court which plays a major role in the initiation and enforcement of various forms of family litigation associated with separation and divorce. While the demand on the court was manageable, the court's procedural system functioned well. More recently, however, a tremendous increase in service demand has created a serious backlog of cases, the delay between the initiation of litigation and court appearance has risen rapidly and, in general, strained the civil court system (Elkin, 1973).

* Howard H. Irving, D.S.W., is a Professor at the Faculty of Social Work, University of Toronto, and the Research Director of the Conciliation Project at the Provincial Court (Family Division), Toronto, Ontario.

Michael Benjamin, M.A., is a Family Sociologist, in the Department of Sociology, University of Toronto, Toronto, Ontario.

Peter E. Bohm, M.S.W., is a Doctoral Candidate at the Faculty of Social Work, University of Toronto, and a Research Assistant for the Conciliation Project at the Provincial Court (Family Division), Toronto, Ontario.

Grant Macdonald, M.S.W., and a Doctoral Candidate at the Faculty of Social Work, University of Toronto, and a Research Assistant for the Conciliation Project at the Provincial Court (Family Division), Toronto, Ontario.

These problems have been accompanied by a growing concern within the legal and social service communities that the adversary system is neither appropriate nor helpful for many couples seeking judicial solutions to their marital difficulties (Kronby, 1972: 123; Wheeler, 1974: 12). The main basis for dissatisfaction is that the adversary system escalates conflict between couples (Coogler, 1977) while exacerbating the emotional trauma already associated with separation or divorce (Irving & Irving, 1974; Weiss, 1975).

Nor should this be surprising. Legal ethics require that lawyers represent their clients with vigor and determination. This recommends that lawyers often take extreme and unnecessarily divisive positions (Coogler, 1977; Weiss, 1975: 265); frequently this involves their advising their clients to engage in conflict escalating behavior (McHenry et al., 1978). Consequently, the process of marital dissolution continues to be structured as a contest between opponents (Eisler, 1977; Elkin, 1977). Paradoxically, this serves to defeat the purpose for which the Family Court was created — the informal solution of marital and family problems — and suggests that adversarial court procedures may be contraindicated with respect to many family problems.

These remarks are not intended to imply that the Family Court no longer has an important and continuing role to play in family litigation. Rather, they suggest, first, that there are many families for whom adversarial court procedures are neither appropriate nor helpful; and, second, that alternative approaches to marital conflict and dissolution need to be found to complement the judicial process.

Conciliation counselling has been proposed as one such alternative. Essentially, this involves a neutral third party counselling persons whose marriage is in distress or has already broken down (*i.e.* separation, divorce). Accordingly, it may be defined as "a form of family intervention involving one or both spouses seen separately or together and designed to achieve one or more of the following outcomes: (1) reduce the level of real or perceived conflict between spouses; (2) facilitate communication between spouses, either in general terms or about specific issues problematic for them; (3) transform an amorphous problem into a resolvable issue; (4) suggest problem-solving strategies as a viable alternative to litigation; (5) provide the most efficient use of the legal system; and (6) optimally, help the spouses achieve a written agreement concerning one or more disputable issues or problems." (Irving *et al.*, 1979: 14-15). Ideally, these outcomes are intended to soften the trauma traditionally associated with marital dissolution as well as reduce the private and public expense typically attendent on it.

Proponents of this approach assume that persons experiencing various family problems can benefit from third party intervention (Elkin, 1973) and that even when reconciliation is impossible, conciliation counselling may minimize whatever emotional damage will be done

(Lightman & Irving, 1976). Further, assuming that this approach is superior to the traditional adversary system, they have argued for the widespread implementation of a conciliation counselling service (CCS) (Weiss, 1975: 112; Davidson, 1975: 14; Irving & Gandy, 1975; Sonne, 1978; Hays, 1978).

The empirical bases of this argument are twofold. First, some support comes from the social psychology literature concerning bargaining and negotiation. In that context, several investigators report evidence that co-operative strategies work better than competitive ones in the prevention or the resolution of conflict (Rubin & Brown, 1975: 263; Deutsch, 1973: 252). Whereas the former promote trust and compromise, the latter engender suspicion and conflict. While persuasive and interesting, as laboratory efforts, these data at best provide only indirect support for the conciliation approach.

A second source of support comes from a handful of clinical projects employing this approach. Thus, Elkin (1962, 1963, 1973) in Los Angeles (California), the Alberta Conciliation Service (1975) in Edmonton (Alberta), Weiss and Collada (1977) in San Jose (California) and the Frontenac Family Referral Service (1979) in Kingston (Ontario) all claim service effectiveness. While these studies have collectively made an important contribution, they remain problematic insofar as they are all primarily descriptive, fail to report operationally defined outcome measures, are non-comparative in design and/or suffer from sampling limitations.

While such efforts are, of course, encouraging, the fact remains that no research study currently exists which provides empirical support for the outcome effectiveness of conciliation counselling as an intervention strategy, either alone or in comparison to alternative (*i.e.* more traditional) intervention approaches. What appears to be needed is an exploratory study of conciliation counselling employing a comparative research design.

In response to this need, the Toronto Conciliation Project began operation in 1976. The Project was situated in the Provincial Court, Family Division, located in the Municipality of Toronto (Ontario) and was funded under the auspicies of Health and Welfare Canada and the Ontario Ministry of the Attorney General. The Project initiated two interlocking studies. The results of the first study, Study 1, have only recently been published (Irving *et al.,* 1979) while this report presents the findings of the second study, Study 2.

Briefly, Study 1 compared the outcome effectiveness of two counselling services attached to the Family Court. The first, the traditional intake service (TIS), while oriented to brief crisis counselling and subsequent referral, also sought to help clients understand and resolve their marital problems without recourse to the court, if possible. The second, the Conciliation Counselling Service (CCS), while oriented to problem resolution and the achievement of agreement between spouses, also made subsequent referrals when this was deemed necessary.

Clients were assigned to the TIS and the CCS groups on a quasi-random basis. Upon arrival at the Family Court, each potential client was issued an intake slip comprising the individual's name, the date and their arrival time. The client with the earliest arrival time was assigned to whichever service had a worker available following a baseline interview.

Two selection criteria were employed for sampling purposes: (1) all clients were first-time users of the court service; and (2) all clients agreed to participate in the research project.

Over a period of nine months (February 1 to October 31, 1977), a total of 228 clients met the above criteria; 122 were assigned to the TIS group compared to 106 assigned to the CCS group. Typically, clients in both groups were white females in their early thirties who had little education, had serious problems concerning financial support and/or physical abuse and were separated from their husbands and living with their children as unemployed housewives on a rather meager income.

The two services offered these clients differed in four ways. The CCS sought to enhance co-operative behaviour between spouses in conflict and to help them use the resources of the legal and social service systems to their best advantage. To these ends, conciliation counsellors were all holders of an M.S.W., had relatively small caseloads, worked flexible hours (including one evening per week) and attended a special in-service training programme consisting of 12 three hour sessions. In contrast, the TIS was designed primarily as a means of brief crisis intervention and so sought to determine appropriate referral and to expedite the client's use of the court's legal services. To these ends, intake counsellors all had undergraduate degrees*, had relatively large caseloads and worked only during standard business hours (*i.e.,* 9 a.m. to 5 p.m.); they were given no special training.

Within this context, evaluation of the outcome effectiveness of the CCS and the TIS took place in four sequential phases summarized in Figure 1.

Phase 1 involved the collection of baseline data. Immediately *prior* to meeting with an intake worker or a conciliation counsellor, each client was interviewed in a private office by one of six experienced and specially trained research interviewers by means of a 39-item Interview Schedule. These interviewers had no clinical responsibilities; their sole involvement with the court was restricted to data collection in the present study.

Phase 2 concerned evaluation of the service delivery process. To this end, workers maintained a running record of each case by means of repeated completion of a 14-item Interview Record Questionnaire and, upon termination of each case, completion of a 40-item Termination Record Questionnaire.

---

* There was an exception; one TIS counsellor had an M.S.W. degree.

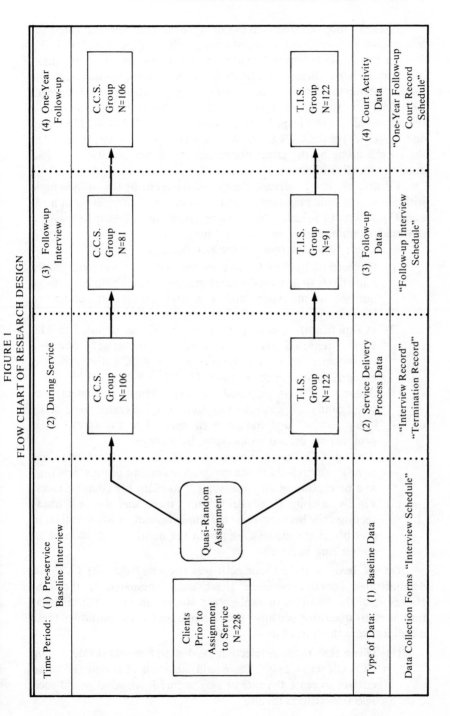

FIGURE 1
FLOW CHART OF RESEARCH DESIGN

Phase 3 concerned folow-up evaluation of service clients and began at least six weeks after termination; on average, clients were interviewed via a 76-item Follow-up Interview Schedule twelve weeks after the termination of service. While considerable difficulty was encountered in locating clients for a follow-up the perseverance of the research interviewers was rewarded; 172 (75%) of the original sample of 228 clients were successfully reinterviewed on follow-up. This represented 72% (n=91) of the TIS group and 78% (n=81) of the CCS group. Almost all interviews were conducted in the client's home by the same interviewer (whenever possible) who had done the baseline interview.

Finally, phase 4 concerned the use of the court by the study sample within one year following termination. This involved completion of a 13-item Court Record Schedule by an experienced court worker following a thorough examination of the Family Court files.

In capsule form, the results were as follows:

(1) Counselling by the CCS as opposed to the TIS was significantly more likely to involve the participation of both spouses, a greater number of interviews and a greater amount of cumulative interview time.

(2) A significantly greater proportion of CCS as opposed to TIS clients reported that they were "much better" following counselling; in addition, significantly more CCS clients reached an agreement with their spouse (21.7% vs 8.2%).

(3) Among CCS as opposed to TIS clients, agreement was significantly related to the number of problems rated "serious" or "very serious" and having been referred to the service by a professional or, more especially, by a lawyer.

(4) Among CCS as opposed to TIS clients, agreement was significantly related to the cumulative amount of interview time and perception of an improvement in client life circumstances.

(5) Finally, among CCS clients only, there was a direct linear relationship between reported improvement in life satisfaction and life circumstances, and both the number and duration of counselling interviews.

On the basis of these findings, it was suggested that the CCS had demonstrated superior outcome effectiveness compared to the TIS. However, in the tradition of exploratory studies, this research raised at least as many questions as it answered. Among the most important of these questions were the following:

(1) Given that random selection yielded an agreement rate among CCS clients of only 22%, would inclusion of specific selection criteria increase the rate of agreement? If so, what would such selection criteria involve?

(2) While the achievement of an agreement is an important first step in avoiding the negative effects of the adversary system, it is of relatively little help if such agreements do not endure. What proportion of agreements stand the test of time, say a period of at least one year? What impact, if any, does this have on usage of the judicial system?

(3) Demonstrated client outcome effectiveness is a prerequisite for the widespread implementation of CCS's. However, another is their acceptance by members of the legal community, especially by lawyers. Accordingly, do lawyers who have had some contact with the CCS believe that it benefits them and their clients? or does it hinder them in the performance of their role?

These essentially pragmatic questions served as the foci of Study 2, which was divided into three parts. Examining the outcome effectiveness of conciliation counselling through the application of selection criteria was the primary objective of Part 1. Attention to the issues of agreement durability (as measured by court recidivism) and lawyer evaluation were the objectives of Parts 2 and 3, respectively.

In what follows below, the methods used in data collection are briefly described. Next, the results are reported in summary form. Finally, these findings are discussed, with a special emphasis on various policy implications which may be derived from them.

PART 1

Sample selection and evaluation setting

The findings of Study 1 (Irving *et al.,* 1979) indicated that the outcome effectiveness of the CCS could be considerably enhanced by using a selected as opposed to a random sample. Accordingly, based on Study 1 data, four selection criteria were employed for sampling purposes:

1. Both spouses agree to participate in counselling. This means that the marital dyad was the primary unit of analysis.

2. Referral to the services must be made by either a judge or a lawyer. With respect to the latter, agreement to refer their client to the CCS must involve the lawyers of both spouses.[1]

3. Both spouses must be able to speak and read English with some level of fluency.

4. Both spouses must agree to participate in the research project, at least during phases 1 and 3.

Over a period of ten months (September, 1978 to June, 1979), a total of 193 out of 352 Court client couples (55%) met the above criteria and so were designated as the CCS study sample.

All service delivery to and baseline evaluation of the study sample was conducted in the offices of the Provincial Court, Family Division, located in the Municipality of Toronto. The majority of follow-up interviews were conducted in the homes of the respondents.

Service evaluation procedure

Evaluation of CCS outcome effectiveness took place in four sequential phases, summarized in Figure 2.

Phase 1 involved the collection of baseline data. Upon arrival at the CCS office, client couples were met by the receptionist who was trained to explain the purpose and confidential nature of the study. She recorded the clients' file numbers and names on two separate copies of a 41-item Client Question Form and asked them to fill it out privately while in the waiting room. In order to minimize the possibility of bias, throughout this and all subsequent phases of the study, data were collected from each spouse separately.

Apart from descriptive data, the Form contained two specific research instruments designed and/or selected to provide a baseline for comparison with later follow-up measures, specifically, the Life Satisfaction Questionnaire (Part 8), modified from Campbell *et al.* (1976), and the Problem Severity Index (Part D). The former consisted of 10 semantic differential[2] items, each of which consisted of a pair of polar adjectives (*e.g.* "boring" *vs* "interesting"). Clients were asked to rate where they would place their present life circumstances on a six-point scale within the two extremes. The eight items[3] most highly intercorrelated (Campbell *et al.*, 1976) were combined to provide a Life Satisfaction Index.[4]

The latter instrument, the Problem Severity Index, was made up of problems common to people using the Family Court. This list of problems was compiled with the help of the staff of the CCS and the Traditional Intake Service.[5] Clients were asked to rate each of the problems listed (*e.g.* custody dispute) on a 5-point Likert-type scale ranging from "Not a problem for me" to "A very serious problem for me". Following the work of Krupinski *et al.* (1972), the problem list was grouped, for analytic purposes, into four content areas:

1.   Abuse of spouse: physical and verbal.
2.   Financial problems: support from spouse, managing money, shortage of income, inadequate housing.
3.   Child-related problems: arguments over child rearing, behavioural problems of children, getting children to take sides.
4.   Personal or interpersonal problems: loneliness, sleeplessness, sex, alcohol.

Prior to its use (*i.e.* prior to Study 1), the Client Question Form

FIGURE 2
FLOW CHART OF RESEARCH DESIGN

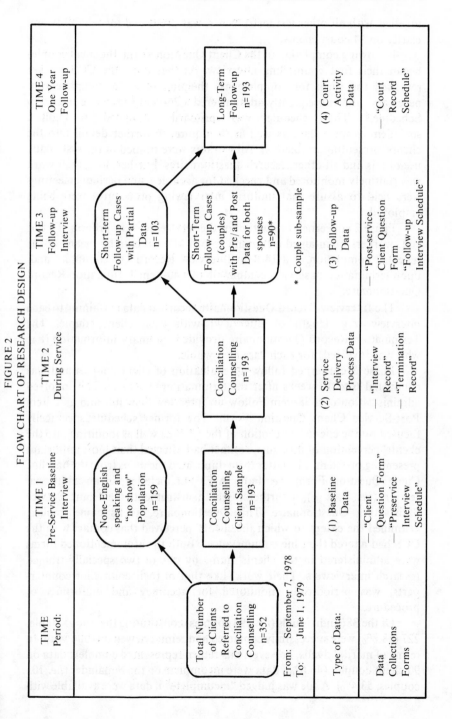

TIME Period:	TIME 1 Pre-Service Baseline Interview	TIME 2 During Service	TIME 3 Follow-up Interview	TIME 4 One Year Follow-up

None-English speaking and "no show" Population n=159

Short-term Follow-up Cases with Partial Data n=103

Long-Term Follow-up n=193

Conciliation Counselling n=193

Short-Term Follow-up Cases (couples) with Pre/and Post Data for both spouses n=90*

Conciliation Counselling Client Sample n=193

Total Number of Clients Referred to Conciliation Counselling n=352

From: September 7, 1978
To: June 1, 1979

* Couple sub-sample

Type of Data:	(1) Baseline Data	(2) Service Delivery Process Data	(3) Follow-up Data	(4) Court Activity Data
Data Collections Forms	— "Client Question Form" — "Preservice Interview Schedule"	— "Interview Record" — "Termination Record"	— "Post-service Client Question Form" — "Follow-up Interview Schedule"	— "Court Record Schedule"

together with all other test instruments, was pre-tested for reliability and clarity on 34 court clients.

Following completion of the Client Question Form, the client couples began their first counselling interview. At that time, the CCS worker reviewed the form for completeness (helping them to complete it if necessary) and subsequently administered a 26-item Preservice Interview Schedule.[6] The schedule was primarily designed to collect sociodemographic data as well as to inquire, in further detail, into the clients' presenting problem(s). All workers were trained in the systematic use of this and all other research questionnaires. Furthermore, their work was routinely monitored and checked for accuracy, and periodic meetings were held to assure that uniform interviewing procedures were being employed.

Phase 2 concerned evaluation of the service delivery process. To this end, workers maintained a running record of each case by means of the repeated completion of a 14-item Interview Record Questionnaire and, upon termination of service, completion of a 40-item Termination Record Questionnaire.

The Interview Record Questionnaire recorded data pertaining to each interview (e.g. length of interview) with each client couple. The Termination Record Questionnaire provided summary information (e.g. who was involved) for each case as a whole.

Phase 3 concerned follow-up evaluation of client couples and was conducted 6 to 12 weeks after the termination of service. This involved administration of a 38-item Follow-up Interview Schedule and a 72-item Post-Service Client Question Form. The former schedule specifically focused on the clients' perception of the CCS as well as inquiring into the clients' perception of how such contact had affected their most important presenting problem. The latter form duplicated the items from the baseline Client Question Form (i.e. Parts A-E) but included, in an additional section (i.e. Part F), a further research instrument, the Court Service Satisfaction Questionnaire. This Questionnaire, as its name implies, examined the extent to which the clients' perceived that contact with the CCS had altered their life circumstances. Both the aforementioned forms were administered in the clients' home by one of two specially trained research interviewers. Their work, like that of their counsellor counter-parts, was periodically monitored for accuracy and uniformity of procedure.

Of the 386 individuals (i.e. 193 couples) constituting the study sample, 227 (58.8%) were successfully contacted and reinterviewed on follow-up. In terms of marital dyads, however, this return represented complete data on 90 client couples (46.6%); data were incomplete on the remainder (i.e. 103 couples; 53.4%). A file was judged "incomplete" if data were available with respect to only one spouse on follow-up or if one or both spouses failed to respond to 20% or more of follow-up interview items.

Finally, phase 4 concerned the use of the court by the study sample within one year following the termination of service. This involved completion of a 13-item Court Record Schedule by an experienced court worker based on a thorough search of the Family Court records. The schedule, developed with the assistance of a CCS worker, was designed to determine the frequency and type of litigation with which each of the study client couples were involved. In addition, at this time, all counsellors were interviewed by the senior investigator. These interviews were relatively informal and open-ended; they focused on the counsellors' general impressions of conciliation counselling, especially the most effective means of helping client couples reach agreement.

Data analysis

As stated above, while data were available with respect to 193 couples, a complete data file existed for 90 of them. On the grounds that collapsing complete and incomplete files together would seriously compromise the validity of any pre-post comparisons[7], such comparisons were limited to the "complete couple" subgroup only; "partial couple" data were disregarded for this purpose. In order to ascertain that this procedure did not yield a sociodemographically biased subsample, partial and complete subgroups were compared statistically. Virtually no statistically significant differences were detected.

Available data were of two types, qualitative and quantitative. With respect to the latter, data were coded, punched on standard cards and "edited" for computer analysis using the Statistical Package for the Social Sciences (Nie *et al.*, 1975). Comparative analysis of data which achieved either a nominal (*i.e.* yes/no) or ordinal (*i.e.* less than/greater than) level of measurement (in the form of a cross-tabulation table) involved the use of the Chi Square test (written X^2) of independence. Analysis of interval data (*i.e.* "mean" or average scores) involved use of the T-test for independent samples (Glass and Stanley, 1970). For both tests, an alpha level of 0.05[8] was employed as the acceptable level of statistical significance.

With respect to qualitative data, these were initially examined by inspection. Wherever the data exhibited some clustering or redundancy, client responses were categorized, collapsed, quantified (in percentage terms) and subjected to statistical analysis using the same procedures as described above.

PART 2

In addition to court follow-up, the durability of agreements was also examined at one year follow-up. At that time, a 50% random sample was selected from among CCS client couples who reached agreement and for whom complete data were available (n=61). Of these (n=30), 16 couples together with 9 single clients agreed to participate.

Initial contact was made by letter. This advised them that they would soon be contacted by telephone for their assistance in completing a Telephone Follow-Up Questionnaire. This consisted of 20 items focusing on: (1) their current marital status; (2) the current status of their conciliation agreement; and (3) their evaluation of and attitudes towards the CCS. All items were either of the Likert type or were of the multiple choice variety. The questionnaire was administered by a group of five graduate social work students as part of a research methods course under the supervision of the senior author.

Because of the small sample size, data analysis did not differentiate between single and couple clients; rather, analysis focused on the responses of the 41 clients seen as single individuals.[9]

PART 3

In order to determine lawyers' evaluation of the CCS, a list of 75 lawyers was first compiled each of whom had referred at least one client to the CCS during the period 1978-79 inclusive. Following contact with these lawyers, 52 (69.3%) agreed to participate and provided usable data.

Each of the lawyers in question was mailed a copy of the Lawyer Questionnaire accompanied by a cover letter explaining the purpose of the study and asking for their assistance. This was followed two weeks later by a telephone call advising them when the questionnaire would be picked up.

The questionnaire consisted of 13 items focusing on: (1) the level of the respondents experience with the CCS; (2) their evaluation of that experience; and (3) their recommendations for the future of the CCS. All items were either of the Likert type or the multiple choice variety. The questionnaire was administered by a group of six graduate social work students as part of a research methods course under the supervision of the senior author.[10]

RESULTS

The results of Study 2, Parts 1 to 3, are each presented below in summary form. For ease of presentation, the results of Part I are divided into four sections concerning client characteristics, service characteristics, outcome and follow-up, respectively. By convention, findings described as "significant" will have met or surpassed the alpha level of 0.05 while findings reported as "substantial" will be greater than 0.05 but less than 0.10.

PART I

(a) Baseline data

Baseline data provide the basis for constructing a capsule picture of the "typical" CCS client couple. Such couples were in their 30's (59%), had been married for more than five years (80%), had at least two children (66%) and reported that this was the first marriage for both spouses (87%). In response to longstanding problems (3-9 years: 81%),[11] most spouses had been separated at least twice in the past (51%) and were currently separated (72%) and living apart (85%), this arrangement having been in place for up to a year (67%). While most women worked on a full- or part-time basis (55%) — typically at clerical (45%) or semi-skilled (19%) occupations — a large proportion (45%) stayed at home to care for the children and remained financially dependent upon their husbands. Most of the latter, like their wives, had a high school education (65%) and worked on a full-time basis (85%) at a skilled (23%) or semi-skilled (24%) occupation, with 52.3% of working women earning an average of $8,000 or more and 70.1% of working men earning an average of $12,000 or more.[12]

Turning to their subjective state, couples reported a moderate level of life satisfaction[13] ($\bar{x}$=4.0) and a low level of marital satisfaction[14] (20-75% depending on the specific issue). This was especially true of wives who consistently reported higher levels of marital conflict than their husbands. While spouses reported "serious" problems in all problem categories, most rated either custody (25%) or access (27%) as the single most important problem which brought them to court. While various categories of persons had been contacted about these difficulties, lawyers were seen by both spouses to have been the most helpful (37%) and it was their lawyer (44%) or the judge (47%) who referred them to the CCS.

(b) Service data

On arrival at the CCS, client couples typically had 4-6 counselling interviews[15] (47%) in which they were seen separately as well as together (55%), with children included on at least one occasion (23%). Counselling tended to involve a combination of morning, afternoon and evening visits (41%) and cumulatively involved six or more hours (51%). The decision to terminate service was usually made by a joint decision of the client couple and the counsellor (78%).

In addition, there was general consensus among counsellors that especially aggressive outreach was required with respect to client couples in which one spouse felt correctly or incorrectly, that the other spouse would not be interested in attending counselling.

(c) Outcome data

The outcome of counselling was strongly positive in several respects. The majority of couples:

(1) reached an agreement (70%), typically in written form (82%); of these, a small proportion also reconciled (12%);

(2) reported that they had completely (54%) or partially (28%) accomplished what they sought to achieve in relation to their most important problem. For example, one wife noted that, as a result of counselling, the "door was open for discussion. It became clear that we (the kids and I) would have to move out. (It also) clarified the custody issue and allowed me to save some dignity.";

(3) agreed that in regard to the total situation, things had either gotten "better" or "much better" (76%) since counselling had begun; this sentiment was aptly expressed by a wife who commented that, as a result of counselling, "I understand better the problems and questions that (may) arise and can cope with them to ensure that my son is not drastically affected." However, counselling also benefited individuals psychologically, as this wife states: "I have more time to myself and I am not as angry with my husband. (Also, my daughter now sees her father, something I had refused before.)";

(4) reported that in comparison to baseline marital conflict over such things as bringing up the children, financial matters, life goals, in-laws, child support and access was considerably reduced; this was especially true of wives who, since they were initially most dissatisfied, showed the most dramatic pre-post decreases (*e.g.* wife: custody 67% to 35%; husband: custody 57% to 47%); the quality of such change is poignantly described by the following comment by a husband: "Up to conciliation, (my) wife and I had been unable to sit down and talk things (out) without arguing in front of the baby. (The) counsellor helped us to act more maturely." Similarly, a couple jointly commented, "(Counselling was) a great experience that brought us closer together.";

(5) exhibited a substantial decrease in the proportion of spouses who still reported a number of "serious" problems (*e.g.* wife: custody 75% to 39%; husband: custody 64% to 52%); in this context, for example, one husband reported that "at least now there is a chance my children will know I'm concerned enough about them that I will seek help (for my problem) in order to be able to see them regularly." Similarly, a wife noted that the CCS "was very good in that although my husband and I didn't accomplish as much as I had hoped, I think we did prevent going to court.";

(6)   agreed that they had positive feelings about their contact with the CCS (75%); as one wife commented, "I feel more people should know about (the) service and be able to use it. It (was) an excellent opportunity to sit down with a third party and work things out. It would have been good to have come to conciliation before (going to) court.";

(7)   agreed that they would return to the CCS if the need arose (80%); thus, as one wife commented, "if there are any problems I would rather go to conciliation than (the) court or lawyers." Similarly, a husband stated that "if my wife was willing to go (back), I would."

(8)   agreed that conciliation was the main reason for any changes they had accomplished (59%) and suggested that its success was primarily attributable to improvements in communication, trust and understanding (35%), achievement of an agreement (12%) and/or reduced conflict and emotional tension (17%); thus, one husband noted that counselling "took (the) selfishness out of me (and) helped me (to) understand my wife." Another husband commented that counselling was "an educational experience which generates trust." Similarly a third husband stated that "my wife and I are not trying to make life difficult for each other anymore. We spend our energy on mutual concern for each other and our child." Finally, a wife observed that, as a result of counselling, "(this is the) first time in five years my husband and I have not argued on (our) son's well-being", while another wife states that "my visits with the children are more relaxed (now). I sense that reaching an agreement has lessened (the) tension (level) and (the) children are responding accordingly."

(9)   two additional findings are worthy of note based on counsellor interviews: (a) most counsellors felt that agreement was especially difficult, if not impossible, among client couples in which the spouses remained emotionally attached to each other; such couples were characterized by one spouse heavily invested in continuing the relationship while the other spouse was equally desperate to end the relationship; this combination almost invariably resulted in protracted arguing; intense emotionality and a high level of irrationality, conversely, client couples for whom separation or divorce was a mutual goal tended to reach agreement easily and with relatively little conflict; and (b) there was consensus among counsellors that reaching an agreement was made much easier if the lawyers in question were supportive of this end; in contrast, lawyers who were disinterested in the process or who persisted in adopting an adversarial approach substantially reduced the probability that an agreement would be reached.

(d) Interaction effects

In addition, client variables and service variables were examined in terms of their interaction with outcome variables. The findings were as follows:

Client Variables

(1) agreement was significantly related to: (*a*) rating custody and access as "a mild problem for me" (see tables 1A & 1B); (*b*) accomplishing what they set out to with respect to their most important problem; (*c*) stating that they found their lawyer or the court most helpful with respect to their difficulties; (*d*) stating that the CCS influenced change for the "better"; and, (*e*) feeling "better" about the problem(s) that brought them to the court in the first place;

(2) satisfaction with alimony, maintenance, access and custody judgment that life circumstances had gotten "better" or "much better" following counselling and improvement in life satisfaction were all significantly associated with reporting that a range of issues, especially those pertaining to children, were rated as "mild" problems;

(3) dissatisfaction with alimony and maintenance was significantly related with having been referred to the CCS by a judge as opposed to a lawyer;

TABLE 1A Seriousness of Custody Problem By Agreement		
Agreement		
Yes	No	Total
Seriousness of Custody Problem %	%	%
Mild	64.7	18.2	53.3
Moderate	5.9	19.1	6.7
Serious	29.4	72.7	40.0
Total	100.0 (34)	100.0 (11)	100.0 (45)

$X^2 = 7.39973$, df=2, p « .02

TABLE 1B Seriousness of Access Dispute Problem by Agreement		
Agreement		
Yes	No	Total
Seriousness of Access Dispute Problem %	%	%
Mild 53.3	28.6	45.5
Moderate 30.0	7.1	22.7
Serious 16.7	64.3	31.8
Total 100.0 (30)	100.0 (14)	100.0 (44)

$X^2 = 10.28462$, df=2, p « .006

(4) judgment that life circumstances had gotten "better" was also significantly related to: (a) having seen a lawyer within three months of referral to the CCS; (b) reporting that they felt "better" or "much better" about the problems that brought them to the court; (c) having accomplished what they wanted to with respect to their most important problem; and (d) agreeing that the CCS was primarily responsible for any changes that occurred; and

(5) improvement in life satisfaction was also significantly related to reporting that they found their lawyer "most helpful" in resolving their difficulties.

Service Variables

(1) agreement was significantly related to: (a) having included a child in counselling at least once (see Table 2) and (b) having attended four or more interview sessions for a total of between four and eight hours of cumulative interview time;

(2) judgment that life circumstances had gotten "better" or "much better" was significantly related to: (a) having attended three or more counselling sessions and (b) that these sessions included morning, afternoon and evening visits; and

(3)   improvement in life satisfaction was significantly associated with attending three or more counselling sessions.

			TABLE 2 Times Child Seen in Counselling By Agreement		
		Agreement			
		Yes	No		Total
Times Child Seen		%	%		%
0		53.3	80.8		61.6
1		28.3	15.4		24.4
2+		18.3	3.8		14.0
Total		100.0 (60)	100.0 (26)		100.0 (80)

$X^2 = 6.18954$, df=2, p « .04

(e)   One year court follow-up

A final concern related to court activity at one year follow-up. These data revealed that:

(1)   most client couples (see Table 3) returned to court (71%) one or more times during the year following counselling; and

(2)   most of this activity (80%) pertained to those issues which brought them to court originally such that their return to court was "automatic".[16]*

(3)   further examination of these date revealed that: (a) return to court with respect to issues which arose after counselling was terminated, was substantially related with having first seen a lawyer within 4-6 months of referral to the CCS; (b) return to court two or more times with respect to the original issue was significantly associated with the client's judgment that their life circumstances had gotten "worse" (see Table 4); reporting that contact with the CCS had made "no difference" to their problems; and, judging that financial support was a "moderate"

---

*   In actual fact very few people return to court regarding their agreement; most returned for reasons that were considered automatic (that is, not related to further litigation).

to a "very serious" problem; (*c*) return to court, irrespective of the issue in question, was significantly related to judging that life circumstances had gotten "worse" and having first seen a lawyer 4-6 months prior to referral to the CCS. In addition, while return to court *per se* was statistically unrelated to agreement, inspection of these data showed that client couples who failed to reach agreement were twice as likely as those that did to return to court four or more times (17% *vs* 9%).

TABLE 3 Court Activity At One Year Follow-Up			
	%		%
	Yes	No	Total
Return to Court	71.1	28.9	100.0 (50)
Number of Court Dates Related To Original Issue(s)	0-1	2+	Total
	70.8	29.2	100.0 (90)
Number of Court Dates Related to Subsequent Issue(s)	0-1	1+	Total
	79.8	29.2	100.0 (90)

TABLE 4 Number of Court Dates Related to Original Issue(s) By How Things Compare			
	How Things Compare		
	Better	Worse	Total
Number of Court Dates Related to Original Issue(s)	%	%	%
1	80.7	55.2	72.1
2+	19.3	44.8	27.9
Total	100 (57)	100 (29)	100 (86)

$X^2 = 5.02228$ (corrected), df=1, p « .02

PART 2

Agreement at one year follow-up

Findings with respect to one year follow-up of clients who reached an agreement were as follows:

(1)   A minority of clients (22%) had reconciled, all within three to six months following the termination of counselling;

(2)   most clients (92%) felt they had a clear understanding of the terms of their agreement and, in addition, felt that this was also true of their spouse (76%);

(3)   although many clients reported having some problems with their agreement, only a handful (9.8%) returned to court over the matter;

(4)   a substantial proportion of clients (40%) had made changes to the terms of their agreement, especially with respect to access; most of these (74%), however, had made these changes informally, that is, outside the court system, and most (79%) were mutually acceptable;

(5)   all clients sought some help in keeping the terms of their agreement; however, this seldom involved formal agencies or organizations (*e.g.* police 1.9%; family or marriage counsellor 7.6%, clergyman, 1.9%, psychiatrist 3.8%); rather, most clients relied on either their lawyer (25%), family or friends (19%) or their family doctor (13%), most (75%) found such support helpful;

(6)   most clients reported that they were either "satisfied" or "very satisfied" with the terms of their agreement (*e.g.* custody 69%; access 69%);

(7)   most clients were either "somewhat satisfied", "satisfied" or "very satisfied" with their total agreement (81%);

(8)   the majority of clients (62%) did not feel pressured to reach an agreement; of those that did, most felt that they would have liked more time in counselling as well as follow-up contact (a service not now provided by the CCS); and

(9)   finally, a majority of clients (53%) stated that in the year following counselling, their overall family situation had "improved".

PART 3

Lawyer's evaluation

With respect to lawyer evaluation of the CCS, the findings were as follows:

(1) a large proportion (49%) of the respondents had had a good deal of contact with the CCS, having referred anywhere from 4 to more than 29 clients to the service during the period 1978-79 inclusive;

(2) most referred cases primarily concerned with either custody (85%) or access (89%);

(3) most (82%) recommended that the CCS be continued on the grounds that it helped clarify issues (52%), narrow issues (56%) or facilitate dispute resolution (60%);

(4) with respect to the issues of access and custody, most respondents reported that the CCS was either "very helpful" (70%) or "helpful" (62%); with respect to other issues, such as property disputes, the majority of respondents felt that it either had no effect (27%) or stated that they "didn't know" (62%);

(5) most respondents recommended that the CCS be continued in its present form (78%) on the grounds that it "always" or "frequently" helped avoid unnecessary litigation (69%), better prepared the client to understand the issues (76%), allowed the client to use their services more appropriately (82%) and reduced the client's emotional turmoil (80%);

(6) most respondents agreed that they would recommend the service to other lawyers (79%) and felt that it operated best as a court-based service, located either in the Family Court (46%) or in the Supreme Cout (43%);

(7) most felt that the CCS could be most helpful to their clients either on first contact with a lawyer (22%) or prior to making the decision to proceed with litigation (39%);

(8) most felt that the goals and/or functions of the CCS were not in conflict with their role as a legal adviser (84%) insofar as dealing with legal problems was their area of expertise while dealing with the emotional aspects of divorce was better handled by the CCS;

(9) in their qualitative responses, respondents noted that the service provides conciliation counselling for clients who would otherwise be unable to afford private counselling;

(10) finally, with respect to the future, most respondents recommended that with respect to contested cases, clients be informed of the availability of the CCS either by the judge (59%) or by a court-initiated letter (47%).

Implications and conclusion

We began this study with three objectives:

(1) to discover the effect(s) of applying conciliation to a selected as opposed to a random sample of client couples;

(2) to inquire into the durability of conciliation counselling agreements at one year follow-up;

(3) to examine the evaluation of the CCS by lawyers who have had experience with the service.

The answers to these questions provided by the findings discussed above are clear and unequivocal. Specifically, they suggest that the CCS provides at least seven major benefits, either to the client couples who use it or to the lawyers referring clients to it.

First, a substantial majority of client couples either achieved a written agreement or reconciled and resumed living together. These outcomes accounted for 70% of all client couples for whom a complete data set were available. Moreover, these agreements typically concerned custody, access or support, the very issues which the majority of couples regarded as their most important problem. These findings are strikingly at variance with those of Study 1 and strongly suggest that the outcome effectiveness of conciliation counselling is enhanced by the use of a selected sample.

Second, agreements achieved during the course of counselling tended to endure, at least as of our last follow-up at one year. Perhaps even more important, the maintenance and/or modification of these agreements was typically achieved informally, without recourse to the courts. It must be noted, of course, that these findings are in some doubt in the light of the small sample from which they were derived. However, the random nature of that sample provides at least some basis for accepting their validity. If so, they attest to the quality of CCS outcome effectiveness and suggest that the CCS not only benefits client couples who use it, but also the court system by helping to avoid unnecessary, wasteful and expensive litigation.

Third, in the same context, a group of respondents best qualified to judge the judicial benefits of the CCS, namely a group of lawyers (N=52) experienced with the operation of the service, unequivocally stated that not only did the CCS save the court time and money by avoiding unnecessary litigation, but it also saved both lawyers' and clients' time by encouraging them to make better use of legal services. It is hardly surprising, therefore, that most lawyers strongly supported the continued operation of the CCS and noted that it did not conflict with their own legal functions.

Fourth, both clients and lawyers claimed benefit from the CCS insofar as it helped narrow and clarify issues in dispute between couples in conflict. It is not unreasonable to believe that the ambiguity surrounding many of the issues client couples bring to their lawyer derives from the intersection of the substantive and the emotional dimensions of conflict. In this context, the lawyers observation that the CCS was better suited than they in dealing with emotional tension helps to explain why issue clarification appears to be regularly associated with conciliation counselling. To the extent that a prerequisite for problem-solving is clear communication, it also helps to explain why the CCS appears to avoid many of the difficulties associated with the traditional adversary approach to divorce litigation.

Fifth, client couples consistently reported that counselling achieved its beneficial results by means of a twofold process: reducing conflict and emotional tension while simultaneously facilitating better communication and mutual understanding. While these data help explain the reduced judicial involvement of CCS clients, it also highlights the qualitative aspects of divorce litigation, namely, the intense and prolonged emotional turmoil typically associated with it. To the extent that such turmoil clouds judgment and intensifies hostility, it can often prolong conflict and worsen an already traumatic situation. In this context, reaching an agreement as a result of conciliation counselling is incidental; its primary benefit is subjective in the form of relief from emotional distress.

Sixth, by its combination of objective (*i.e.* agreement) outcome and subjective relief, conciliation counselling is strongly associated with significant improvements in life circumstances and/or marital satisfaction. This may have various meanings for the client couples in question, including improved mutual regard among married couples or assured child support and visitation for couples who are separated or divorced. Whatever the details, these data imply that such clients show an increased ability to cope with their life exigencies, the opportunity to get some satisfaction out of life and the possibility of achieving new or revised life goals, all novel achievements for many of these couples troubled for years prior to counselling.

Finally, reduced use of the court, better use of legal expertise, and so on, all imply that the CCS should be a cost effective method of handling pre- or post-divorce dispute resolution. Unfortunately, objective data in support of this expectation were beyond the scope of the present study. However, a Staff Report (1979) indicates that during the period of Study 1, the CCS was indeed effective in this way, yielding $155 in public saving per case. Insofar as the outcome effectiveness of that study was considerably lower than that of the present study, it is only reasonable that Study 2 can be expected to have improved in cost effectiveness over its predecessor. This reasoning finds further support from a recent study of Bahr (1980) who, among other things, examined the cost effectiveness of eight conciliation projects most of which were in the United States. Based on his analysis, Bahr concluded that, in the United States alone, widespread implementation of conciliation counselling (which he called "divorce mediation") would yield $98 million annually in combined public and private savings. These data, taken together with our own, suggests that widespread implementation of conciliation counselling should yield a comparable level of savings in Canada.

These benefits of conciliation counselling are significant and their importance cannot be underestimated. However, this is not to suggest that the CCS, in its present form, has reached its optimal level of functioning. Rather, data from the present study suggest a number of changes and raise a number of as yet unanswered questions.

One such issue concerns the strong relationship between agreement and reporting that a variety of concerns were "mild" problems. This finding is significant for its consistency, as variable after variable displayed the same relationship, and its marked contrast with Study 1, in which problem severity was associated with agreement. This difference between the two studies is amenable to alternative interpretations. It is possible, for example, that differences in sample selection rendered the two studies noncomparable, with Study 2 having relatively few cases that exhibited many very serious problems.[17] Alternatively, the relationship between agreement and problem severity may in fact be that of a U-curve, with a high level of agreement among clients with either mild or very severe problems. Irrespective of the interpretation selected, however, this finding suggests, first, that the operation of sample selection criteria is crucial to the optimal performance of the CCS; second, that the amenability of the CCS to client couples with very severe problems warrants investigation within the context of a selected sample; and finally, that "mild problem type" warrants examination as an additional sample selection criterion in the future operation of the CCS.

A related issue concerns the relationship between lawyer referral and agreement, especially with respect to custody and access. This raises two issues. First, lawyers are clearly of the opinion that certain of their clients will benefit from the CCS while others will not do so. It would be extremely valuable to know the bases of this selection. While lawyers have stated that the CCS is most beneficial with respect to cases of custody and access, the fact that they were frequently unable to say whether or not the CCS was beneficial with respect to other types of cases (*e.g.* property and maintenance) leaves the matter in doubt; it clearly warrants further research.

Second, lawyers have argued that the earlier in the judicial process their clients make contact with the CCS the better. These data were not available in the present study. However, previous work by the Frontenac Referral Service (1979) provides empirical support for this contention. This suggests that this variable be given a great deal more attention in the future than it has received in the past. In turn, this requires, first, a concerted future effort to advise lawyers and their clients of the availability of this CCS, and, second, more aggressive future efforts at casefinging.

A further issue concerns the service program offered by the CCS. At present, service tends to be relatively brief and does not involve follow-up contact beyond the point of service termination. In this context, however, clients have reported dissatisfaction with the short time available in which to reach agreement and have stated a desire to receive follow-up contact. While there is as yet no empirical basis for believing that such extended service would either increase the proportion of client couples reaching agreement or enhance the durability of agreements signed, these possibilities are clearly worth investigating. While this would necessarily involve increased fiscal expenditure, the possibility of increased cost effectiveness as a result justifies at least temporary efforts in this direction.

A related issue concerns the association between agreement and having children involved in the counselling process. All too frequently divorce litigation is seen as a matter pertaining exclusively to the marital dyad. Consequently, child involvement, when and if it does occur, is typically regarded as incidental to the main focus of counselling. This perspective, however, overlooks two insights long available to family counsellors, namely, that (1) an integral aspect of family life is the interdependence between and among constituent members, and (2) all family members actively participate, either directly or indirectly, in the development and maintenance of family problems (*e.g.* Minuchin *et al.*, 1978: ch. 2). It follows that the involvement of all family members must also relate to problem resolution preceding change. This suggests the need for a shift in the focus of conciliation from the marital to the family unit. This would recommend that, unless specifically contra indicated, counsellors encourage the involvement of all family members on the grounds that it may significantly contribute to increased outcome effectiveness.

Still a further issue concerns the rather delicate topic of the relationship between counsellor expectations and outcome. Traditionally, description of a counsellor as a change agent or helper is left unqualified. This assumes that once a client has been accepted in the counselling process, all counsellors are equally zealous in their efforts to achieve a positive outcome and that they do not differentiate between clients in terms of the probability of their achieving such an outcome. The recent work of Stapleford and Bell (1980), however, with respect to marital separation counselling, clearly calls these assumptions in doubt. Their data indicate that (1) counsellors have quite definite, if implicit, expectations concerning which clients are likely to be most amenable to their treatment efforts, and (2) this has a highly significant impact on outcome, with poor outcomes associated with clients with whom the counsellors did not expect to succeed. While the collection of comparable data was beyond the scope of Study 2, our subjective impression is in keeping with Stapleford and Bell's results. This suggests that worker expectations is a component of conciliation counselling that merits research attention.

A final issue concerns the association between agreement and clients having accomplished what they set out to with respect to their most important problem. For many clients, this marked a dramatic departure from what they had become accustomed to over the several years preceding counselling, years filled with turmoil, uncertainty and failure. That counselling tended to improve their morale and their life circumstances is clear. Whether it impacted similarly on their level of self-esteem and self-perception remains in doubt — although tantalizing bits and pieces of subjective data suggests that it does. If so, this suggests that conciliation counselling may have long term effects hitherto unsuspected, effects that may pay off both for the client as well as for the judicial system. This is yet another area requiring future research investigation.

In light of the foregoing discussion, we may conclude by suggesting that, while there is much yet to be done, the data we have examined in this study indicate that the CCS is a viable and useful adjunct or alternative to the adversary system in relation to problems of marital conflict and dissolution. We therefore recommend its widespread implementation and continued systematic evaluation in the strongest possible terms.[18]

APPENDIX 1

Recommendations for the Establishment of Conciliation Court Services

1. It is helpful for such a service to be imbued with the legal status and authority of the court system.
2. The service should be located within the court, so that they may be closely connected and to give the service greater credibility. This is especially important for lawyers making referrals.
3. Ideally the service should be provided on a state or province-wide basis and be jointly funded by state or province and federal levels of government.
4. A conciliation counsellor should be available at all times to see an immediate referral following pre-trial conferences or referrals from judges.
5. There should be an advisory board made up of representatives from the professional and client communities.
6. A director of conciliation services should be appointed who is responsible to the chief judge or his designee.
7. Conciliation counselling should be made available to all who wish to make use of it, even before formal proceedings are instituted.
8. The service should perform both intake (initial screening) and dispute resolution functions in order to eliminate fragmentation and duplication of service.
9. There should be a conciliation term composed of social workers aided by consultation from lawyers, psychiatrists, and psychologists, as well as staff from the area's pre-dominant social and ethnic groups.
10. The nature of the service should be short-term (approximately one to six interviews) and crisis-oriented, with dispute resolution as the mode of approach.
11. The service should be voluntary, but the court, through the use of its influence, should urge strongly that the service be used.
12. Conciliation counsellors should have professional backgrounds in the psychological and social sciences with experience in family counselling and negotiating skills.

13. An intensive in-service training program should be established to provide seminars in the socio-legal implications of family law.
14. Students from various disciplines should be affiliated with the service for part of their clinical training.
15. In order to allow clients to discuss their problems openly, conciliation counsellors should be granted privileged communication.
16. There should be opportunities for both mediation and arbitration depending upon the conciliator's assessment.
17. A research design should be developed prior to the establishment of a conciliation service, so that the service may be evaluated as it continues and so that further recommendations may be made.[19]

REFERENCES

Alberta Conciliation Service, Demonstration Project #558-1-12, National Health and Welfare Canada, 1975.

Bahr, S. Unpublished manuscript, Brigham Young Univ., 1980.

Brown, P., Manela, R. "Client Satisfaction with Marital and Divorce Counselling", The Family Coordinator, July 1977, 294-303.

Campbell, A., Converse, P.E., and Rodgers, W.L. The Quality of American Life, N.Y.: Russell Sage Foundation, 1976.

Carter, H., and Glick, P.D. Marriage and Divorce: A Social and Economic Study, Cambridge: Harvard U. Press, 1970.

Chiancola, S.P. "The Process of Separation and Divorce: A New Approach", Social Casework, 1978, 59(8), 494-499.

Chiriboga, D.A., and Cutler, L. "Stress Responses Among Divorcing Men and Women", Journal of Divorce, 1977, 1(2), 95-106.

Conciliation Project of the Provincial Court (Family Division) Questions Raised by the Address of the Attorney General at the Conciliation Conference, Toronto, Canada, October 1978 (unpublished).

.... (Pamphlet): "Conciliation Services", 1978.

Coogler, O.J. "Changing the Lawyer's Role in Matrimonial Practice", Conciliation Courts Review, September 1977, 15 (1), 1-8.

Danziger, K. Introduction. In K. Danziger (ed.). Readings in Child Socialization, London: Pergamon, 1970.

Davidson, R. Marriage and Family Law in Ontario, Vancouver and Toronto: International Self-Counsel Press Ltd., 1975.

Deutsch, M. The Resolution of Conflict, New Haven and London: Yale University press, 1973.

Elkin, M. "Short-Contact Counselling in a Conciliation Court", Social Casework, 1962, 43, 184-190.

Elkin, M. "Conciliation Courts: The Reintegration of Disintegrating Families", The Family Coordinator, Vol. 22, No. 1, January 1973, 63-72.

Frontenac Family Referral Service, Couples in Crisis. Kingston, Ontario: Frontenac Family Referral Service, 1979.

Glass, G.V., and Stanley, J.C. Statistical Methods in Education and Psychology, Prentice-Hall, N.J., 1970.

Glick, P.C. "A Demographer Looks at American Families", in A.S. Skolnick and J.H. Skolnick (eds.), Family in Transition, 2nd ed., 1977, 90-108.

Goldstein, J., Freud, A., and Solnit, A.J. Beyond the Best Interests of the Child, 1973, London: The Free Press.

Gurman, A.S. "Effects and Effectiveness of Marital Therapy: A Review of Outcome Research", *Family Process*, 1973, *12*, 145-170.

Haynes, J.M., "Divorce Mediator: A New Role", *Social Work*, 1978, 23(1), p. 5-9.

Holmes, T.H. and Rahe, R.H. "The Social Readjustment Rating Scale" Journal of Psychosomatic Research, 1967, *11*, 213-218.

Holmes, T.S., and Holmes, T.H. "Short Term Intrusions into the Lifestyle Routine", Journal of Psychosomatic Research, 1970, *14*, p. 121-132.

Howard, K.I., Orlinsky, D.E. "Psychotherapeutic Processes", Annual Review of Psychology, 1972, *23*, 615-668.

Hudson, W., and Glisson, D. "Assessment of Marital Discord in Social Work Practice", Social Service Review, Vol. 50, No. 2, 1976, 293-311.

Hunt, M. *The World of the Formerly Married*, N.Y.: McGraw-Hill Book Co., 1966.

Irving, H. *Divorce Mediation*, Toronto: Personal Library Pub., 1980.

Irving, H. *The Family Myth*, Toronto: Copp-Clark, 1971.

Irving, H., and Bohm, P. "A Social Science Approach to Family Dispute Resolution", Canadian Journal of Family Law, 1978, *1* (1), 39-56.

Irving, H.H. et al, *A Comparative Study of the Family Court Services*, Ontario Ministry of the Attorney General, 1979.

Irving, H.H., and Gandy, J. "Family Court Conciliation Project: An Experiment in Support Services", Reports of Family Law, Vol. 25, 1977, 47-53.

Irving, H.H., and Irving, B.G. "Conciliation Counselling in Divorce Litigation", Reports of Family Law, Vol. 16, 1974, 257-266.

Kiesler, D.J. "Experimental Designs in Psychotherapy Research", in A.E. Bergin and S.L. Garfield (eds.), *Handbook of Psychotherapy and Behaviour Change*, N.Y.: Wiley, 1971.

Kressel, K., Deutsch, M., Jaffe, N., Tuchman, B., and Watson, C. "Mediated Negotiation in Divorce and Labor Disputes: A Comparison", Conciliation Courts Review, 1977, *15*(1), 9-12.

Kronby, M.C. *The Guide to Family Law*, Toronto: New Press, 1972.

Krupinski, J., Marshall, E., and Yule, V. "Patterns of Marital Problems in Marriage Guidance Clients", Journal of Marriage and the Family, February 1970.

Ladbrook, Dennis "The Health and Survival of the Divorced", Conciliation Courts Review, Vol. 14, No. 1, September 1976, 21-23.

Lidz, T., *The Family and Human Adaptation.* N.Y.: Inter. Univ. Press, 1963.

Lightman, E.S., and Irving, H.H. "Conciliation and Arbitration in Family Disputes", Conciliation Courts Review, 1976, *14* (2), p. 12-21.

Macklin, E.D. "Nonmarital Heterosexual Cohabitation," Marr. Fam. Rev., 1978, 1(#2), 1-12.

Markus, N. Staff Participation in Organizational Change, Dissertation, University of Toronto.

Martin, P. *Marriage and Marital Therapy*, N.Y.: Brunner/Mazel, Publishers, 1978.

McRae, B.C., and Fish, M.L.R. "Separation and Divorce Counselling in Canada", The Social Worker, 1978, *46* (4), 99-101.

Minahan, A., and Pincus, A. "Conceptual Framework for Social Work Practice", Social Work, 1977, *22* (5), 347-352.

Minuchin, S., Rosman B. and Baker L., *Psycho-somatic Families: Anorexia Nervosa in Context*, Cambridge, Mass., Havard Univ. press, 1978.

Mowrer, E.R. *Domestic Discord Its Analysis and Treatment*, Chicago: University of Chicago Press, 1928.

Nett, E.M. The Changing Form and Functions of the Canadian Family: A Demographic View, in K. Ishwaran (ed.) *The Canadian Family*. Rev. Ed. Toronto: Holt, Rinehart and Winston, 1976.

Nie, N.H., Hull, C.H., Jenkins, J.G., Steinbrenner, K., and Bent, D.H. *Statistical Package for the Social Sciences*, N.Y.: McGraw-Hill, 1975.

Ontario Association of Family Services, Client Satisfaction Survey, Toronto (unpublished manuscript), 1976.

Ontario Legislature "Bill 59, An Act to Reform the Law Respecting Property Rights and Support Obligations Between Married Persons and in Other Family Relationships", 2nd Session, 31st Legislature, 27 Elizabeth II, 1978.

Osgood, C.E., Suci, G.J., and Tannenbaum, P.H. *The Measurement of Meaning,* University of Illinois, 1957.

Paul, G.L. "Strategy of Outcome Research in Psychotherapy", Journal of Consulting Psychology, 1967, 31, 109-118.

Paykel, E.S., Prusoff, B.A., Uhlenhuth, E.H. "Scaling Life Events," Arch. Gen. Psychiat., 1971, 25, 240-247.

Ramey, J. "Experimental Family Forms in the Family of the Future," Marr. Fam. Rev., 1978, 1 (#1), 1-9.

Rubin, J.Z., and Brown, B.R. *The Social Psychology of Bargaining and Negotiation,* New York: Academic Press, 1975.

Shulman, L. *The Helping Process,* University of British Columbia, 1977.

Sigal, J.J., Barrs, C.S., and Doubilet, A.L. "Problems in Measuring the Success of Family Therapy in a Common Clinical Setting: Impasse and Solutions", Family Process, 1976, *15* (2), 225-234.

Skolnick, A.S., and Skolnick, J.H. Introduction, *Family in Transition,* Boston and Toronto: Little, Brown and Company, 1977 ed.

Smith, L.L. *Crisis Intervention Theory and Practice,* Millburn, New Jersey: R.F. Publishing, Inc., 1975.

Sonne, J.C. "On the Question of Compulsory Marriage Counseling as a Part of Divorce Proceedings", Family Coordinator, 1974, Vol. 23, 303-305.

Spanier, G.B. "Measuring Dyadic Adjustment", Journal of Marriage and the Family, 1976 February *38* (1), 15-25.

Staff Report, Toronto Project of the Provincial Court (Family Division) 1980.

Stapleford, J. and Bell, N., *Marital Separation Counselling and the Uncoupling Process,* Toronto: Family Service Assoc. of Toronto, 1980.

Statistics Canada, Population: Demographic Characteristics, Marital Status, 1976, Census of Canada, Ministry of Industry, Trade and Commerce: Ottawa, 1978, 1-17.

Statistics Canada, *Vital Statistics, Volume II, Marriages and Divorces, 1975,* Ottawa: Statistics Canada Health Division, Published by authority of the Minister of Industry, Trade and Commerce, 1977.

Weiss, R.S. *Marital Separation,* N.Y.: Basic Books, Inc., Publishers, 1975.

Weiss, R.S. "The Emotional Impact of Marital Separation", The Journal of Social Issues, 1976, Vol. 32, No. 1, 135-146.

Weiss, W.W., and Collada, H.B. "Conciliation Counselling: The Court's Effective Mechanism for Resolving Visitation and Custody Disputes", The Family Coordinator, 1977, *26* (4), 444-447.

Wheeler, M. *No-Fault Divorce,* Boston: Beacon press, 1974.

---

1 While the initial suggestion that the client couple use the CCS was occasionally made by someone outside the judicial system (*e.g.* a social worker), the couple was not accepted as a referral unless the lawyers representing both spouses agreed that this was an appropriate course of action. In this sense, third party "referrals" involved less than 5% of the study sample.

2 Developed by Osgood *et al.* (1957), the semantic differential is a method for exploring the connotative meaning of concepts.

3 The two items excluded were "easy" vs "hard" and "free" vs "tied down."

4 The index score was computed by summing the scale scores for the 8 items in question and then deriving a mean score, with index scores having a range of 1 to 6. Some items were reverse scored so that higher scale scores reflected greater life satisfaction.

5 The Traditional Intake Service pre-date the establishment of the CCS in 1976. It is primarily concerned with crisis counselling Family Court clients with the aim of helping them use the court appropriately.

6 In less than 10% of cases, this data collection sequence was altered in response to client crisis circumstances.

7 Such a procedure would have constituted a threat to external validity by raising the possibility of comparing quite different groups on pre and post test measures.

8 Statistical significance at the 0.05 level means that there are about 5 chances out of 100 that the observed differences between two group scores is not "real", but simply due to chance variation. Consequently, whenever the derived probability is less than 0.05 (written $p < .05$), the two groups being compared are probably different in terms of the variable(s) in question.

9 The students in question were Karen Kutner, Bayla Cheskes, Randi Davies, Edith Reiman and Lori Hoffman.

10 The students in question were Birgit Fraser, Heather Lisner-Kerbel, Tom MacNeil, Kathryn Munro, Kitty Soni and Susan Stern.

11 Client couples had been coping with their problem(s) for 5.9 years, on average, before coming to the CCS.

12 On average, $6,000 per year for all women and $13,000 per year for all men.

13 Clients were asked to rate where they placed their present life circumstances on a 6 point scale.

14 Clients were asked to rate their "Degree of Satisfaction" with their present marriage (e.g. "I feel that my spouse treats me badly.").

15 Of these, the first session was typically devoted to the collection of research data. Client couples had 5.1 interviews on average.

16 This is intended to indicate that couples return to court because their case was delayed, remanded or was pending.

17 Out of 90 client couples in Study 2 with respect to whom a complete data set was available, only 18 (20%) reported having four or more problems rated "serious" or "very serious". This compares to 53 (50%) CCS clients in Study 1.

18 For a series of recommendations concerning the means by which this might be accomplished, see Irving (1980: 191-192).

19 From Irving Divorce Mediation (1980: 191, 192).

Joint Custody of Children
Following Divorce

H. Jay Folberg*
and
Marva Graham**

The topic of joint custody has provoked both skepticism and praise, but little legal analysis. This article analyzes the law of joint custody as well as its history, terminology and use. The expressed concerns of attorneys, judges, and others are critically examined before suggesting broad criteria for joint custody and advocating that it be decreed more often.

INTRODUCTION

Increasing numbers of parents are attempting to continue their joint role as parents following divorce by exercising joint custody over their children.[1] The subject has received considerable attention in the press[2] in social science journals,[3] and to a lesser extent, in legal publications.[4] There are several new popular books advocating joint custody[5] and counseling workshops and interdisciplinary conferences now frequently address the topic.[6] Three states have recently passed legislation that explicitly recognizes joint custody.[7] Additional states are considering bills supporting the concept of joint custody.[8]

Nevertheless, there is significant opposition to joint custody among members of the legal profession. Attorneys may rebuff clients who wish to try joint custody, and judges often refuse to award it.[9] This opposition ignores research findings documenting the importance of post-divorce cooperation and involvement of both parents. There is also evidence that

---

*   Professor of Law, The Lewis and Clark Law School. B.A. 1963, San Francisco State College; J.D. 1968, University of California, Berkeley.
** Third year law student, The Lewis and Clark Law School. B.A. 1956, Lewis and Clark College; M.A.T. 1963, Reed College.
*** Initially published in Vol. 12, No. 2. University of California Davis Law Review and included in this publication with the permission of The Regents of the University of California which owns the copyright in this article and to whom any request for the use of this material must be directed.

sole custody awards often result in substantial problems for children, parents and the legal system. Joint custody, however, is an issue attorneys and judges will have to face with increasing frequency.

CUSTODY TERMS

Both the forms of custody following divorce and the terms which describe them are vague and overlapping. The lack of standard definitions and the courts' tendency to use certain terms interchangeably[10] have created confusion. Legal periodicals reporting custody cases at times have augmented the confusion by categorizing a case in one area of custody with headlines applicable to another category.[11] Because of this lack of definitional clarity, arguments that might validly be advanced against one form of custody are sometimes used to discourage a different custody form. This article, therefore, discusses and defines at the outset common custody arrangements and indicates judicial attitudes toward each form. The four forms of custody discussed here are sole custody, divided custody, split custody, and joint custody.

(a) Sole custody

The most commonly approved form of custody upon dissolution is an award of sole custody to one parent with visitation rights to the non-custodial parent.[12] The non-custodian, by informal agreement, may have a voice in important decisions affecting the child, but ultimate control and legal responsibility rest with the custodial parent.[13]

(b) Divided custody

Divided custody allows each parent to have the child for a part of the year. This form of custody may also be referred to as alternating custody. Each parent has reciprocal visitation rights under this arrangement, and each exercises control over the child while the child resides in his or her custody.[14]

Although courts routinely divided custody upon parental request until the beginning of the twentieth century, divided custody has generally been disapproved in this century.[15] Courts have based their disapproval primarily on the theory that shifting a child from home to home results in no real home, no stable environment and no permanent associations for the child.[16] Courts also disapprove of divided custody because they believe that it creates confusion for the child as to who has authority, which leads to disciplinary problems.[17]

Despite the generally negative attitude toward divided custody, appellate courts have upheld such awards when the facts of a particular case have warranted a division of custody.[18] Courts sometimes have found the disadvantages of divided custody did not outweigh the child's right to the love and affection of both parents.[19] Courts most often award divided custody which provides for residence with one parent during the school year and the other during vacations.[20] When parents' homes are widely separated, making frequent visits impractical, courts have sometimes approved divided custody.[21] On the other hand, some courts have justified divided custody on grounds that both parents live in the same area. In these cases, the courts view the proximity as minimizing the strains that divided custody might place on the children.[22]

The ages of the children have also influenced the courts. Courts generally maintain that young children are best left in the sole custody of one parent.[23] When parents are able to agree to divide custody, however, and the agreement is incorporated into the divorce decree, an appellate court may refuse to modify custody if there is evidence that the young child is enjoying good health, making good progress, and benefiting from a continuing relationship with both parents.[24]

There is no clear line between "sole" custody with liberal visitation rights and "divided" custody.[25] Courts unwilling to countenance divided custody may reconcile the goal of stability for the child with the goal of association with both parents by upholding a non-custodial parent's right to extensive visitation.[26] Thus, in some cases, the only significant difference between two forms of custody may be the labels placed on them.

(c) Split custody

Yet another custody form is to award custody of one or more of the children to one parent and the remaining children to the other.[27] The policy of the law has generally been to keep siblings together because "A family unit is struck a vital blow when parents divorce; it is struck an additional one when children are separated from each other."[28] Courts, therefore, refuse to grant split custody absent compelling reasons.

(d) Joint custody

Finally, courts can award custody to the parents jointly.[29] The term "joint custody" as used here goes beyond the concept of "divided custody," although the terms are sometimes used interchangeably.[30] Joint custody is also referred to as joint parenting, co-custody, shared custody, or co-parenting.[31] Its distinguishing feature is that both parents retain legal responsibility and authority for the care and control of the child, much as in an intact family.[32] While in divided custody only the parent with physical custody retains these incidents, "joint custody" upon divorce is defined as an arrangement in which both parties have equal rights and responsibilities to the minor child and neither party's rights are superior."[33] In New York, where the concept of joint custody has been more extensively developed by case law than in other states,[34] a trial court stated that "joint custody means giving to both parents an equal voice in the children's education, upbringing and general welfare."[35]

Disagreement exists among writers as to the proportionate time arrangement required for joint custody. Some writers have suggested that the term "joint custody" should be reserved for near equal time arrangements,[36] others have pointed to the flexibility that joint custody allows as one of its strongest attributes.[37] Other authors view the distinguishing trait of joint custody as allowing each parent to interact with his or her child in everyday situations rather than "visit" them.[38] In some states, notably California, courts have frequently awarded joint legal custody to both parents but specifically assign physical custody to one parent.[39] The courts have been inclined in such cases to consider the parent who has physical custody as the "true" custodian of the child or children.[40]

HISTORICAL PERSPECTIVE

A review of the history of custody decisions illustrates how the law concerning custody has changed to accommodate the needs of the day.[41] New theories of child development and changing family structures have led courts to reexamine their custody preferences.[42] This historical review is necessary to better understand why the curent judicial bias against joint custody is ripe for scrutiny and change.

In England, the common law regarded children as their father's property.[43] The presumption that the father was "the person entitled by law to the custody of his child" was irrefutable.[44] The English rule of paternal preference does not appear to have been so strictly applied in nineteenth-century America.[45]

The dramatic social and economic upheavals of the nineteenth century reshaped the dynamics of the family. Industrialization changed a rural, agrarian society into an urban society. Accompanying the transition to wage labor was a separation of the home and work place which placed fathers in factories and plants, while mothers generally remained at home as the primary nurturers of the children.[46] The specialization of parental function that the industrial revolution fostered helped create the concept of the nuclear family as the foundation of society.[47]

The nineteenth century also saw significant changes in the status of women and children. The early women's rights movement brought women enfranchisement, greater political power and laws granting women rights to own property rather than be property. Concurrently, the nineteenth century brought changes in the attitude of society towards children.[48]

Society's acceptance of child development theories that viewed children as evolving human beings led to placing a higher value on the importance of maternal care, which undermined the paternal custody assumption.[49]

Consequently, the common law preference for fathers in custody disputes gave way to a preference for mothers as custodians, particularly of young children.[50] Most state courts, at one time or another, adopted a judicial presumption favoring mothers as custodians of their children.[51] Although early cases extolled the father-child relationship[52] the pendulum's swing in favor of mothers elicited even more lyrical extremes of judicial bias.[53]

Judges also began to speak of the child's needs as the paramount consideration in awarding custody. The resulting best interests "test" was not so much a fixed formula as it was a general approach to custody decisions.[54] The "best interests of the child" has become the cornerstone of most state custody statutes.[55]

Later case law[56] and more recently state statutes[57] sought to define the best interests approach by listing specific factors courts should consider in awarding custody. Although many statutes may direct that the factors be given equal weight,[58] courts appear to give their greatest attention to the child's need for stability and continuity of relationships and environment.[59] The interpretation of "stability and continuity" attributed to the influential book *Beyond The Best Interests Of The Child*[60] slowed acceptance of alternative forms of custody.[61]

Just as the early women's right movement influenced family structure and custody considerations, the contemporary equal rights movement has again altered the balance. The movement's emphasis on equality in the marketplace, greater independence for women to pursue professional goals and less sexual stereotyping has led to greater participation by fathers in the parenting function in intact families.[62] With fathers more likely to have been involved in the day-to-day care of their children,[63] there is less reason to assume that, upon divorce, an award of custody to the mother will give the child greater "continuity and stability" than an award to the father.

While early research on child development stressed the maternal role, recent research has emphasized the importance of the role that fathers play in their children's development.[64] In the past courts usually granted an award of custody to the father only on a showing that the mother was unfit.[65] More recently, courts have indicated a willingness to award custody to fathers when the facts of the case appear to make such an award appropriate.[66]

Fathers, perhaps encouraged by what they perceive as a more friendly judicial climate, are seeking custody in greater numbers.[67] They are also challenging the constitutionality of the tender years presumption[68] and other perceived obstacles to fair judicial treatment in custody decisions.[69]

Fathers are uniting to support each other's custody battles and to press for legislative changes.[70]

Convenient presumptions, first for the father, then for the mother, are no longer available as a short cut to a court in arriving at the most appropriate custody determination. When parents disagree about custody, judges are now in the perplexing bind of trying to predict, with limited information and no existing consensus, which of two fit parents would best guide a child toward adulthood.[71]

There is scant data available documenting the effect of divorce on children,[72] and existing psychological theories are not reliable for purposes of prediction.[73] Longitudinal research on the empirical effects of different custody patterns is sadly rudimentary and provides few predictative tools,[74] with one notable exception: *researchers are finding that the key variable affecting satisfactory adjustment of children following divorce is the extent of continuing involvement by both parents in child rearing.*[75] *Similarly, divorces having the least detrimental effect on the normal development of children are those in which the parents are able to cooperate in their continuing parental roles.*[76] One researcher states the point more affirmatively: if parental cooperation can be freed from the marital tension that may have adversely effected the child, then the divorce may present a positive developmental influence.[77]

Parental cooperation can not easily ordered or decreed, but it can be judicially encouraged and endorsed.[78] "Winner take all" custody decisions tend to exacerbate paental differences[79] and cause predictable post divorce disputes as parents try to strike back and get the last word.[80] Judges,[81] attorneys,[82] and legal scholars[83] are recognizing that parents themselves can best decide the most appropriate arrangement for the care and custody of their children upon divorce. Court connected counseling,[84] mediation,[85] and arbitration[86] are increasingly available to help families make their own decisions about child custody.

JOINT CUSTODY AND CONTROL DURING MARRIAGE

The least disruptive custody arrangement following divorce is likely to be the one most resembling the custody and control exercised before divorce. Custody and control between parents during marriage has received little judicial scrutiny because courts and legislatures have been reluctant to intercede in such matters during marriage.[87] Traditionally the intact family has been viewed as a self-governing unit,[88] with parental rights and obligations vested primarily in the father.[89] The modern statutory trend has been to equalize parental rights. Today in the intact family the father and mother generally have joint and equal rights to the custody, care, and services of their children.[90]

Parental "custody" during marriage is seldom defined in statutes or cases.[91] Where it is defined, it embraces a bundle of rights and obligations.[92] The parents have an obligation to protect and care for their children,[93] to control and discipline their children[94] to provide necessary medical care,[95] and to make decisions regarding the education and religious training of their children.[96] The authority and responsibility regarding children are generally not differentiated between the parents.[97] Although fathers were primarily responsible for supporting children at common law, modern case law and statutes have tended to make the parental support obligation joint and several.[97.1] Reciprocally, the parents jointly have a right to share the childrens' services and earning.[98] These rights are not unrestricted. The state will intervene in the affairs of an intact family unit to protect the children's welfare.[99] This state power is explained as stemming from the Crown's prerogative as *parens patriae* to protect subjects unable to protect themselves.[100]

JOINT CUSTODY FOLLOWING DIVORCE

When a marriage ends, the courts in all states have the task of determining the future care and custody of any minor children.[101] At this point, they must sort out and assign the bundle of parental rights and obligations that have probably been undifferentiated in the intact family.[102] The belief that a court must award custody to one of two fit parents complicates the task.[103] In most states the mother and father, by statute, are equal contenders for custody of their children.[104] Even though the parent awarded "custody" usually has less than the full bundle of rights that existed in the intact family,[105] the non-custodial parent generally ceases to have authority to make significant decisions or to engage in long-range planning for the children.[106] The non-custodial parent retains authority over day-to-day decisions made during visitation periods while the children are in that parent's possession.[107]

(a) De facto joint custody

Following divorce, some parents informally agree to share their parental responsibility much as they did prior to divorce. Often this *de facto* joint custody comes as a gradual development.[108] The parents may then ask the court to give legal sanction to the ongoing arrangement. A circuit court judge in Oregon summed up what must be a common judicial experience:

> We have had joint custody, I think, forever. Not because the Court thinks it is necessary to decree joint custody, but because parents went ahead despite what the decree said and did what was best ... I've had a number of cases in court where they wanted a final stamp of approval, but for a number of years

they had gone ahead and done what was best for the children and the best thing for themselves without paying too much attention to what the Court decree said.[109]

(b) Stipulated joint custody

Joint custody is most often decreed when the parents present an executed separation agreement to the court for approval and include within their agreement a plan for joint parenting.[110] Just as there are no statistics on the number of families operating under some sort of *de facto* joint custody arrangement, there are no published statistics on the incidence of joint custody decrees. The number of reported appellate cases involving joint custody is not an accurate indicator of the incidence of joint custody decrees because the reported cases generally only arise from the litigation of continuing disagreements — the antithesis of cooperative parenting. One noted legal commentator indicates that joint custody currently constitutes a small minority of court approved custody arrangements but states that courts are under pressure from parents to permit "joint legal and physical custody, and they are awarding joint custody in a somewhat larger number of cases."[111] In a review of 1,922 divorce cases in San Diego, California, 72 couples (less than 4%) were listed in the court records as having been awarded joint custody.[112] A recent survey in Portland, Oregon, where joint custody is recognized by statute, also found a 4% incident of joint custody.[113] Despite this evidence that joint custody decrees are rare, Harriet Whitman Lee, who worked with the Consumer Group Legal Services in Berkeley, California, estimated that "more than half of the divorcing couples who come in . . . ask for joint custody these days."[114] Current statistical information on custody arrangements cannot document the number of joint custodial families, but the number is increasing as information about this custody alternative becomes more wide-spread,[115] and as court-connected counseling becomes more readily available.[116]

(c) Court ordered joint custody

In addition to *de facto* joint custody and to joint custody granted pursuant to a separation agreement, courts have occasionally awarded joint custody when neither party,[117] or only one party,[118] has requested it. Court ordered joint custody, however, is controversial. In *Braiman v. Braiman* Chief Judge Breitel of the Court of Appeals of New York made these comments about court ordered joint custody: "It is understandable . . . that joint custody is encouraged primarily as a voluntary alternative for relatively stable, amicable parents behaving in a mature civilized fashion . . . As a court-ordered arrangement imposed upon already embattled and embittered parents, accusing one another of serious vices and wrongs, it can only enhance familial chaos."[119]

Yet, in at least one Michigan case, a court accepted the recommendation of the children's court appointed attorney to award joint custody, although neither parent had requested it.[120] The decision was based on the court's finding that neither parent alone was a sufficient parent. This case, thus, runs counter to the general prerequisite that before considering joint custody there must be a determination that both parents are fit.[121]

No state statutes specifically prohibit joint custody[122] but advocates perceive a need for a clear expression of public policy on joint custody. Legislative proposals have run the gamut from simply recognizing the legality of joint custody orders, to creating a strong presumption favoring joint custody.[123] To date, no state has gone beyond a simple recognition of the court's authority to decree joint custody.

JOINT CUSTODY STATUTES*

(a) Oregon

Some Oregon courts had been awarding joint custody prior to the passage in 1977 of legislation explicitly authorizing such action. These courts apparently found authority for these decrees within the wording of the then-existing post-dissolution custody statute.[124] Support to amend the statutes to explicitly recognize joint custody came from parents who had *de facto* joint custody and feared court disapproval, from fathers who felt that despite the supposed equality extended them in the custody statutes courts continued to favor mothers in custody awards, and from professionals who felt that joint custody should be clearly available in appropriate post-dissolution situations.[125]

Two bills providing for joint custody were introduced in Oregon; one in the House of Representatives and one in the Senate.[126] The House bill, the stronger of the two measures, was tabled.[127] The Senate bill that became law, unlike the tabled House version, does not expressly encourage joint custody, nor does it set forth criteria for awarding it. It simply states that the court has the power to decree for the "future care and custody of the minor children of the marriage *by one party or jointly* as it may deem just and proper."[128] The statute does not specifically define joint custody.

---

* Following submission of this article, California Senate Bill 477 was signed by Governor Brown on July 3 and became effective January 1, 1980. The bill, referred to in notes 175, 304, 329, 334 *infra* and elsewhere, amends § 4600 of the California Civil Code and adds a new section to create a conditional presumption in favor of joint custody. In addition, it authorizes joint custody on a discretionary basis in other circumstances and provides items to be considered in the modification of a joint custody decree. The California legislature specifically declared in the bill "that it is the public policy of this state to assure minor children of close and continuing contact with both parents after the parents have separated or dissolved their marriage."

(b)   Wisconsin

Wisconsin's new joint custody statute became effective on February 1, 1978. Unlike the Oregon statute, it offers a definition of joint custody. The definition adopts a joint custodial rights and responsibilities concept, stating: "... Joint custody under this paragraph means that both parties have equal rights and responsibilities to the minor child and neither party's rights are superior."[129]

Prior to the passage of this bill, some Wisconsin judges and family court commissioners had read Wisconsin's custody statute as permitting joint custody, while others had found joint custody precluded.[130] The resulting inconsistencies in decisions among and within the counties led drafters to introduce a clarifying amendment.[131] As in the Oregon experience, part of the push for the legislation in Wisconsin came from the "grass roots."[132] A Family Court Counselor was quoted as saying that divorcing couples had become more assertive in seeking control over the custody determination and that "more parents were seeking joint custody in various forms, and they were facing discouragement from their lawyers, judges, family court commissioners and marriage counselors."[133]

(c)   Iowa and other states

Iowa also amended its post-divorce custody statute to authorize an award of joint custody where justified in 1977. The statute now reads:

> When a dissolution of marriage is decreed, the court may make such order in relation to the children, property, parties, and the maintenance of the parties as shall be justified. The order may include provision for joint custody of the children by the parties.[134]

Other states with post-divorce custody statutes that expressly accommodate joint custody include North Carolina and Maine.[135]

JOINT CUSTODY CASE LAW

The question of whether a particular state statute provides authority for an award of custody jointly or whether the court must select from between two fit competing parents usually depends on the court's interpretation of general statutory custody language. Few reported cases contain discussions of the propriety of joint custody awards under typical custody statutes. But in a recent New Jersey case, the court specifically addressed the question of whether the New Jersey post-divorce custody statute gave the court authority to order joint custody. The New Jersey statute provides that:

> [T]he court may make such order as to the alimony or maintenance of the wife, and also as to the care, custody, education and maintenance of the

children, or any of them, as the circumstances of the parties and the nature of the case shall render fit, reasonable and just. . . .[136]

In finding that this statute contained authority for joint custody, the court stated:

> Clearly, this legislative grant of authority would include the authority to order "joint", "divided" or "split" custody. Assuming, therefore, that the circumstances of the parties and the nature of the case render an award of joint custody, "fit, reasonable and just," there is no reason why such an order should not be entered.[137]

In New York the statute does not expressly provide for joint custody. It merely provides that the divorce court "must give ... direction, between the parties, for the custody ... of any child of the parties, as ... justice requires, having regard to the circumstances of the case and of the respective parties and to the best interests of the child."[138] New York courts have not hesitated to infer from this language the power to give custody jointly to both parents where appropriate. As one judge reasoned, "[t]his court has the power to award custody to either parent, and so can give such custody jointly to both parents."[139]

Missouri appellate courts, on the other hand, have held that Missouri's seemingly broader statute precludes joint custody. There the statutes direct that upon dissolution of a marriage:

> The court shall determine custody in accordance with the best interests of the child. The court shall consider all relevant factors including: (1) The wishes of the child's parents as to his custody; (2) The wishes of a child as to his custodian; (3) The interaction and interrelationship of the child with his parents, his siblings, and any other person who may significantly affect the child's best interests; (4) The child's adjustment to his home, school, and community; and (5) The mental and physical health of all individuals involved.[140]

The court said that a 1949 Missouri case's statement that "In the very nature of things general custody must be awarded to one parent as against the other ..."[141] correctly interpreted Missouri's custody laws.[142]

The research of Foster and Freed, indicates that "it is only in a minority of states that one finds decisions or rules which are prejudicial to the viable alternative of joint custody ..."[143] One of the minority states is Vermont. In a recent Vermont Supreme Court decision, the court established a presumption that joint custody is against the best interests of the child. A finding of special circumstances indicating that such an award would be in the child's best interest is necessary to overcome this presumption.[144]

ATTITUDE OF ATTORNEYS, JUDGES AND BEHAVIORAL EXPERTS

Increased use of joint custody is inhibited not only by a lack of clear statutory authority and by some negative precedent in case law, but by a prevailing attitude of pessimism about its use by the professionals divorcing parents encounter. Parents who have sought joint custody have encountered attorneys with a negative attitude about joint custody, even when the couple has agreed on the custody issue.[145] One parent reported:

> My former husband and I waged a more difficult battle with the lawyers than we did with one another; they wanted one or the other parent named as custodian.[146]

In one popular handbook directed to parents contemplating or experiencing divorce, the attorney authors make the following statements against joint or divided custody:

> Particularly for younger children, the instability of this sort of arrangement is bound to be upsetting. In early development, psychologists are agreed, routine has an important emotional function in a child's growth. The repeated uprooting from friends and schools is another source of disturbance. For a child faced with a situation that is already bewildering, this pillar-to-post life can be nothing more than an additional and possibly overwhelming burden.[147]

A "Shared-Custody Primer" recently printed in New West magazine warns fathers to "Interview prospective attorneys as to their views on shared custody before offering a retainer. Be prepared for opposition and even scorn."[148]

Perhaps one reason for the negative attitude of attorneys is their recognition that many judges frown on joint custody awards. Materials distributed at an orientation workshop for new judges sponsored by the Oregon Judicial College included the following admonition — even though the Oregon Legislature had recently passed legislation making the alternative of joint custody an express part of the law:[149]

> Joint custody is an abomination to the Court, a nightmare to the children and a fruitful source of subsequent controversy.[150]

In a case before the Oregon Court of Appeals that did not directly concern joint custody, a comment in the dissent shows that the same arguments advanced against divided custody tend to be used against joint custody:

> Joint custody is the least attractive alternative facing a court. It succeeds in dividing not only the legal responsibilities but also the practical aspects of child rearing and shifts the parental role in the eyes of the children on a constant basis.[151]

A dissenting judge in an earlier Washington case expressed a similar attitude toward joint custody:

> I cannot agree with the majority that the custody should be awarded jointly to the parents. It has been my experience as a trial judge that joint custody does not bring satisfactory results. Divided responsibility ends too often in constant bickering between the parents, each trying to exert authority — all to the detriment of the children.[152]

One explanation offered to explain the hostility of some judges toward joint custody is that successful joint parenting is not visible to those involved in litigating contested cases.[153] Judges encounter only the failures of joint custody and perhaps extrapolate from that experience a pessimistic view of its possibilities.[154]

Considerable disparity exists in behavioral experts' attitudes toward joint custody. Professor Foster and Dr. Freed caution that joint custody has received its most serious setback, not from attorneys or courts, but from behavioral experts.[155] The initial task for proponents of joint custody, state Foster and Freed, is to overcome the professional bias of child behavior experts.[156] Perhaps typically, the "experts" are not in agreement. The most ardent supporters of joint custody are, themselves, behavioral scientists.[157] Other behavioralists and mental health professionals are skeptical and believe joint custody will create unresolved adjustment difficulties for children and may represent an unhealthy continuing relation between the parents.[158]

These behavorial experts, however, have been quick to label as "unhealthy" any deviation from that which has been regarded as normal or that which is considered novel.[159] Thomas Szasz, the noted iconoclastic psychiatrist, has stated that "the characteristic tendency of modern society is to brand as sick that which is merely unconventional."[160] There may be a tendency to shame people into abiding by conventional norms in divorce by suggesting anything to the contrary is a barometer of emotional disturbance.[161] However, some authors in the mental health profession have noted this suggestion is a fallacy and counter that parents can better fulfill their roles toward children if "freed from conjugal misery."[162] Moreover, "a child's relationship with his or her parents ... does not depend on the parents' marital status."[163]

ANALYSES OF JOINT CUSTODY CONCERNS

Those opposed to joint custody raise many questions concerning the viability of such arrangements. Many of these apprehensions, however, merely reflect distrust of the unfamiliar. Examination of these concerns reveals that the feared disadvantages of joint custody are generally unfounded or no worse than the disadvantages of other forms of custody.

(a) Can parents cooperate after divorce?

The adversary nature of fault divorce helped ensure that parents would be pitted against one another and that the only surviving relationship between them would be one of animosity, if not hatred. All but a few states have now recognized the futility of requiring a finding of fault for divorce and have enacted some form of "no-fault" divorce reform to help reduce the scars left by an adversary contest.[164] To the extent that divorce laws and procedures still impose an adversary model on the parents in matters of custody, they create a self-fulfilling prophecy which ensures that divorced parents cannot cooperate together. One noted family law attorney summed up this frequently heard concern: "It's asking a lot to expect two people who could not get along in marriage to suddenly share decision making for a child's education, religion and every day activities."[165] Perhaps too often we assume that divorcing people will not be able to agree and cast divorcing parents in the role of enemies.[166]

In arguing for joint custody as a way around this "custody trap," June and William Nobel conclude,

> [I]f custodial care were to be considered a joint responsibility in divorce, as it is in marriage, there would be less opportunity for enmity to replace cooperation. ... Arguments about child upbringing, financial needs, and the like go on in virtually every marriage, normal or otherwise. These arguments do not have to become more shrill upon separation. In fact, removing the irritating factor of two unloving people living together can probably make them both more responsive to the needs of the children.[167]

Mel Roman and William Haddad, authors of *The Disposable Parent,* concluded that joint custody may work to minimize parental conflict. They explain that because a joint custody arrangement can meet each parent's needs more completely, rancor diminishes.[168] Another writer reaches much the same conclusion, stating that once the pressures of the day to day marriage relationship are eliminated, the possibility of being a successful parent increases.[169]

Although there has been a frequent suggestion that joint custody can work only for couples with an amicable relationship, the pertinent inquiry should be whether the parents are able to isolate their marital conflicts from their role as parents.[170] There is increasing evidence that a couple which makes a commitment to share custody of their children is able to cooperate even though they do not like each other. In researching for her book, *The Custody Handbook,* Persia Woolley talked with parents who are co-parenting. She found that "although many sharing parents became friends after they had been sharing for a while, many others did not ... It is not necessary to like each other as people even though they trust each other as parents."[171] In studying fathers who have joint custody, another researcher found that many of the fathers had hostile relationships with their ex-wives and avoided seeing them for long periods of time, using the child's school as the drop-off point for scheduled exchanges. But despite the hostilities, the fathers reported that they had been able to separate out their marital problems from their role as parents.[172]

Some have suggested that joint custody makes cooperation between parents possible because it eliminates the need for and the likelihood of power plays between them. Rather than a one-sided decision that places power in the sole custodian and creates in the imbalance a need to strike back, recognition of the equal rights of the parents "discourages power plays, use of strategy, and neutralizes the power of the custodial parent."[173] With the power more equally divided, the possibility of using the children as pawns decreases.[174]

An award of joint custody may create an additional incentive for parental cooperation. The Director of the Conciliation Court of Los Angeles County, Hugh McIsaac, is of the opinion that an award of joint custody makes the motivation for cooperation greater because a breakdown of the arrangement will likely result in an award of sole custody to the parent who did not precipitate the failure.[175] Perhaps the best evidence that divorced parents can share parenting is found in statements made by parents with joint custody arrangements. Their statements demonstrate that the high priority they place on their continuing involvement in their child's life has made it mandatory to find a way to work together.[176]

Even if parents can cooperate following divorce, there is an expressed concern, particularly among mental health professionals, that joint custody is requested by parents who are not yet ready to fully dissolve their relationship and are unable "to separate in a healthy way."[177] This concern may be lying in wait for would be joint custody parents who escape the doubts of those who believe divorced parents can not cooperate, only to be told that their desire to cooperate as parents cloaks an underlying need to perpetuate their marital relationship. Perhaps for some, joint custody is but a way station enroute to some other arrangement.[178] However, in studying the relationship that exists between divorced parents who are participating jointly in raising their children, one research concluded that the parents studied had the ability "to continue a co-parenting relationship while terminating, both legally and emotionally, a spousal relationship."[179]

Patterns of parental relationships following divorce are undergoing significant change.[180] Divorce research in the 1950's and 1960's treated divorce as a singular event that destroyed the family and resulted in a "broken" or "single-parent home."[181] A new concept of the post-divorce family is emerging that views divorce not as a single event but as a crisis in the life cycle or process of a family that requires a rearrangement of the interdependent relationships.[182] As one writer put it, "Divorce does not end relationships in post-divorce families it changes them."[183] Another author observes that "the very decision of divorce may be a family's way of trying to salvage the family by putting the pieces together in different ways."[184] Of the many possible family patterns that can emerge after divorce, one is the establishment of a maternal and a paternal household still connected by the bonds of the parents to the children and the children to the parents.[185]

(b) Should only the "Best Interests of the Child" be considered?

The dominant legal doctrine that custody will be awarded in the best interest of the child[186] has tended to focus attention on the child without acknowledging the implicit fact that the child's best interest is interdependent with and to a large measure a by-product of the best interest of all family members.

(i) Mothers

Although researches have rarely systematically studied the impact of divorce on adults,[187] what information there is tends to show that most post-divorce mothers with sole custody feel their children overburden and imprison them.[188] Further, there is evidence that mothers with sole custody become emotionally and physically exhausted,[189] as well as socially isolated.[190] It is not surprising then that in a study of joint custody parents, the mothers reported that the greatest advantage they saw in joint custody was the sharing of responsibility for the children.[191]

The mother with sole custody not only has the primary responsibility for the children, but most likely finds it necessary to supplement spousal support and child support by working outside the home.[192] Often she must either return to school to upgrade her skills or settle for a low-paying unskilled job. Freedom from continuous parental responsibility makes it more likely that she will be able to reach a point of self-sufficiency that is personally satisfying. Further, public policy may mandate such self-sufficiency.[193]

Even though a mother may feel that she does not want the sole responsibility for a child after divorce, she may hesitate to divulge this "selfishness" and "unnaturalness."[194] Most strongly stated, "in our society, not to want to be a mother is to be a freak, and not to be a blissful mother is to be a witch."[195] Although society's attitude may be changing, the potential social and psychological consequences to a mother who is not prepared to fight for the custody of her children are ominous.[196] The notion remains strong that if a woman is not given sole custody of the children, there must be something radically wrong with her.[197]

Yet not all mothers really want custody of their children upon divorce, and more have mixed feelings about custody. An award of joint custody may help assuage the guilt the mother may experience if the children are awarded to the father's sole custody and forestall the negative speculation about the mother that the children would likely learn from those around them. More importantly, it may allow the mother to retain more than "visitor" status and serve to actively involve her in the parenting role.

Something other than an "all or nothing" or "win or lose" alternative may encourage both parents to actively work together in the child's best interests, rather than to fight to protect themselves. It has been observed that "If the mother (or father) didn't feel threatened with loss, each would be in a healthier position for give and take."[198]

(ii) Fathers

If mothers feel "overburdened" following divorce, fathers usually are not sufficiently "burdened". Attention in recent years to the effects of divorce on fathers[199] has exploded the myth that fathers walk away from divorce and from their families unscathed and carefree. In her unpublished doctoral dissertation on Fathers, Children, and Joint Custody, Judith Greif reported that her research showed that after divorce men experienced stress that sometimes caused physical problems, depression, and a severe sense of loss.[200] In the usual pattern, fathers lose wife, home and children, and end up with only visitation rights and support obligations. Some men become so overwhelmed by these difficulties that sooner or later they just give up and stop seeing their children.[201]

Another study of fathers revealed that fathers often continued to have almost as much face-to-face interaction with their children immediately after divorce as fathers in intact homes, but that non-custodial fathers became increasingly less available to their children over a period of time.[202] In explaining why the non-custodial fathers tended to fade out of their children's lives, this study stated that

> ... (Fathers) could not endure the pain of seeing their children only intermittently and by two years after divorce had coped with this stress by seeing their children infrequently although they continued to experience a great sense of loss and depression.[203]

In a panel presentation by joint custody parents one father explained why it had been important to him to have joint custody.

> I think built into the legal system that favors giving custody to the woman, there's a tendency to cause the father to feel that he's not really a father. He's a "good fellow" or a "good friend". There's a tendency to make you walk away. I know I felt this so I'm sure that other men who do not have this right [joint custody] must.[204]

In the same study that reported that women see joint custody's greatest advantage as a sharing of responsibility, the men studied saw the greatest advantage as an "opportunity for the child to maintain contact with both parents."[205] Whereas the artificial structure of "visiting" the children does not foster a normal parental relationship between father and children,[206] to the extent that joint custody allows interaction in normal day-to-day living situations, even fathers who were somewhat uninvolved with their children prior to divorce are able to become "nurturing" parents.[207] Experts in child development often stress the importance of a male as well as a female role model for children in daily activities.[208] Although we have in the past glorified the role of the mother in raising children, there is no psychiatric evidence or longitudinal behavioral studies that establish the superior parenting ability of one sex or the other.[209] As stereotyped sex roles have broken down, fathers have become more involved in rearing their children in intact families, and it is no longer a natural assumption that upon divorce the mother is the only "nurturing" parent, even of very young children.[210]

(c) Do "stability" and "continuity" require custody to only one parent?

The greatest current obstacle to an award of joint custody is the assumption that joint custody will detrimentally affect the child because the child will be "shuttled" between the parents. As previously discussed, joint custody does not necessarily require "shuttling" the child between two homes.[211] This concern, however, is also based on the theory that the kind of attachment to a "psychological parent" that is necessary for the growth of a healthy child cannot be achieved without the certainty and stability that is thought best promoted by complete custody to one parent.[212]

One might ask at the outset why a guideline seeking stability and continuity does not logically imply continuing, as nearly as possible, the same relationship between child and parents that existed before the divorce.[213] Evidence supports the fact that children, who often exhibit an extraordinary measure of common sense, show a great tenacity and desire to continue existing relationships with both parents.[214] Some experts believe that joint custody, by reducing the child's feelings of rejection and abandonment, as well as supplying continued positive role models, is conducive to the child's emotional stability.[215]

The book *Beyond The Best Interests Of The Child* is often cited in support of arguments against joint custody. The eminent authors of that influential work assert that "children have difficulty in relating positively to, profiting from, and maintaining contact with two psychological parents who are not in positive contact with each other."[216] Though the book does not directly address, or even mention, the issue of joint custody, the authors appear to assume that divorced parents can not be in positive contact with each other. They proceed to make that assumption self-fulfilling by recommending that custody be expeditiously and permanently awarded to the parent most likely to be the "psychological parent," without opportunity for modification.[217] They further assert that the child's stability would be best served if the non-custodial parent is stripped of his or her legal rights to the child:

> Thus, the non-custodial parent should have no legally enforceable right to visit the child, and the custodial parent should have the right to decide whether it is desirable for the child to have such visits.[218]

The elimination of the ongoing relationship between the child and one parent is designed, paradoxically, to protect the no more important psychological relationship "between the child and the custodial parent."[219] The authors appear to disclaim responsibility for this radical proposal by, in effect, placing the blame at the feet of the parents for legal consequences far more severe than their actual parenting relationship may justify:

> [T]he state neither makes nor breaks the psychological relationship between the child and the noncustodial parent, which the adults involved may have jeopardized. It leaves to them what only they can ultimately resolve.[220]

This stark treatment afforded the non-custodial parent by Goldstein, Freud and Solnit has been criticized by many, including Professor Henry H. Foster, Jr. who stated:

> In short, at the whim of the custodial parent, all contact with the other parent would be foreclosed. Such a position ignores the child's needs and desires, as well as those of the other parent, and in the name of continuity and autonomy encourages spiteful behavior. Given such power, one can visualize the blackmailing, extortion, and imposition which might be visited upon the non-custodial parent who wants to maintain contact with his or her child.[221]

Rather than fostering cooperation between the parents, the guidelines developed in *Beyond The Best Interests Of The Child* promote a situation where parents are pitted against each other in a "winner take all" battle. A high premium is placed on gaining physical custody at the first available moment so that a history of "continuity" can commence. Vying for control over the child at the earliest stage of separation becomes essential and the parent who maneuvers the child into his or her possession at the time of the custody hearing will have a strong advantage.[222]

The guidelines offered in *Beyond The Best Interests Of The Child* encourage the parents to sever their personal and parental relationship rather than offer emotional support to one another throughout the child-rearing years.[223] This notion may have fit within the earlier concept of divorce as the death of the family, but is irreconcilable with a concept of the post-divorce family as a reorganized, but still interdependent unit. It also contradicts the emerging model of parents divorcing one another without becoming divorced from their children.[224] Many courts now instruct divorcing families that "parents are forever."[225]

Beyond The Best Interests Of The Child equates stability with keeping the child in one environment. In answering the contention that joint custody will destroy stability Dan Molinoff, a joint custody father who has written about his battle for joint custody, stated:

> What sharing parenthood offers is a new, different kind of stability . . . I have spent three years helping to make this type of arrangement work and can attest to the fact that two homes have been far better for our sons than one broken one. I think it is certainly more damaging for a child to have only minimal contact with an absent parent than it is to have two sets of clothes, books and toys.[226]

Those who have studied joint custody families have sought to weigh the advantages for children of two psychological parents against the problems created by two homes in order to answer the persistent question of whether two homes undermine stability. Judith Greif concluded that the concern over the disruption of having two homes was more a concern of others than of joint custody families themselves.[227] Alice Abarbanel observed four shared custody families in California and found that the children felt "at home" in both environments and that the children saw themselves as living in two homes.[228] Her research showed that it had taken the families a period of time to evolve the time schedule that worked best for them and, while each maintained enough flexibility in the schedule to allow the parents to cooperate in covering vacations and sickness, all found a certain predictability and stability in the schedule as a benefit.[229] Abarabanel found that the children of the families studied did in fact have "two psychological parents, not one."[230]

In a Wisconsin study, Nadine Nehls reported that her research results showed there are problems regarding a child's transition between two houses.[231] This problem did not appear, however, to be a by-product of any particular time arrangement and was present where the child lived primarily with one parent, much as in sole custody with visitation rights, as well as where time was more equally split between two homes. She concluded that this area needs further study and joined many others in hoping that research on the effects of different custodial arrangements will be forthcoming to help determine if joint custody is more or less advantageous than sole custody for fathers, mothers and children.[232]

Although having one environment may be an important element for the security of a very young child, other students of child behavior have emphasized that children's needs change at different ages.[233] Joint custody provides a mechanism that allows the parents to adjust living arrangements as the child's needs change. Parents are usually in a better position to know their child's needs than are any outside "experts."[234] If parents have a structure that allows them to admit the need for change and then make their own mutual decisions without jeopardizing their future custodial rights, they and the children can be expected to benefit.[235]

(d) Does joint custody require close geographical contact?

The location of the parents' homes is a frequently mentioned factor to be considered in determining whether an award of joint custody is appropriate.[236] However, it is apparent that the "geographical closeness" required for joint custody is a by-product of a number of factors: age of the children, school arrangements, location of other members of the child's network of supporters (grandparents, cousins, friends), ease and availability of transportation, and the family's financial resources. It may be more accurate to speak in terms of the logistics of joint custody rather than geographical limits.[237]

It was evident in the panel discussion of parents with joint custody arrangements previously cited that parents with joint custody arrangements must be aware of the distance between their residential locations and the effect of moving. Several parents had turned down favorable opportunities to move to other areas in order to stay near the other parent and the children.[238] However, if it is accepted that the major distinguishing characteristic of joint custody is shared responsibility for major decisions effecting the child, including where the child will live, then close geographical location is not essential.[239] Certainly in our mobile society, joint custody agreements might anticipate a more from the vicinity and provide a process for dealing with it.[240] At a minimum, the agreement should acknowledge that any material change of circumstance may require reconsideration, negotiation, mediation, or arbitration of its terms. Failing those, the courts remain available for modification if the change is considered substantial.[241]

The experience of one family, in adjusting their joint custody arrangement to accommodate the 10,000 mile move of the father and son from California to England, is told in a recent magazine article.[242] It illustrates that parents can effectively resolve unanticipated major moves and separations if the best interests of their child is the central consideration within the reality and limitations of their own circumstances. The story also illustrates that the distinguishing feature of joint custody is shared decision making and not geographical proximity.

(e) Can many families afford joint custody?

At the present time joint custody appears to be limited primarily to sophisticated couples who are frequently both professionals.[243] The Nehls study found that joint custody parents tended to be well educated and have relatively high income levels.[244] Nehls speculates that limited access to information about joint custody might explain the correlation between education and income levels and the use of joint custody.[245] One judge has acknowledged that joint custody parents have to have money and that where it has worked, the parties have often been professional people.[246] A family therapist and researcher who has long specialized in the problems of divorcing families and is an advocate of joint custody has observed, however, that no one needs to have a house, a yard and an extra bedroom to be a co-parent. "Those are just accoutrements. It is the childrens' sense of belonging and of territory that makes a home. If you have a sleeping bag rolled up in the closet, that's enough."[247]

It was clear from testimony given at the Oregon Legislative Hearings on joint custody that knowledge of the possibility of using joint custody is not widespread.[248] In fact, one of the express reasons offered for passing new legislation when the legal possibility for joint custody already existed was to increase the group of people who know of and recognize the possibility of using joint custody.[249] As information about joint custody becomes more widely disseminated, one would expect its use to increase throughout all parts of society. Susan Whicher, a Colorado attorney who heads a special American Bar Association committee on joint custody has stated:

> [L]egally it's terrifying for a lot of lawyers and judges, but by the end of the 1980's it will be the rule rather than the exception.[250]

As was discussed earlier in this article, non-custodial parents tend to stop seeing their children after divorce.[251] Support payments from non-custodial parents also are often short lived.[252] Empirical studies place the range of non-compliance with child support orders after only one year following the divorce decree from 62 percent in Wisconsin to 47 percent in Illinois.[253] The same studies report that within one year following divorce no support payments at all were received from ex-husbands in 21 percent of the Illinois cases and 42 percent of the Wisconsin cases. At the conclusion of 10 years following divorce 79 percent of the fathers in Wisconsin had ceased paying any support and 59 percent in the Illinois study had quit.[254] An even higher percentage were not in full compliance but made partial payments.[255]

Children are inevitably the losers when child support is in arrears.[256] A chicken and egg dilemma is often posed as to whether visitation restrictions and a lack of parental cooperation concerning visitation invites non-support,[257] or whether non-support causes opposition to regular visitation. The two areas, each of obvious importance to the children, are inexorably connected.[258]

One of the most positive attributes of joint custody is its potential for avoiding the problem of non-support arising out of bitterness over the custodial decision.[259] Not only does regular contact with the children create an incentive to provide for their needs, but participating in routine activities of feeding, clothing, housing and caring for children realistically brings home to both parents the escalating expenses of rearing them and promotes more flexible attitudes. Additionally, the likely increased contact between co-parents makes each more aware of the financial capabilities of the other and breeds sensitivity to what each can monetarily contribute.[260] Parents who can rely on each other for more than just economic help are more apt to be understanding of the financial pinches that most sometime encounter.[261]

Joint custody thus helps free both parents to pursue educational and financial improvement. If the joint custody arrangement is able to allow the mother (or in some cases the father) to improve earning capacity and is flexible enough to allow them both to work more than do most sole custody arrangements, then both parents may better be able to contribute to the childrens' financial needs.[262] Such mutuality of contribution enhances cooperation, fosters independence and provides the children with greater security as well as a more positive view toward each parent.[263] Joint custody appears to open up the total human and financial resources of both parents for the benefit of their children as well as themselves.

Monetary resources alone, however, do not determine the affordability of joint custody. The traditional pattern of divorce is likely to disrupt the relationships that the child had with the non-custodial parent's side of the family.[264] Although we have focused our attention on the central participants of a divorce, mothers, fathers, and their children, there is a growing recognition that court orders may also cut off grandparents from their grandchildren.[265] Just at a point when a child is faced in most sole custody decisions with the loss of a parent, he also must bear the loss of grandparents and other relatives. Harry M. Fain, President of the American Academy of Matrimonial Lawyers, pointed out that a "grandparent's love can fill the deep, emotional void created in the lives of children whose parents are separated or divorced ... they can connect a child with the deeper roots of his history."[266] Margaret Mead stated it most succinctly: "[e]veryone needs to have access both to grandparents and grandchildren in order to be a full human being."[267]

Visitation time of the non-custodial parent may not reflect the number of children involved. It may be very difficult for a non-custodial parent to fine time alone with any one of the children. But one by-product of co-parenting is that divorced families are better able to arrange schedules so that one child has time alone with each parent.

Some joint custody families find that the children "have more of their parents' individual time and attention than most kids do."[268] When the child is with them they clear the decks for parenting. Joint custodial parents may have fewer actual hours with their children then when the family was intact, but they have noted that the time they have is of a higher quality.[269]

Although the development of the nuclear family has tended to seclude the family from the wider family,[270] in many subcultures "parenting" is not reserved for only mothers and fathers, but an entire network of relatives and friends are called upon to raise the children.[271] Particularly when parents divorce, there is reason not only to preserve the network of friends and relatives that the child has had, but also since the chances are very high that both parents will be working, we should encourage an opening up of the family system to welcome other's help. Joint custody provides a better opportunity for preservation of contact with a greater number of supporters than does sole custody. For this reason, joint custody may in fact be the optimum option upon divorce for the poor as well as the rich.[272]

(f)   Will the reactions of others defeat joint custody?

Society seems to have very set notions about the roles that the participants in a divorce should play. The great American "soap opera," as divorce has been called,[273] also assigns certain role scripts to the family and friends of those who divorce. Not only does joint custody tend to destroy the soap opera aspects of the drama and deprive participants of their opportunity to mourn or console the parties, it may place friends and relatives on stage with no script.

Even if family and friends are willing to give up the old roles, they may have to overcome a feeling that there is something unsavory about divorced people being able to get along well enough to cooperate in the raising of their children. As Margaret Mead stated:

> Among the older generation, there is some feeling that any contact between divorced people somehow smacks of incest; once divorced, they have been declared by law to be sexually inaccessible to each other, and the aura of past sexual relations makes any further relationship incriminating.[274]

Fathers participating in joint custody arrangements may find that their involvement in the daily tasks of child rearing raises questions about their manhood in the minds of some. Daniel Molinoff, who was one of the trail blazers for joint custody fathers, described his experience as follows:

> Most of my relatives and friends also thought I had made the wrong decision. Most of the uncles and aunts, none of whom had been divorced or separated from their children during their marriages, thought Michael and Joel were "better off with their mother." "Mothers take care of children," they said, "not fathers."
>
> My friends didn't like the idea of my having custody either, but for different reasons. Most of the men I knew were angered by what I was doing. The married men, who were not taking as active a part in the upbringing of their children as I was, saw my arrangement as a threat to their marital

tranquility, to the system, to Manhood ... As for the women I knew ... they couldn't understand why I'd want to cook and clean for my children ... other women, including neighborhood mothers and my sons' teachers, considered me the village villain.[275]

Women who are co-parenting, on the other hand, often feel that they are being criticized for not being proper mothers if they are willing to "let" the children's father "have" the children rather than keep the children in their exclusive domain.[276]

Joint custody families may encounter difficulties with schools and teachers. One joint custody parent reported that no matter how carefully she described their shared arrangement, the school continued to cast her alone in the role of the care-taking parent.[277] School notices and communications to parents are often addressed "Dear Mother."[278] School personnel may have difficulty accepting the fact that on certain days they should call the father if the child becomes ill at school.

The mechanics of communicating with the school may be an irritation, but a more substantive problem is that the child may find the subtle influences of the classroom geared to an intact nuclear family model. Not only does the picture of mom, dad, sister, brother, dog and cat prevail in many school books, it may still be the picture in the minds of many teachers. Some children may have difficulty in not fitting this model.[279]

Because joint parenting may be a more complicated and currently unconventional way to raise children after divorce than having the children remain with the mother or father,[280] parents who choose to be co-parents must be prepared to explain their arrangement and enlist the cooperation of their families and the schools, as well as friends, in order to help the arrangement work.[281] Of course, it is often no less easy for children and custodial parents in more traditional divorce arrangements to explain the continual absence of one parent.

(g)   If parents can cooperate, does it matter what the decree says?

The fact that parents have been informally working out what amount to "joint custody" arrangements, probably for as long as the concept of post-divorce custody awards has existed, prompts some to ask, "So what's in a term?" Certainly some of the agitation for joint custody involves a search for status as a legal custodian, as much as a search for a new or different living pattern. Parents, and, in particular, fathers, want legal recognition of their right to participate in their child's life and assurance that the other parent does not have unequal power. Rather than arrive at joint custody by circumventing the court order and accepting a judicially imposed fiction, there is a desire to have the court order match reality. Moreover, a divorce decree is a public document to which children who increasingly want to learn the circumstances of their parents' divorce and their legal relationship to each parent may later refer.[282]

It is indeed curious that judges and attorneys would argue for disregard of a court order[283] or tell people who desire to conform their conduct to the language of the law that what the court pronounces in its decree is without factual consequence. Even the most cooperative of parents sometimes need legal definition of their rights, responsibilities, and the parameters of their parenting relationship. It belies the integrity of our judicial system and the credibility of its pronouncements to expect parents to pretend that a custody decree means something different than what it says. This is particularly true when the court maintains the power of contempt when its decrees are not followed as written.

At times of stress or conflict, parents may also need the incentive of a realistic decree to achieve continuing compliance with the terms of their agreement. Giving one of two "equals," all the legal power contained in a court order stacks the deck against mutual coperation in the face of what might otherwise be minor, but inevitable, parental friction. The decree then serves as a disincentive for continuing accord and mutual accommodation. Fair negotiation during the dynamics of family reorganization requires equal legal power and sanctions. Neither parent should have the right, when both are capable, to "give" or "take" custody at their whim.

Including a provision for joint custody in the decree not only gives legal recognition to the equal-status of the parents, but also provides a standard of expected behavior to guide the parents following divorce. Carol Bruch, writing about her intriguing proposal for "dual parenting orders", first develops the importance to the child and to the parents of continuing involvement and then emphasizes the role that court orders can effectively play in shaping patterns of behavior.[284]

Perhaps it is a question of whether our legal system should encourage parents to attempt to work within the system with its civil safeguards and dignity, or outside of it by their own devices. Requiring parents who are given no choice but to utilize the courts to dissolve their marriage and fix their custody rights and obligations to arrange their relationship contrary to the courts written pronouncements because its forms and conventions do not meet the reality of their situation and needs is a classic case of the tail wagging the dog.[285]

Finally, formal custody decrees are necessary because private agreements concerning custody and child support which contradict a decree are of questionable validity and are not likely to be enforced if not approved or incorporated by the court.[286] Unilateral decisions which violate the parties' private joint custody agreement cannot be prevented if the decree provides for custody to one parent. A father with informal joint custody, for example, does not ordinarily have any right to make decisions regarding his child's education.[287] The reluctance of some courts to prevent custodial parents from moving out of state with the child may leave a non-custodial parent with a non-decreed joint custody arrangement powerless to prevent the child from being permanently removed from the home jurisdiction.[288]

Joint custody will normally require different support and financial obligations than sole custody.[289] Both parents are entitled to know what financial arrangements they can rely on in attempting to meet their legal obligations, rather than trying to second guess, at their peril, whether a judge might later reject or enforce their understanding.[290]

There is always the possibility that joint custody and its accompanying finances will require court modification if a change in circumstances occurs.[291] Modification can not be intelligently considered if the original decree does not accurately reflect the situation and legal relationships at the time of the divorce. Decrees incorporating the joint custody agreement provide some standard for a court to later determine, if necessary, whether both parents have lived up to their bargain for the benefit of the child.[292]

(h) Do joint custody decrees result in more modification problems?

Some opposition to joint custody is based on a fear that joint custody decrees will consume more time for modification than traditional awards of sole custody.[293] Certainly, reported cases evidence that some joint custody decrees do come back to court[294] as do decrees of sole custody.[295] In reality, there is no such thing as a "permanent" custody order.[296] Statistics are not available to compare the proportion of modification requests stemming from joint custody awards as opposed to sole custody awards.

There is, however, some evidence based on judicial experience that less, not more, modification battles result from decrees of joint custody. Commissioner John R. Alexander of Santa Monica, California, estimates that in the past two and a half years he has had at least a dozen cases before him in court where the couples have stipulated to joint custody. None of these couples, so far as he knows, have reached an impasse over their children's upbringing that have brought them back to court. He suggests that this lack of "legal pathology" indicates that the principal of joint custody is working better in practice than many domestic relations lawyers and judicial officers might expect.[297]

One attorney who has negotiated and secured for his clients many joint custody decrees has written that these decrees, when based on a mediated or negotiated settlement have a low "recidivism rate" and rarely come back for redetermination.[298] This attorney, Stephen Gaddis, urges inclusion of a mediation or arbitration provision in the initial joint custody agreement as an alternative to resolve a parental deadlock.[299] Such a provision, stresses Gaddis, is appropriate "because an important part of the joint custodial process is to encourage private decision making rather than litigation."[300] If mediation fails, arbitration is another available mechanism that couples can include in the joint custody agreement.[301]

Other attorneys, as well as Gaddis, include provisions in their joint custody agreements for periodic review of its terms by the parties,[302] or review and renegotiation upon the happening of listed contingencies, such as remarriage, co-habitation, or a move from the geographical area.[303] When these events occur, they often result in practical concerns as well as substantial emotional reactions that make fighters out of parents who previously cooperated. For this reason, the agreement may provide that the parents will seek counseling[304] or advice on how others have handled these issues. Periodic review of the joint custody arrangement, counseling, mediation or arbitration should provide effective alternatives to modification motions for most parents who have demonstrated their proclivity to avoid court proceedings by stipulating to joint custody or who the court has found are capable of cooperating together in the best interests of their children.[305]

If joint custody should fail or require modification, the proceeding should be no more burdensome or harmful than modification of sole custody decrees. The same mechanisms available to one are available to the other. Each requires a material change of circumstances before modification can be ordered.[306] The remarks of a California judge considering a request for modification of spousal support are even more apt in regard to modification of child custody:

> One of the paradoxes of our present legal system is that it is accepted practice to tie up a court for days while a gaggle of professional medical witnesses expounds to a jury on just how devastating or just how trivial a personal injury may be ... Yet at the same time we begrudge the judicial resources necessary for careful and reasoned judgments in this most delicate field — the break up of a marriage with its resulting trauma and troublesome fiscal aftermath. The courts should not begrudge the time necessary to carefully go over the wreckage of a marriage in order to effect substantial justice to all parties involved.[307]

(i) Are decrees of joint custody enforceable?

Decrees of joint custody are enforceable, though they may present some unique issues and consequent uncertainty. The more delineated the parental rights and responsibilities in a joint custody decree, the more subject it is to traditional enforcement procedures. If the decree establishes "residential care," with one parent for certain periods of time, for example, that parent has a right to require return of the child from the other parent as agreed and resist a modification of joint residential custody in the absence of a material change in circumstances.[308] Similarly, typical provisions for child support, college expenses, insurance coverage and tax exemptions can be enforced as in any other decree.[309]

When the joint custody decree does not contain specific provisions as to how decisions regarding education, religious training or medical care are to be made and a parental deadlock occurs, some courts may first require the joint custodial parents to confer and try to reach agreement, or participate in mediation.[310] If necessary, the court may, upon the presentation of evidence, make a decision for the parents without altering the joint custody arrangement.[311] Other courts may allow a unilateral decision by the residential parent[312] or declare the joint custody a failure and decree one parent as sole custodian with the right to unilaterally make decisions.[313]

In considering a modification of joint custody to sole custody, the conduct of one parent in unilateraly frustrating or violating the joint custody arrangement may influence the court in choosing which parent shall have sole custody.[314] This potential consequence may increase even more the motivation for parental cooperation and serve a preventive function.[315] It may also, however, lead to punitive modifications to sole custody and give rebirth to a consideration of "fault" which is, arguably, not relevant to a custody modification.[316] Punitive decrees are of questionable validity, at least for purposes of out of state enforcement.[317]

Living in the same geographical area is not essential to a workable joint custody arrangement,[318] but restrictions against geographical moves with the child, particularly out of state, are common in joint custody agreements and decrees.[319] The very nature of joint custody requires parents to confer and, if necessary, negotiate over where the child shall live when one parent moves and what other adjustment to the joint custody pattern will be necessary.[320] Such provisions restricting moves, whether by prohibition or by requiring a joint decision, have come under attack on practical and constitutional grounds.[321] They, too, may lead to punitive changes of custody for their violation, but they serve an important preventive function in at least requiring negotiation.[322]

A joint custody decree which does not provide that one parent is the residential parent or which contains no restriction against moving the child's residence is undertermined custody for purposes of interstate enforcement under the Uniform Child Custody Act. If one of the parents moves and takes the child, the other parent has no direct enforcement remedy under the Act in the second state.[323] The only available judicial mechanism would be a motion to modify custody to provide the aggrieved parent a legal right to retain the child. If the decree does not establish with which parent the child is to reside, self-help is available to either parent, though this antithesis of cooperation would obviously mark the end of the joint custody arrangement.

CRITERIA FOR DECREEING JOINT CUSTODY

Joint custody is not for everyone.[324] The indiscriminate use of joint custody as a "cop out"[325] or to avoid hurting one parent[326] would be to substitute one evil for another. For some the anger and frustration surrounding divorce is too great an immediate obstacle to the cooperation required to make joint custody work.[327] For those whose divorce was precipitated by severe differences over how the children should be raised or who have, in fact, harmed their children by consciously using them as weapons in their private war, joint custody may be only a perpetuation of unacceptable and damaging parental conduct. There are, sadly, some parents who do not care for their children and others who are incapable because of pathological disturbances or marginal capacities of participating in reasoned decision making for their children. In many cases the divorce may have been marked by one parent's lack of involvement in caring for and making decisions about the children. However, it defies reason and what we know of human potential to think that those capable of joint custody constitute less than 4 per cent of the divorcing population.[328]

It has been suggested that a presumption be established in favor of joint custody.[329] At least one appellate court has recently acknowledged a presumption against joint custody.[330] Other courts, while not articulating such a presumption, appear to rule against joint custody for a similar reason.[331] Presumptions of the past, first for the father, then for the mother, have not worked well.[332] It does not seem wise to create a presumption for joint custody in all cases; it might serve as a disincentive for careful fact finding if custody is contested.[333] Perhaps a legislatively declared "preference" for joint custody is a workable middle ground, however, these terms are but labels, the effect of which may be dependent on statutory wording and court interpretation.[334]

When parents do agree upon joint custody, however, it should be decreed.[335] The courts should not stand in the way of parental efforts to share responsibility for their children following divorce. The parents know, better than a judge, what each is capable of and how they can best meet the needs of their children within the reality of divorce. Court dockets are sufficiently full of cases where parents disagree; the court should not create conflict where the parents do agree. The fact that stipulated joint custody may on occasion not work does not justify the time, expense, agony and potential error of judicial inquiry into the parents joint decision to continue their basic parental roles following divorce any more than courts should second guess parents prior to divorce. Should disagreement later occur, the courts will be available, as needed, to sort out parental rights and decide upon custody.

Concerns about agreements arrived at by "compromise" or

"overreaching" are generally misfounded. All agreements represent some degree of compromise and patterns of dominance, manipulation, or overreaching during divorce are likely no different than during marriage. There is no indication that these elements occur any less frequently in agreements of sole custody, which are generally not questioned by courts. Courts may wish to satisfy concerns about these issues by requiring parents seeking joint custody to first obtain professional divorce counseling or to utilize the services of a divorce mediator.[336] Agreements reached through attorneys representing each parent and, in those states requiring it, counsel for the child, should also answer these concerns.

This is not to suggest that it is inappropriate for courts to scrutinize stipulated joint custody agreements to assure that the financial and care arrangements have been adequately considered and are realistic. The general criteria for approval of joint custody, however, should be based on the unique features of joint custody, rather than the more restrictive criteria for divided custody.[337] Courts can utilize this same set of criteria in deciding when to encourage joint custody when parents do not initially agree upon a custody resolution. Indeed, if a court is careful in finding that the facts exist which satisfy the joint custody criteria set forth below, courts should consider ordering joint custody in contested custody cases.

An award of sole custody to one of two parents competitively seeking custody runs a high risk of coming back to haunt the court in motions for modification, contempt, non-support, and a myriad of other manuevers that parents embittered over a custody fight may devise.[338] Though court ordered joint custody may be more likely to fail than when parents agree, ordered joint custody is not necessarily more prone to failure than an order of sole custody following a divisive court contest. The potential benefit to the child is greater because a court ordered joint custody decree may help parents discover their potential for shared parenting and require them to do more for their children rather than less.[339] It is too often forgotten that one of the most noble functions of laws and courts is to establish models for conduct expected of people.[340]

Joint custody benefits children and parents by continuing the active involvement of both parents in the child's life through shared authority similar to that during the marriage. Courts should decree joint custody when (1) both parents are fit; (2) both parents wish to continue their active involvement in raising the child; (3) both parents are capable of making reasoned decisions together in the best interests of the child; and (4) joint custody would disrupt the parent-child relationship less than other custody alternatives.

A finding of parental fitness assures that the child will not be subjected to the care of a parent incapable or unwilling to provide for the child's needs and to protect the child from harm. If there is no evidence of abuse or neglect and no allegation to the contrary, a finding of fitness would normally present no difficulty.[341] A finding of parental fitness protects both parents, in the event either later contends for sole custody. The court's attention in considering a request for modification could then be focused only on evidence following the initial decree of joint custody.

If one parent, though fit, does not wish to be actively involved in raising the child following divorce, there is little reason to go further.[342] Stipulated agreements of joint custody should meet the requirements of this criteria without further evidence, as would separate petitions or motions by both parents for sole custody. Inclusion of this criteria, which will in most cases be a "given," creates a risk that it will be used as a battleground for testing sincerity or comparing degrees of love for the child. However, it does provide the court with the opportunity to focus the parents' attention on the need of both parents to actively involve themselves on a continuing basis with the child. It also provides some standard for modification should one parent later "drop out" or otherwise fail to meet his or her joint parental responsibility.

Even if the parents in the emotional heat of their divorce have not made reasoned decisions together in the best interests of their child, the judge may find that they are capable of doing so. If the parents, outside of the divorce setting, have each demonstrated that they are reasonable and are willing to give priority to the best interest of their child, then the judge need only determine if the parents can separate and put aside any conflicts between them to cooperate for the benefit of their child. The judge must look for the parents ability to cooperate and if the potential exists, encourage its activation by instructing the parents on what is expected of them.[343] In the increasing number of jurisdictions offering court connected counseling, professional guidance is readily available and can be a condition of joint custody.[344]

The court may wish to consider the pre-divorce parenting pattern in determining which available custody alternative would be the least disruptive. A father, or a mother, who prior to divorce has not actively participated in caring for the child or in making major decisions on behalf of the child, may not be in a position to actively do so following divorce without a disruptive effect. The child's needs for continued involvement with paternal and maternal relatives and friends may also be a factor. Though a child's residence need not be shifted as a result of joint custody, the court should weigh the practical effect of a parent's relocation or change of lifestyle and should structure the custody arrangement to minimize any disruptive effect on the child. Finally, the court should view joint custody not in comparison to an idealized intact family, but rather relative to the less than ideal alternatives of sole custody litigation and disposable parents.

CONCLUSION

Joint custody has been brought to the attention of attorneys and judges by parents who seek to divorce their spouse, but not their children. Limited social science data indicate that joint custody may often best serve the needs of children to remain actively involved with both parents following divorce. The law has reluctantly responded by allowing joint custody in limited circumstances and expecting the worst. The cases frequently refer to joint custody as a modern Solomon, dividing the child in two,[345] rather than recognizing it as an opportunity to avoid cutting off half the child's family and to allow the child the continuing benefit of both parents.

Joint custody is no cure-all for the agony of divorce and the often difficult adjustment it requires of children and parents. It is, however, preferable to the divisiveness inherent in decreeing custody to one parent or the other. Joint custody will work in more cases than now thought possible. Responsibility rests with attorneys, judges and others involved in the process of divorce to inform clients of this positive alternative to the isolation of sole custody and the bitterness of custody litigation.

---

1 Divorced parents who formally obtain joint custody remain a relatively small minority, but some predict they will eventually become the majority. See note 248 and accompanying test, *infra.*

2 Baum, "The Best of Both Parents," N.Y. Times, Oct. 31, 1976 (Magazine) at 44-48; Dullea, "Joint Custody: Is Sharing the Child a Dangerous Idea?" N.Y. Times, May 24, 1976, at 24, col. 1; Fager, "Co-parenting: Sharing the Children of Divorce," San Francisco Bay Guardian, Feb. 3, 1977, at 7, col. 1; Holly, "Joint Custody: The New Haven Plan," Ms. Magazine, Sept. 1976, at 70-71; Huerta, "Joint Custody: Co-Parenting After Divorce," Los Angeles Times, Jan. 30, 1979, Part IV at 1, col. 2; Kellogg, "Joint Custody," Newsweek, Jan. 24, 1977, at 56; Klemesrud, "Parents Move, Children Don't Under Pact," The Oregonian (Portland, Ore.), Feb. 20, 1978, § C, at 1, col. 3; Levine, "Parents Agree to Joint Custody," The Christian Science Monitor, May 5, 1975, at 18; Molinoff, "For this Father, Joint Custody is Tough, Satisfying," Capital Times (Madison, Wisc.), Oct. 30, 1975, at 33, col. 1; Molinoff, "Joint Custody: Victory for All?," N.Y. Times, March 6, 1977, at § 22, at 18, col. 1; Molinoff, "After Divorce, Give Them a Father, Too," Newsday, Oct. 5, 1975; Reiner, "Joint Custody Lets Parents be Parents," Oregon Statesman and Capital J., (Salem, Ore.), April 23, 1978, at E-1, col. 5; "One Child, Two Homes," Time, Jan. 29, 1979, at 61; Ware, "Joint Custody: One Way to End the War," New West, Feb. 26, 1979, at 42.

3 Cox & Cease, "Joint Custody," 1 Fam. Advocate 10 (1978); Eder, "Shared Custody of Children: An Idea Whose Time Has Come," Conciliation Courts Rev., June 1978, at 23; Grote & Weinstein, "Joint Custody: A Viable and Ideal Alternative,"1 J. Divorce 43 (1977); Gaddis, "Joint Custody of Children: A Divorce Decision-Making Alternative," Conciliation Courts Rev., June 1978, at 17; Roman, "The Disposable Parent," Concilation Courts Rev., Dec. 1977, at 1; Roman & Haddad, "The Case For Joint Custody," Psych. Today, Sept. 1978, at 96; Stack, "Who Owns the Child?" 23 Soc. Prob. 505 (1976); Woolley, "Shared Custody," 1 Fam. Advocate 6 (1978).

4 A comprehensive article, "Joint Custody — A Viable Alternative," by the respected

scholarly team of Henry H. Foster and Doris Jonas Freed was serialized in three parts by the New York Law Journal: Nov. 9, 1978, Nov. 24, 1978, Dec. 22, 1978, condensed in Trial, May 1979, at 26; the initial issue of the Fam. Advocate, a journal by the ABA Family Law Section (Summer 1978) featured the topic "Joint Custody" and contained a number of articles on the subject, which are referred to individually herein. See also Ramey, Stender & Smaller, "Joint Custody: Are Two Homes Better Than One?" 8 Golden Gate U.L. Rev. 559 (1979); Brah, "Joint Custody," 67 Ky. L.J. 271 (1979).

5   See M. Roman & W. Haddad, *The Disposable Parent* (1978). The forceful advocacy of Roman and Haddad has provoked considerable discussion and comment. See also M. Galper, *Co-Parenting: A Source Book for the Separated or Divorced Family* (1978); R. Cassidy, *What Every Man Should Know About Divorce* (1977). For a most helpful comprehensive treatment, see P. Woolley, *The Custody Handbook* (1979).

6   1978 Annual Conference, Association of Family Conciliation Courts, Vancouver, British Columbia, Canada, Workshop, Joint Custody (May 20, 1978); Conference of the Association of Conciliation Courts, Ft. Lauderdale, Fla., Joint Custody Workshop (Dec. 7-9, 1978); Workshop on Joint Custody sponsored by Washington Association of Family Courts and the Oregon Association of Conciliation Courts, in Kelso Washington (October 14, 1977); Panel on Joint Custody of Children, American Orthopsychiatric Association Annual Meeting, in San Francisco, Calif. (March 27-31, 1978); Annual Meeting of National Council on Family Relations, Philadelphia, Pa. (Oct. 19-22, 1978).

7   Or. Rev. Stat. § 107.105 (amended 1977); Wis. Stat. Ann. § 247.24 (amended 1977) (West Cum. Supp. 1977-78); Iowa Code Ann. § 598.21 (amended 1977) (West 1979).

8   As of this writing, joint custody bills are being considered in Michigan (S.B. 1976), California (S.B. 477 and A.B. 1480) and Massachusetts (House Bills 1617, 2387, 2394 and 2411). Some of these bills simply authorize joint custody, others would establish it as a preference or create a presumption of joint custody. In Oregon, where joint custody is now explicitly allowed by statute, legislation is pending that would establish a presumption for joint custody. (HB 2538) In answers received from 45 states to the author's survey of pending legislation, it was apparent that confusion exists as to what joint custody means. For that reason the survey results may be inaccurate.

9   The appropriateness of using words such as "award" in "custody" decrees is questionable, but they are used here for introductory convenience. There is need to develop new terms. See *e.g.,* Elkin, "The Language of Family Law is the Language of Criminal Law," Conciliation Courts Rev., Sept. 1975, at iii.

10   See *e.g., Kilgore v. Kilgore,* 54 Ala. App. 336, 308 So. 2d 249 (1975) where terms "split", "divided" and "alternating" are used interchangeably to describe one custody situation.

11   See *e.g.,* 3 Fam. L. Rep. (BNA) 2678 (1977) where *Roth v. Roth,* an alternating custody case, is headlined as "Joint Custody".

12   See Mnookin, "Child Custody Adjudication: Judicial Functions in the Face of Interminancy," L. & Contemp. Prob., Summer 1975, at 233; Cox & Cease, "Joint Custody," 1 Fam. Advocate 10 (1978).

13   See also note 12 *supra.* 1 A. Linde, Separation Agreements and Ante-Nuptial Contracts, § 14 (1967).

14   See note 13 *supra.*

15   Cases discussing "divided" and "alternating" custody are collected in the following annotations: Annot., 92 A.L.R. 2d 695 (1963); 27B C.J.S. 2d *Divorce* § 308D (1959); 24 Am. Jur. 2d Divorce and Separation § 799 (1966).

16   See *e.g., Smith v. Smith,* 257 Iowa 584, 133 N.W. 2d 677 (1965). Stability and continuity of relationship as the most important elements in determining the best interests and welfare of the child were forcefully supported by the publication in 1973 of the influential work *Beyond The Best Interest of the Child, infra* note 60. Quotations from this work appear in a number of reported cases, see *e.g., Ellenwood and Ellenwood,* 20 Or. App. 486, 491, 532 P. 2d 259, 262 (1975).

17 See *e.g., Phillips v. Phillips,* 153 Fla. 133, So. 2d 922 (1943).

18 See *e.g.,* Note, "Divided Custody of Children After Their Parents Divorce," 8 J. Fam. L. 58 (1968).

19 See *e.g., Mueller v. Muller,* 188 Va. 259, 49 S.E. 2d 349 (1948).

20 See *e.g., Reynolds v. Reynolds,* 45 Wash. 2d 394, 275 P. 2d 421 (1954).

21 See *e.g., Maxwell v. Maxwell,* 351 S.W. 2d 192 (Ky. 1961).

22 See *e.g., Grant v. Grant,* 39 Tenn. App. 539, 286 S.W. 2d 349 (1954).

23 But see *Lutker v. Lutker,* 230 S.W. 2d 177 (Mo. Ct. App. 1950) where the court affirmed an award of divided custody of a two-year old noting that both parents were devoted to the child, both homes were suitable for the child's growth, and the homes were not far from one another.

24 See *Flanagan v. Flanagan,* 195 Or. 611, 247 P. 2d 212 (1952). However, where it appeared that the agreement was reached during a period of great turmoil and where the wife had not been represented by counsel, the appellate court modified divided custody and gave sole custody to the mother in *Whitlow v. Whitlow,* 25 Or. App. 765, 550 P. 2d 1404 (1976).

The *Flanagan* decision has been criticized for upholding divided custody where there was evidence that the child was upset by the alteration between homes. Note, *supra* note 18 at 64.

25 Because parents can exercise great leeway over dividing a child's time under a traditional "sole" custody order, some have questioned the need for a "joint" custody order, *infra* section VIII(G).

26 The liberal visitation rights upheld in *In re Marriage of Powers,* 527 S.W. 2d 949 (Mo. Ct. App. 1975) are discussed in 42 Mo. L. Rev. 136 (1977).

27 1 A. Linde, *supra* note 13.

28 *Ebert v. Ebert,* 38 N.Y. 2d 700, 704, 346 N.E. 2d 240, 243 (1976). But see *In re Hagge's Marriage,* 234 N.W. 2d 138 (Iowa 1975) which affirmed a division of the siblings with three boys to live with their father while their sister was placed in the mother's custody.

29 Joint custody has, however, frequently been disapproved by courts. See discussion in section VII *infra.*

30 See Bodenheimer, "Progress Under the Uniform Child Custody Jurisdiction Act and Remaining Problems: Punitive Decrees, Joint Custody and Excessive Modification," 65 Calif. L. Rev. 978, 1009 (1977).

At a conference on current developments in child custody held in New York City, Justice Felice Shea observed that often counsel do not make it clear what custody form they are asking for. She asked that the concepts of shared decisional power and equal custodial time be kept separate: 5 Fam. L. Rep. (BNA) 2144 (1978).

31 The various terms in use to describe this type of custody arrangement are listed in M. Galper, *supra* note 5 at 16 (1978). Professor Carol Bruch uses the term "dual parenting" in a provocative article which nicely separates legal custody from a proposed obligation of each parent to share time with the child and the imposition of sanctions for failure to do so. Bruch, "Making Visitation Work: Dual Parenting Orders," 1 Fam. Advocate 22 (1978). Another term is suggested by the title of a recent report that asks for public hearings in the state of New York on joint custody and related topics, W. Haddad & M. Roman, *No-fault Custody, Special Report to Honorable Speaker Stanley Steingut, The Assembly, State of New York,* (July 1978). Yet another term is proposed by Gaddis & Bintliff, *Concurrent Custody A Means of Continuing Parental Responsibility After Dissolution,* AFLC Joint Custody Handbook at A11 (1979). They would use the term "concurrent custody" as a "general term which encompasses several varying arrangements, each of which legally affirms the continued parental role involvement in the upbringing of children by both parents after separation or divorce." Joint custody is seen as one variety of "concurrent custody". Although each of the alternatives has some

merit we have chosen to continue using the term joint custody in this Article rather than further proliferate the literature and confound research by adopting still another phrase. Cases and statutes most frequently use the term joint custody and though its meaning may vary, we will attempt to use it consistently and provide a definition of greater clarity.

32 See Cox & Cease, *supra* note 12. See also Foster & Freed, "Joint Custody — A Viable Alternative," N.Y.L.J., Nov. 9, 1978 at 4, col. 3, where the authors nicely distinguish joint authority for decisions from physical custody.

33 Wis. Stat. Ann. § 247.24(b) (West Cum. Supp. 1978-79).

34 See text accompanying notes 138-139, *infra*.

35 *Odette R. v. Douglas R.*, 91 Misc. 2d 792, 795, 399 N.Y.S. 2d 33, 36 (1977).

36 M. Roman & W. Haddad, *supra* note 5, at 175 state:
    ... [J]oint custody is that post divorce custodial arrangement in which parents agree to equally share the authority for making all decisions that significantly affect the lives of their children. It is also that post divorce arrangement in which child care is split equally or, at the most discrepant, child care resolves itself into a two-to-one split.

37 Grote & Weinstein, *supra* note 3, at 45 state:
    Joint custody simply does not mean that one person is to have a child for six months and the other for another six months, though it can mean a sharing of the living arrangements. Joint custody is more than an arrangement wherein one child resides with two parents — it is a flexible and open arrangement for living, sharing, and loving. No one model is adequate to describe the possibilities opened by joint custody arrangements to post divorce families. ..."

38 Woolley, *supra* note 3 states:
    I have defined shared custody as any method that permits the children to grow up knowing and interacting with each parent in an everyday situation, whether that comes about by splitting the time on a fifty-fifty basis each week or by having the children go live with the other parent for several years or more.

39 See *e.g., Gudelj v. Gudelj*, 41 Cal. 2d 202, 259 P. 2d 656 (1953).

40 Commenting on such arrangements, one judge stated: "(J)oint or divided custody decrees generally give both parents legal responsibility for the child's care, but when physical or actual custody is lodged primarily in one parent, custody may be joint in name only." *Dodd v. Dodd,* 93 Misc 2d 641, 645, 403 N.Y.S. 2d 401, 403 (1978).

41 For a general history of custody see Foster & Freed, "Life with Father: 1978," 11 Fam. L.Q. 321 (1978). See also Derdeyn, "Child Custody Contests in Historical Perspective," 12 Am. J. Psych. 133 (1978).

42 Foster and Freed trace the change in judicial attitudes which first uniformly favored fathers then shifted radically to a preference for mothers who, until quite recently, prevailed in at least 90% of the cases. Foster & Freed, *supra* note 41, at 3.

43 Foster & Freed, *supra* note 32.

44 *King v. DeManneville,* 102 Eng. Rep. 1054, 1055 (K.B. 1804). A noted exception and bellwether of later trends was the refusal of a court in 1817 to give the poet Percy Shelley custody of his children because of his "vicious and immoral atheistic beliefs." *Shelley v. Westbrooke,* 37 Eng. Rep. 850 (Ch. 1817).

45 Mnookin, *supra* note 12, at 234. But see, Derdeyn *supra* note 41, at 1370.

46 M. Roman & W. Haddad, *supra* note 5, at 29-30.

47 Stack, *supra* note 3, at 506.

48 For a unique study that uses paintings and diaries to trace the origin of the modern family and the development of a concept of childhood see P. Aries, *Centuries of Childhood* (1962).

49 Derdeyn, *supra* note 41, at 1371. Mnookih, *supra* note 12, at 234, reports that:
    in 1839 the English Parliament modified the absolute rule of paternal preference for

legitimate children by passing the so-called Talfourd's Act, which gave a mother the right to custody of infants under the age of seven years, An Act to Amend the Law Relating to the Custody of Infants, 2 & 3 Vict. c. 54 (1839); and later for infants of any age. An Act to Amend the Law as to the Custody of Infants, 36 & 37 Vict. c. 12 (1873).

50 The origin of the "tender years presumption" is also placed with the passage of Talfourd's Act in 1839, which permitted chancery to award custody to the mother if the children were less than seven years of age. Mnookin, *supra* note 12, at 234.

Although it has generally been agreed that preschool children are included, the age when the presumption ends is unclear. H. Clark, *The Law of Domestic Relations in the United States* 585 (1968).

51 An extensive collection of cases containing a tender years presumption is cited in Roth, "The Tender Years Presumption in Child Custody Disputes," 15 J. Fam. L. 423, 432-33 (1975).

52 See *e.g.*, *Magee v. Holland,* 27 N.J.L. 86, 88-89 (1858):

Every father blessed with that natural affection which God, in His infinite wisdom and goodness, has implanted in the heart of man, that the care of his offspring may be a pleasure, rather than a burden, knows the value of those little offices which the young prattler can offer with filial affection.

53 See *e.g.*, *Tuter v. Tuter,* 120 S.W. 2d 203, 205 (Mo. Ct. App. 1938): "There is but a twilight zone between a mother's love and the atmosphere of heaven, and all things being equal, no child should be deprived of that maternal influence unless it be shown there are special or extraordinary reasons for so doing." and *Jenkins v. Jenkins,* 173 Wis. 592, 181 N.W. 826, 827 (1921):

For a boy of such tender years nothing can be an adequate substitute for mother love — for that constant ministration required during the period of nurture that only a mother can give because in her alone is duty swallowed up in desire; in her alone is service expressed in terms of love.

54 The enunciation of the "best interests test" is usually credited to Justice Brewer in an 1881 Kansas decision which awarded custody of a 5-year old girl to her grandmother who had raised her rather than to her father. The judge wrote that though the father had a natural right to custody, the paramount consideration was the welfare of the child: *Chapsky v. Wood,* 26 Kan. 650 (1881).

55 See *e.g.*, Mo. Rev. Stat. § 452.375.

56 See *e.g.*, *Tingen v. Tingen,* 251 Or. 458, 459, 446 P. 2d 185, 186 (1968) where the Oregon Supreme Court stated:

In determining the best interests of a child in a custody dispute the court ought to consider all the relevant factors. These, as we see them would generally include: (1) the conduct of the parties; (2) the moral, emotional and physical fitness of the parties; (3) the comparative physical environments; (4) the emotional ties of the child to other family members; (5) the interest of the parties in, and attitude toward, the child; (6) the age, sex, and health of the child; (7) the desirability of continuing an existing relationship and environment; and (8) the preference of the child.

57 See *e.g.*, *Minn. Stat. Ann.§* 518.17 (West Cum. Supp. 1978):

The best interests of the child means all relevant factors to be considered and evaluated by the court including:

(a) The wishes of the child's parent or parents as to his custody;

(b) The reasonable preference of the child, if the court deems the child to be of sufficient age to express preference;

(c) The interaction and interrelationship of the child with his parent or parents, his siblings, and any other person who may significantly affect the child's best interests;

(d) The child's adjustment to his home, school, and community;

(e)The length of time the child has lived in a stable, satisfactory environment and the desirability of maintaining continuity;

(f) The permanence, as a family unit, of the existing or proposed custodial home; and

(g) The mental and physical health of all individuals involved.

The court shall not consider conduct of a proposed custodian that does not affect his relationship to the child.

58 See e.g., Or. Rev. Stat. § 107.137 which lists relevant factors and then directs: "The best interests and welfare of the child in a custody matter shall not be determined by isolating any one of the relevant factors. ...."

59 See e.g., Reflow v. Reflow, 24 Or. App. 365, 373, 545 P. 2d 894, 899 (1976) "[C]ontinuity in one unchanging family environment, especially for young children, is probably the most important single element necessary to a child's wholesome development."

60 J. Goldstein, A. Freud & A. Solnit, Beyond the Best Interests of the Child (1973) [hereinafter cited as Goldstein, Freud & Solnit].

61 See section VIII(c) infra.

62 Quinn, "Fathers Cry for Custody," Juris Doctor, May 1976, at 42.

63 For one account of family switching roles in child care and household responsibilities see J. McCready, Kitchen Sink Papers (1975); see generally M. Young & P. Willmot, The Symmetrical Family (1973).

64 Recent research is summarized in Roth, supra note 51, at 448-57.

65 Oster, "Custody Proceedings: A Study of Vague and Indefinite Standards," 5 J. Fam. L. 21 (1965).

66 The award of his two children to Dr. Lee Salk by a New York Court in 1975 on a finding not that his wife was unfit but that he was "better fit" was seen as a breakthrough for fathers in Solomon, "The Fathers' Revolution in Custody Cases," Trial, Oct. 1977, at 33.

67 See Quinn, supra note 62. More than 1.5 million single parent homes are now headed by fathers, though it is not known what number of these are a result of divorce custody decrees: 5 Fam. L. Rep. (BNA) 2143 (Dec. 19, 1978). Judicial attitudes may be improving, but in interviews conducted for her doctoral dissertation, Dr. Jill Sanford found judges held a continuing bias for mothers in custody disputes and a suspicion of motives of fathers who sought custody, e.g. saving child support. Fathers seeking custody were seen as "selfish" while mothers not seeking custody were seen as "abandoning their children." Dr. Sanford concluded that men wanting custody would have "to somehow prove sincerity, in addition to proving ability to parent." Kapner & Frumkes, "The Trial of a Custody Conflict," Fla. B.J. March 1978, at 174.

68 In State ex rel. Watts v. Watts, 77 Misc. 2d 178, 350 N.Y.S. 2d 285 (1973) for example, a New York court rejected the tender years doctrine as sex discrimination. Noting Supreme Court decisions that find different treatment based on sex "suspect" and subject to the strictest level of judicial scrutiny, the Watts court reasoned that the tender years presumption could stand only if it served a compelling state interest. The court acknowledged that the best interests of the child might well be a compelling state interest. But taking judicial notice of contemporary thought about child development that rejects the stereotyped presumption that children of tender years belong with the mother, the court concluded that the necessary nexus between a compelling state interest and the tender years presumption was not present and, therefore, different treatment based on sex was unconstitutional. Contra, Gordon v. Gordon, 577 P. 2d 1271 (Okla. Sup. Ct. 1978), cert. denied, 99 S. Ct. 185 (1978).

69 The Texas Fathers for Equal Rights recently brought an unsuccessful class action suit against all the district court judges in the state on a theory that Texas law invades their constitutionally protected parental rights by failing to allow joint custody of children

post-divorce, where joint custody is in the children's best interests. The federal district court found the plaintiffs lacked standing because they failed to show that the alleged defect in the law caused them injury. In *dictum* the court stated that Texas law does not prohibit joint custodies where parents agree to joint custodies and that a compelling interest in avoiding undue interference by the state in family matters justifies prohibiting joint custody where it is opposed by one parent. *Shelton v. Chrisman,* Civil Action No. CA-3-75-1268-D, Jan. 31, 1979 (N.D. Tex. 1979).

70 Fathers groups have supported efforts to pass measures that would *"encourage"* joint custody. Although three states have recently passed bills that explicitly *recognize* joint custody, see notes 125-135 *infra,* no state has yet accepted the stronger language advocated by some fathers' groups.

71 For an insightful and searching analysis of this problem, see Mnookin, *supra* note 12, at 226.

72 Schlesinger, "Children and Divorce: A Selected Review," Conciliation Courts Rev., Sept. 1977, at 36.

73 See Mnookin, *supra* note 12, at 229, 258-60.

74 "At this point we simply do not know what difference it makes to children of different ages to be subjected to any of the wide variety of possible arrangements." R. Weiss, *Marital Separation* 171 (1975).

75 See Hetherington, Cox & Cox, "Divorced Father," 25 Fam. Coordinator 417, 425-26 (1976). See also Wallerstein & Kelly, "The Effects of Parental Divorce: Experiences of the Child in Later Latency," 46 Amer. J. Orthopsych. 256 (1976); Wallerstein & Kelly, "The Effects of Parental Divorce: Experiences of the Preschool Child," 14 J. Amer. Acad. Child Psych. 600 (1975); Wallerstein & Kelly, "The Effects of Paternal Divorce: The Adolesant Experience," in 3 *The Child in His Family* (E. Anthony and C. Koupernik eds. 1974); and Wallerstein, "Children Who Cope in Spite of Divorce," 1 Fam. Advocate 2 (1978).

76 See Jones, "The Impact of Divorce on Children," Conciliation Courts Rev., Dec. 1977, at 28.

77 Cohen, Coments on Current Divorce Research, presented at Annual Meeting, American Assoc. of Marriage and Family Counselors, San Francisco (1977). See Schlesinger, *supra* note 72, at 39.

78 See, Folberg, "Counseling in the Courts — A Better Way to Resolve Family Disputes," Judge's J., Fall 1975, at 74.

79 See generally J. Noble & W. Noble, *The Custody Trap* 160 (1975).

80 In commenting about the advese effect of repeated post-divorce custody motions, one judge commented "the chances of a child developing emotional problems as they [sic] grow up increases in direct proportion to the thickness of the file involved in a divorce case." *King v. King,* 10 Or. App. 324, 328, 500 P. 2d 267, 269 (1972).

81 See Judge Lindslay, "Custody Procedures, Battlefield or Peace Conference," Conciliation Courts Rev., Sept. 1975, at 1. See also Cantor & Ferguson, "Famil Counseling in the Conciliation Court: An Alternative to Custody Litigation," Conciliation Courts Rev., Sept. 1976, at 1.

82 See Gaddis, "Divorce Decision Making: Alternatives to Litigation," Conciliation Courts Rev., June 1978, at 43. See also O. Coogler, *Structured Mediation in Divorce Settlement* (1978), in which the author, describes in detail a divorce mediation process, including suggested *forms* for joint custody.

83 R. Mnookin, *supra* note 71, at 287-89.

84 See Folberg, "Facilitating Agreement — The Role of Counseling in the Courts," Conciliation Courts Rev., Dec. 1974, at 17. S.B. 477, pending in the California legislature, provides for consultation "with the conciliation court for the purpose of assisting the parties to formulate a plan for the implementation of the joint custody order . . ."

85 See Milne, "Custody of Children in a Divorce Process: A Family Self-Determination Model," Conciliation Courts Rev., Dec. 1978, at 1.

86 See Holman & Noland, "Agreement and Arbitration: Relief to Over-Litigation in Domestic Relations Disputes in Washington," 12 Willamette L.J. 527 (1976). See American Arbitration Association, Family Dispute Services (1972). This pamphlet explains the AAA's process in marital and custody disputes and is available from the AAA, 140 W. 51 St., New York, N.Y.

87 See e.g., People ex rel Sisson v. Sission, 271 N.Y. 285, 2 N.E. 2d 660 (1936); Kilgore v. Kilgore, 268 Ala. 475, 107 So. 2d 885 (1958).

88 See e.g., Matarese v. Matarese, 47 R.I. 131, 131 A. 198 (1925).

89 See e.g., Pyle v. Waechter, 202 Iowa 695, 210 N.W. 926 (1926); Magee v. Holland, 27 N.J.L. 86 (1858).

90 The following are typical of modern statutes: "The father and mother are joint natural guardians of their minor children and have equal powers and duties and neither parent has any right superior to the right of the other concerning the custody of their children." Md. Code Ann. § 1, art. 72A; and ". . . The parents have equal powers rights and duties concerning the minor." Ill. Ann. Stat.. ch. 3 § 132.

    Though most states do not use the term "joint custody" in setting forth the rights of the parents to the care of their children in the intact family, the Kentucky statutes use that term: "The father and mother shall have the joint custody, nurture and education of their minor children . . ." Ky. Rev. Stat. § 405.021(1). See generally Foster & Freed, supra note 40 at 321 (Updated 12 Fam. L. Quart. iii (1978)).

91 H. Clark, supra note 50, § 17.2 at 573 (1968).

92 Based on California statutes, Justice Traynor defined custody as follows: "Custody embraces the sum of parental rights with respect to the rearing of a child, including its care. It includes the right to the child's services and earnings . . . and the right to direct his activities and make decisions regarding his care and control, education, health and religion." Burge v. City of San Francisco, 41 Cal. 2d 608, 617, 262 P. 2d 6, 12 (1953) (citations omitted).

93 See generally Annot., 36 A.L.R. 866 (1925). An early case describes the obligations as follows: "The duty to maintain and protect [one's children], is a principle of natural law." People ex rel. O'Connell v. Turner, 55 Ill. 280, 284 (1870).

94 See Turner v. Turner, 167 Cal. App. 2d 636, 642, 334 P. 2d 1011, 1015 (2d Dist. 1959), where it was stated: "The parent has authority to control the child, and to administer restraint and punishment, in order to compel obedience to reasonable and necessary directions." (citations omitted).

95 See generally Annot., 100 A.L.R. 2d 483 § 6 (1965). See also Singleton v. State, 33 Ala. App. 536, 35 So. 2d 375 (1948).

96 Typical judicial comments on this point include "It is not seriously debatable that the parental right to guide one's child intellectually and religiously is a most substantial part of the liberty and freedom of the parent": Pierce v. Society of Sisters, 268 U.S. 510, 518 (1925) (citations omitted). "As to the mother's failure to train the little girl in the faith of her fathers, that, too, is within the parents' sole control": People ex rel. Portnoy v. Strasser, 303 N.Y. 539, 544, 104, N.E. 2d 895, 898 (1952) (citations omitted). See also In re Guardianship of Faust, 239 Miss. 299, 123 So. 2d 218 (1960).

97 Although it generally has been assumed that the rights of the parents are not differentiated in the intact family, both Australia and Great Britain have passed statutes which allow either parent to apply for orders regarding custodial rights during a marital relationship. Gaddis and Bintliff, Concurrent Custody: A Means of Continuing Parental Responsibility After Dissolution, AFLC Joint Custody Handbook 15 (1979).

97.1 See Freed & Foster, 3 Fam. L. Rep. (BNA) 4052 (1977), which notes that "since 1970, the majority of new state laws make support the obligation of both parents . . ." In regard to the support obligation an Illinois judge stated: "In our opinion the support of a child is a joint and several obligation of both husband and wife ... We recognize that this is contrary to the traditional view that support of a child is exclusively a husband's obligation ... But with the emancipation of women and the change in times, we believe this view to be outmoded as indicated by more modern case law and statutory enactments." *Plant v. Plant,* 20 Ill. App. 3d 5, 7-8, 312 N.E. 2d 847, 849-50 (1974).

98 See *e.g.,* "The mother of an unmarried minor child is entitled to its custody, services and earnings. The father of the child ... is equally entitled to the custody, services and earnings of the unmarried minor." Cal. Civ. Code § 197 (West Cum. Supp. 1979).

99 See *e.g., In re Rotkowitz,* 175 Misc. 948, 25 N.Y.S. 2d 624 (1941).

100 H. Clark, *supra* note 50, at 572.

101 One typical statutes states: "Whenever the court grants a decree of annulment or dissolution of marriage or of separation, it has power further to decree as follows: (a) For the future care and custody of the minor children of the marriage ..." Or. Rev. Stat. § 107.105.

102 See generally, Mnookin, *supra* note 12, at 233.

103 See *e.g., Marriage of Pergament,* 28 Or. App. 459, 462, 559 P. 2d 942, 943 (1977) "When a family is split by dissolution of the marriage the child of necessity can be in custody of only one parent and the custodial parent is given the primary responsibility for rearing the child."

104 See Foster & Freed, *supra* note 40, for discussion and chart of state statutes.

105 H. Clark, *supra* note 50, at 573.

106 See generally, Annot. 66 A.L.R. 2d 1410 (1959) (Religion); Annot., 36 A.L.R. 3d 1093 (1969) (Education).

107 Gaddis, *supra* note 3.

108 Woolley, *supra* note 3, at 6 points out that in many instances tenagers are sent off to live with fathers after several years with mothers; she postulates that if these informal arrangements are included within joint custody statistics, joint custodies, might comprise as much as 35 or 50 percent of custody arrangements.

109 Judge Howard Blanding, Legal Aspects of Joint Custody, Panel Presentation, Conference on Joint Custody, Kelso, Washington October 14, 1977 (Transcript available from authors).

110 The prevalence of such agreements was seen as support for the feasibility of joint custody in Kubie, "Provisions For the Care of Children of Divorced Parents: A New Legal Instrument," 73 Yale L.J. 1197 (1964).

111 Bodenheimer, *supra* note 30, at 1010 (footnote omitted).

112 Ahrons, The Coparental Divorce: Preliminary Research Findings and Policy Implications (Unpublished paper presented at the annual meeting of the National Council on Family Relations, Philadelphia, Pa., Oct. 19-22 1978) at 6. The author found when the 144 persons were contacted that 26 did not have actual joint custody.

113 Oregon Bureau of Labour, "Divorced Women in Portland" 7 (1978).

114 See Dullea, *supra* note 2.

115 See text accompanying note 248, *infra.*

116 In Connecticut a study of the disposition of 221 contested custody cases referred for mediation in fiscal year 1977-1978 showed that in 10% of the mediated cases the couples entered into a shared custody arrangement. Letter from Anthony Salius, Director, Superior Ct., Family Div., Conn., Feb. 15, 1979.

117 See *Odette R. v. Douglas R.,* 91 Misc. 2d 792, 399 N.Y.S. 2d 93 (1977).

118 See *Mayer v. Mayer,* 150 N.J. Super. 556, 376 A. 2d 214 (1977).

119 44 N.Y. 2d 584, 586, 407 N.Y.S. 2d 449, 451, 378 N.E. 2d, 1019, 1021 (1978) (citation omitted).

120 *Stamper v. Stamper,* 3 Fam. L. Rep. (BNA) 2541 (Mich. Circuit Ct., Wayne County, June 16, 1977).
121 See text accompanying notes 311, *infra.*
122 Foster & Freed, "Joint Custody — A Viable Alternative," N.Y.L.J., Nov. 24, 1978 at 4, col. 3.
123 The four bills introduced in Massachusetts in 1979 illustrate the range of statutory possibilities. House bill 2387 requires the Court to recognize agreements reached by parents for joint legal custody and the shared or sole physical custody of the children;" House bill 2411 states "Joint custody shall be encouraged" and lists circumstances where such an award would be appropriate; House Bill 1617 states that "both parents shall share ... custody and domicile ... unless one or both are unfit or one or both abandon the children or voluntarily relinquish shared custody;" and House Bill 2394 directs that where parents have not made a stipulated agreement as to legal custody, "it shall be the presumption of the court ... that legal custody ... shall remain equally with and be equally shared by both parents."
124 Prior to amendment Oregon law read, "Whenever the court grants a decree of annulment or dissolution of marriage or of separation, it has power further to decree as follows: (a) For the future care and custody of the minor children of the marriage as it may deem just and proper." Or. Rev. Stat. § 107.105.
125 Minutes of the House Committee on Judiciary, March 18, 1977 and May 5, 1977; Minutes of the Senate Committee on the Judiciary, March 11, 1977 (Available from the Oregon Legislative Assembly, State Capitol, Salem, Oregon).
126 1977 Or. Laws, Chapter 205 (Senate Bill 446, Or. Senate, Reg. Sess. (1977); House Bill 2532, Oregon Legislative Assembly, Reg. Sess. (1977).
127 House Bill 2532, *supra* note 126, which failed to pass, stated "joint custody shall be encouraged" and included the following list of circumstances under one or more of which joint custody might be appropriate:
   (a) Where there exists an amicable relationship between the parties and they are able to communicate and generally agree with each other concerning joint decisions affecting the welfare of the child.
   (b) Where both parties are employed and the child would benefit by the assumption by both parties of joint responsibility for care and maintenance of the child.
   (c) Where the child is of such age or emotional development that the child would benefit from experiencing the advantages of joint custody.
   (d) The health or the conditions of one party are such that custody of the child by that party alone may be undesirable.
   (e) Where legal conditions exist such that the interests of the child would be best served by joint custody.
   (f) Where the parties live in sufficiently close proximity to each other that the child's life is not disrupted to any significant degree by joint custody.
   (g) Any other circumstances as the court may deem appropriate.
Bills similar to Oregon's HB 2532 have been defeated in California, Massachusetts, and Pennsylvania. See Foster & Freed, "Joint Custody — A Viable Alternative," N.Y.L.J., Dec. 22, 1978 at 2, col. 5.
128 Or. Rev. Stat. § 107.105. (New language is italicized). Other Oregon statutory provisions were amended to recognize the option of joint custody; *e.g.* Ore. Rev. Stat. 107.095 now provides for support "by one party or jointly."
129 Wis. Stat. Ann. § 247.24. (West Cum. Supp. 1978-79). This definition of joint custody is advocated by the authors of this article.
130 Bondenhagen, "Joint Custody of Children and the Wisconsin Divorce Reform Act of 1977" (Unpublished Paper, University of Wisconsin Law School, Dec. 13, 1977) at 22.

131 *Id.*

132 *Id.*

133 *Id.* at 23.

134 Iowa Code Ann. § 598.21 (Supp. 1978-79).

135 N.C. Gen. Stat. § 50-13.2(b) states: "An order for custody of a minor child may grant exclusive custody of such child to one person, agency, organization or institution, or, if clearly in the best interest of the child, provide for custody in two or more of the same...."
Me. Rev. Stat. title 18, § 217 states: "[The judge] may decree which parent shall have the exclusive care and custody of the person of such minor or he may apportion the care and custody of the said minor between the parents, as the good of the child may require".

136 N.J. Stat. Ann. § 2A.

137 *Mayer v. Mayer,* 150 N.J. Super. 556, 561, 376A. 2d 214, 217 (1977). Having found statutory authority to award joint custody, the court then considered whether it was appropriate under the facts of the case. Reasons given to support the joint custody award were (1) the children, ages 13 and 11, were not of such a young age that an award of joint custody would be detrimental to them; (2) the parents would be living one in New Jersey and one in Pittsburgh, Pennsylvania, and if sole custody were given the mother, visitation by the father would be difficult and expensive, and (3) the children were entitled to know, love and respect their father just as much as they know, love and respect their mother. *Id.* at 220.

138 N.Y. Dom. Rel. Law § 240.

139 *Odette R. v. Douglas R.,* 91 Misc. 2d 792, 795, 399 N.Y.S. 2d 93, 95 (1977).

140 Mo. Rev. Stat. § 452.375. This list of factors to be included in determining the best interests of the child was added by amendments in 1973. There has been a trend in the 1970's to articulate such factors in order to bring meaning to the nebulous "best interests of the child" standard for custody awards.

141 *Schumm v. Schumm,* 223 S.W. 2d 122, 125 (Mo. Ct. App. 1949).

142 *Cradic v. Cradic,* 544 S.W. 2d 605, 607 (Mo. Ct. App. 1976).

143 Foster & Freed, *supra* note 127.

144 *Lumbra v. Lumbra,* 394 A. 2d 1139 (Sup. Ct. Vt. 1978). The negative attitude of some courts toward joint custody is not confined to the United States. The Ontario Court of Appeals denounced joint custody except in special cases in reversing an order of a trial court that had granted joint custody where each parent had sought sole custody. Lipovenko, "Court Overturns Order for Joint Custody of Child," The Globe & Mail (Toronto, Canada) March 30, 1979.

145 Woolley, *supra* note 3 at 9 states: "Not only are such arrangements not mentioned, they are usually specifically discouraged ..."

146 Holly, *supra* note 2.

147 R. Moffett & J. Scherer, *Dealing With Divorce* 108-09 (1976).

148 Ware, "Joint Custody: One Way to End the War," New West, Feb. 26, 1979, at 44.

149 See note 127 and accompanying text, *supra.*

150 Oregon Judicial College, Judicial Orientation Workshop, Domestic Relations Outline, III 3(d), (October, 1977), (Unpublished).

151 *Roberts v. Roberts,* 30 Or. App. 1149, 1154, 569 P. 2d 668, 670 (1977) (Dissenting opinion) (Richardson, J.); See text accompanying notes 14-26 *infra,* for a summary of arguments against divided custody.

152 *Wheeler v. Wheeler,* 37 Wash. 2d 159, 170, 222 P. 2d 400, 406 (1950).

153 Gaddis, *supra* note 3 at 19.

154 Although later labeling it "a myth that most American courts are dead set against joint custody", Foster and Freed explained the skepticisim of lawyers and courts as follows: "... [l]awyers and courts encounter custodial failures more often than successful arrangements as to child custody, hence, their pessimism, if not their hostility, towards a

division of control and physical custody, is understandable." Foster & Freed, *supra* note 122, at 4, col. 1, and *supra* note 127 at 2, col. 1.

155 Foster & Freed, N.Y.L.J. Nov. 24, 1978, at 4, col. 2.

156 *Id.*

157 See *e.g.,* M. Roman & W. Haddad, *supra* note 5.

158 See text accompanying notes 211-222, *infra.*

159 See generally S. Gettleman & J. Markowitz, *The Courage to Divorce,* Ch. 4 (1974), which does not specifically address the issue of joint custody, but is an excellent resource to help dispell many myths of divorce and its effect on children.

160 *Id.* at 42.

161 *Id.* at 48.

161 *Id.* at 47.

163 *Id.* at 73.

164 Only Illinois, Pennsylvania and South Dakota now have fault grounds exclusively. Freed & Foster, "Divorce in the Fifty States," 11 Fam. L.Q. 297 (1977) updated in 11 Fam. L.Q. at v. (1978).

165 Harry Fain of Los Angeles, past chairman of the ABA Family Law Section, as quoted in Dullea, *supra* note 2.

166 Woolley, *supra* note 3, at 33.

167 J. Noble & W. Noble, *The Custody Trap* 160 (1975).

168 They report that their own research and two other joint custody studies agree that "joint custody couples show reduced conflict and their children are quite well adjusted." M. Roman & W. Haddad, *supra* note 5, at 116.

169 Woolley, *supra* note 3, at 33.

170 In summarizing circumstances favorable to joint custody, Foster and Freed described the necessary parental relationship as follows: "2. The parties have demonstrated that they are capable of reaching shared decisions in the child's best interests and are able to communicate and to give priority to the child's welfare." Foster & Freed, *supra* note 127 at 3, col. 1. New York City Supreme Court Justice Bentley Kassel described the necessary parental attitude as "the parents must give priority to the child's interest when they communicate." 5 Fam. L. Rep. (BNA) 2143, 2144 (1978).

171 Woolley, *supra* note 3, at 9.

172 Grief, "Fathers, Children, and Joint Custody" 11-12 (Unpublished paper presented at the 1978 Anual Meeting of the American Orthopsychiatric Association, San Francisco, Cal.). See also Grief, "Joint Custody; A Viable Alternative?" Trial, May 1979, at 32.

173 Gaddis, *supra* note 3, at 18.

174 Grief, *supra* note 172, at 11.

175 Interview with Hugh McIsaac, Director of the Conciliation Court, Los Angeles County, California, Feb. 4, 1979. Legislation now pending California to create a presumption for joint custody would allow modification to sole custody upon "... evidence of any substantial or repeated failure of a parent to adhere to the plan for implementing the joint custody decree ..." Calif. S.B. 477.

176 Both M. Galper, *supra* note 5, and M. Roman & W. Haddad, *supra* note 5, contain numerous "testimonials" of joint custody parents that support this conclusion. See also Ware, *supra* note 2. Remarks by parents who participated in a panel presentation, Practical Aspects of Joint Custody at a workshop sponsored by the Washington Association of Family Courts and the Oregon Association of Conciliation Courts, Kelso, Washington, Oct. 14, 1977 (transcript available from authors) showed this same dedication to cooperation. [hereinafter cited as Parents Panel].

177 M. Roman & W. Haddad, *supra* note 5.

178 One might question if parental efforts to "shut the book softly" and utilize joint custody as a transition for children and parents is, in itself, something to be discouraged.

179 Ahrons, "The Coparental Divorce: Preliminary Research Findings and Policy Implications 13" (Unpublished paper presented at the annual meeting of National Council on Family Relations, Philadelphia, Pa., Oct. 19-22, 1978).

180 Meyer Elkin, the founding director of the Los Angeles Conciliation Court, in writing about joint custody, believes that family patterns have changed so rapidly as to make traditional family law "a reflection of another time, another age that no longer exists." Elkin, "Editorial-Reflections on Joint Custody and Family Law," Conciliation Courts Rev., Dec. 1978, at iii.

181 Abarbanel, "Joint Custody: What are We Afraid Of?" 3 (Unpublished paper presented at the 1978 annual meeting of the American Orthopsychiatric Association in San Francisco, Cal.).

182 See Ahrons, *supra* note 179, at 14.

183 Grote & Weinstein, *supra* note 3, at 46.

184 Elkin, *supra* note 180.

185 See Ricci, "Disspelling the Stereotype of the Broken Home," Concilation Courts Rev., Jan. 1976, at 7.

186 Almost every reported child custody decision uses this doctrine as a starting point. Most state statutes listing criteria for custody decisions also concentrate on the "best interest of the child." See *e.g.,* Uniform Marriage and Divorce Act § 402.

187 M. Roman & W. Haddad, *supra* note 5, 50-51.

188 *Id.* at 73-79.

189 *Id.* at 79.

190 Remarks of Helen Mendes, Ph.D, at conference on "The Divorcing Family" at University of Southern California, Jan. 26-27 as reported in Los Angeles Times, Jan. 30, 1979.

191 Nehls, "Joint Custody of Children: A Descriptive Study" 7 (Unpublished, 1978).

192 It is reported that, "About 60% of divorced women work outside the home", "One Child, Two Homes," Time, Jan. 29, 1979, at 61. A recently completed survey in Portland, Oregon found 84% of divorced women worked for pay. Oregon Bureau of Labor, *Divorced Women in Portland* 35 (1978).

193 In Oregon, ex-wives are encouraged to become independent of spousal support within a ten-year period; failure to make "a reasonable effort" to become independent gives grounds to terminate spousal support. Or. Rev. Stat. § 107.407.

194 See S. Gettleman & J. Markowitz, *supra* note 159, at 194.

195 *Id.*

196 See J. Noble & W. Noble, *supra* note 167, at 120-22, in which the authors recount a dramatic case where a mother who decides initially not to seek custody is rebuffed by parents, neighbors and lawyers until she does fight for custody and loses. She then suffers the double whammy of public censure for relinquishing custody and of judicial insult by being found the "less fit" parent.

197 R. Eisler, *Dissolution, No Fault Divorce, Marriage and the Future of Women* 57 (1977).

198 J. Noble & W. Noble, *supra* note 167, at 160.

199 For instance the October, 1976, issue of "Fam. Coordinator" was devoted to materials on fathers and fathering.

200 Greif, *supra* note 172, at 8.

201 E. Atkin & E. Rubin, *Part-Time Father* 29 (1976).

202 Hetherington, Cox & Cox, *supra* note 75, at 421.

203 *Id.* at 427.

204 Parents Panel, *supra* note 176.

205 Nehls, *supra* note 191, at 7.

206 Greif, *supra* note 172, at 7. Fathers with visitation rights have used a variety of terms to describe this limited relationship with their children including "Disneyland Dads,"

"Sugar Daddy," "Week-end father," "Good-time Charlie," and "I feel like a grand-father".

207 *Id.*

208 See *e.g.,* H. Biller, *Father, Child & Sex Role* (1971).

209 A study by the Child Study Institute at the University of Maryland looked at children in the sole custody of mothers and children in the sole custody of fathers and concluded: "Given comparable income, parental adjustment, and parental interests in the child, fathers were seen as equally capable as mothers in providing a home environment conducive to the healthy growth and adjustment of the child." 3 Fam. L. Rep. (BNA) 2745 (1977).

210 See Parke & Swaine, "The Father's Role in Infancy: A Re-evaluation," 25 Fam. Coordinator 365 (1976) and Lamb & Lamb, "The Nature and Importance of the Father-Infant Relationship," 25 Fam. Coordinator 379 (1976). It is estimated that 1,500,000 men now head single parent homes. 5 Fam. L. Rep. (BNA) 2143 (1978).

211 This argument has been used most frequently against divided custody, see section I(B). Although joint custody does not require any particular type of physical arrangement or division of a child's time between the parents, because many joint custody families do divide the child's time, arguments against divided custody are frequently advanced against joint custody.

Woolley, *supra* note 3, found that joint custody families were using a great variety of physical arrangements including alternating weeks, split weeks, alternating days, and "bird's nest" — where the children stayed in the family home and the parents took turns "living in" and "living out." Some families with older children left arrangements completely flexible and worked out schedules as needs of children and parents dictated.

212 See Goldstein, Freud & Solnit, *supra* note 60.

213 See discussion, section III, *supra.*

214 M. Roman & W. Haddad *supra* note 5, at 111. In a recent University of Michigan study on children of divorced parents, the custody arrangement most frequently chosen by 165 children questioned was half the week with one parent and half with the other: 5 Fam. L. Rep. (BNA) 2395 (1979).

215 Elkin, *supra* note 180, at iv.

216 Goldstein, Freud & Solnit, *supra* note 60, at 38.

217 *Id.* at 37.

218 *Id.* at 38.

219 *Id.*

220 *Id.*

221 Foster, "A Review of Beyond the Best Interest of the Child," 12 Willamette L.J. 545, 551 (1976).

222 Many courts have wholly embraced the "Beyond the Best Interests of the Child" thesis in divorce custody cases. See *e.g., In re McClure,* 21 Or. App. 441, 535 P. 2d 112 (1975) in which the Oregon Court of Appeals affirmed the award of custody to the mother who regained physical custody of their two children following recovery from her mental breakdown and then moved the children out of state. Though the children were most recently in the care of the mother, the father had previously cared for them and was found by the court relatively equal in "those factors considered when custody is determined." *Id.* at 444-45. The appellate court, after extensively quoting Goldstein, Freud and Solnit, held "the best interests of the children will be served by the least detrimental alternative of continuing their custody in the mother." *Id.* at 446. The court's acknowledgement of the importance of "leaving the children where they are" regardless of why they have been shifted between mother and father *Id.* at 445, was notice to other divorce litigants that the parent with physical custody at the time of the hearing is likely to "win" permanent custody.

223 Stack, *supra* note 3 at 507.

224 See Folberg, "Facilitating Agreement," Conciliation Courts Rev., Dec. 1978, at 17.

225 The Association of Family Conciliation Courts has distributed more than 130,000 copies of a pamphlet entitled "Parents Are Forever." Ass'n of Fam. Conciliation Courts, Publication Report (1978).

226 Molinoff, "Joint Custody: Victory for All?" N.Y. Times, March 6, 1977, § 22, at 18, col. 1.

227 Greif, *supra* note 172, at 10.

228 Abarbanel, *supra* note 181, at 15.

229 *Id.* at 17.

230 *Id.* at 20.

231 Nehls, *supra* note 191, at 31.

232 *Id.*

233 Batt, "Child Custody Disputes: A Developmental-Psychological Approach to Proof and Decisionmaking," 12 Willamette L.J. 491 (1976).

234 M. Galper, *supra* note 5, at 124.

235 Professor Robert H. Mnookin observes that of possible decision makers, "parents are more appropriate decision makers than some disinterested third part (like a judge) or a professional (like a doctor)" in remarks not directly concerning custody decisions in "Children's Rights: Legal and Ethical Dilemma," 2 The Transcript, No. 3, at 8 (1978) (published by Boalt Alumni Association, Berkeley, California).

236 Although proximity is often mentioned as a prerequisite for joint custody, see *e.g., Lumbra v. Lumbra,* 394 A. 2d 1139 (Sup. Ct. Vt. 1978), the great distance between the parents homes was seen as a reason to award joint custody in *Mayer v. Mayer,* 150 N.J. Super. 556, 376 A. 2d 214 (1977).

237 Foster and Freed speak of the necessary closeness of the parental homes in these terms: "The logistics are such that there is no substantial disruption of the child's routine, schooling, association with friends, religious training, etc. Ordinarily this means close geographical proximity of both parents or a ' bird nest' arrangement." Foster & Freed, supra note 127.

238 Parents Panel, *supra* note 176. Alice Abarbanel observed that "all the parents in this study expressed a commitment to staying in close geographical proximity," Abarbanel, *supra* note 181, at 25.

239 One of the authors has drafted an apparently successful joint custody agreement, accepted by the court, in which one parent resides in Oregon and one in Colorado, and in another case where the residential parent was in Oregon and the other parent, an airline pilot, was anticipating a move to Hawaii.

240 See discussion accompanying notes 318-320, *infra.*

241 See discussion of modification issue, section VIII (H), *infra.* S.B. 477, now pending in the California Legislature, would specifically allow consideration of evidence "... that one parent has established, or is likely to establish, his or her principal residence in another state ..." in motions to modify decrees of joint custody.

242 Ware, *supra* note 2, at 52-53.

243 Bodenheimer, *supra* note 30, at 1011.

244 Nehls, *supra* note 191, at 20-21.

245 *Id.*

246 Remarks of New York Supreme Court Justice Bentley Kassal, Conference on Current Developments in Child Custody, New York, Dec. 2, 1978, reprinted in 5 Fam. L. Rep. (BNA) 2141 (1978).

247 Isolina Ricci, in a presentation entitled "Cooperative Parenting After Divorce: Myth or Reality" given at a conference on the Divorcing Family, University of Southern California, Jan. 27, 1979, as reported in the Los Angeles Times, Jan. 3, 1979, Part IV, at 4, col. 2. Persia Woolley found child sharing arrangements at all economic levels. Letter

to authors dated March 9, 1979.

248 See note 125 *supra.*

249 *Id.*

250 "One Child, Two Homes," *supra* note 2.

251 See notes 202-203 and accompanying text, *supra.*

252 See Annot., 92 A.L.R. 2d 705 (1963).

253 Johnson, "Child Support: Preventing Default," Conciliation Courts Rev., Sept. 1978, at 27, at 31. Johnson compares the higher non-compliance figures from a metropolitan county in Wisconsin, where support payments, apparently, need not be paid through the court, with non-compliance in seven diverse Illinois counties, where support payments were ordered to be paid through the courts. The same figures as those cited above in Wisconsin are cited by R. Moffatt & J. Scherer, *supra* note 147, at 116, though the authors there seem to attribute the figures to New York.

254 *Id.* at 31.

255 It is not entirely clear from the comparative tables used by Johnson, *id.,* if the percent figures listed under "no compliance" included cases in which less than the full amount was contributed.

256 E. Atkin & E. Rubin, *Part-Time Fathers* 90 (1976).

257 See E. Atkin & E. Rubin, *supra* note 256 for a typical scenario of the chain reaction.

258 Though support obligations and visitation privileges are generally independent, there is a trend to legally recognize their interrelationship. See *e.g.,* Or. Rev. Stat. § 107.135 which authorizes a petition to cease support if visitation rights are purposely frustrated. New York family courts have regularly held that child support and visitation rights are interdependent. 3 Fam. L. Rep. (BNA) 1109 (1977). The Utah Supreme Court has also held that visitation is a condition precedent to receiving support. 1 Fam. L. Rep. (BNA) 2208 (1977). *Contra, Comiskey v. Comiskey,* 48 Ill. App. 3d 17, 366 N.E. 2d 87 (1977).

259 Johnson, *supra* note 251.

260 For examples of co-parents' attitudes on flexibility of financial arrangements, see M. Galper, *supra* note 5, at 48-50.

261 Woolley, *supra* note 3, at 9.

262 M. Galper, *supra* note 5, at 17-19.

263 For a handbook that both traces patterns of cooperation and sets out practical guidelines on how to provide greater security for children through shared custody, see P. Woolley, *The Custody Handbook* (1979).

264 S. Gettlemen & J. Markowitz, *supra* note 159, at 93.

265 Some few states now give grandparents standing in their childrens' divorce proceedings. In Wisconsin the 1977 Divorce Reform Act retained the statute allowing the court to award visitation rights to a grandparent where that is in the child's best interests, and expanded it to include great-grandparents as well. Wisc. Stat. Ann. § 247.245. See generally Annot., 90 A.L.R. 3d 222 (1979).

266 As quoted in The Oregonian (Portland, Oregon) Dec. 26, 1977, at 1, col. 1.

267 M. Mead, *Blackberry Winter — My Earlier Years* 282 (1972).

268 M. Galper, *supra* note 5, at 133.

269 Parents Panel, *supra* note 176.

270 Stack, *supra* note 3, at 508.

271 *Id.* at 513.

272 See the argument advanced on this point by M. Roman & W. Haddad, *supra* note 5, at 113-115.

273 Isolina Ricci, marriage and family counselor, as quoted in Huerta, *supra* note 2.

274 M. Mead, Anomalies in American Postdivorce Relationships, *Divorce And After* 121 (P. Bohannan ed. 1971).

275 Molinoff, "After Divorce, Give Them a Father, Too," Newsday, Oct. 5, 1975.

276 M. Galper, *supra* note 5, at 112.

277 Baum, *supra* note 2.

278 Another joint custody father reports that after informing his childrens' teachers that he was sharing joint custody and the children were residing with him, the next notice from the classroom was politely addressed "Dear Parent". The message read, "Please send a pair of your old pantyhose to school with your child . . ."

279 When a child from a joint custody family was asked by her second-grade teacher to draw a picture of her family, the little girl began drawing two houses. Upon correction by the teacher, the child changed her picture to show what the teacher wanted, although the resulting picture did not reflect the reality of her life: M. Galper, *supra* note 5, at 111.

280 Joint custody can encompass arrangements in which the children reside with one parent, except for periods that in sole custody situations would be referred to as visitation. Again, the distinction is the shared authority for major child related decisions and a requirement for open communication and cooperation, see text accompanying notes 29-40 *supra*. In joint custody arrangements where the children regularly reside with one parent, others may or may not know of the shared decision making.

281 A 12-year old boy who spends two days with one parent, then two days with the other and rotates three day weekends in each home did not perceive his unconventional living arrangement as a problem to his friends: "My friends know where to reach me. I just give them the phone numbers and the schedule. It works out okay." Parents of an 8-year old girl, however, who spends summers with her father and the rest of the year with her mother reported that their daughter "has two sets of friends, neither of which has fully accepted her because of her part-time living." "One Child, Two Homes," *supra* note 2.

282 A teenager, Gabrielle Ream, who works with her school's Divorced Kids Group says "I think it's very important to read the (divorce) agreement . . ." Cooke, "Children of Divorced Help Peers With Woes," The Oregonian, (Portland, Oregon) March 21, 1979, at D4, col. 3.

In a somewhat parallel vein, there is a growing trend to recognize the right and interest of adoptees to obtain information from sealed adoption records. See R. Klibanoff, "Genealogical Information in Adoption: The Adoptee's Quest and the Law," 11 Fam. L.Q. 185 (1977).

283 In *Shelton v. Chrisman,* Civil Action No. CA-3-75-1268-D, Jan. 31, 1979 (N.D. Tex. 1979), the court points out that the state itself does not enforce decrees relating to custody. "Notwithstanding the terms of the decree, the parents are generally free to do with their children what they will, if they agree."

284 Bruch, "Making Visitation Work: Dual Parenting Orders," 1 Fam. Advocate 22 (1978).

285 This makes "the law appear an ass", as Mr. Bumbles phrased it in C. Dickens, *Oliver Twist,* Ch. 10.

286 See *Daniel v. Daniel,* 239 Ga. 466, 469, 238 S.E. 2d 108, 110 (1977).

287 For a discussion of the non-custodial parents rights in matters of the child's education, see Annot., 36 A.L.R. 3d 1093 (1970).

288 Bodenheimer, "Equal Rights, Visitation, and the Right to Move," 1 Fam. Advocate 18 (1978).

289 Galper, *supra* note 5, at 48-52.

290 For example, where a father stopped making support payments for a six month period during which he assumed custody of the children so his ex-wife could return to school, a Georgia trial court nonetheless held him in arrears for payments not made during the period the child was with him. The Appellate court refused to uphold the execution but cautioned "we are by no means authorizing blanket modification of divorce decrees by private agreement." *Daniel v. Daniel,* 239 Ga. 466, 469, 238 S.E. 2d 108, 110 (1977).

291 *Id.*

292 See *e.g., Leskovich v. Leskovich,* 385 A. 2d 373, (Pa. Super. Ct. 1978).

120   FAMILY LAW: AN INTERDISCIPLINARY PERSPECTIVE

293 See instructions to judges *supra* note 150 and accompanying text.
294 See *e.g., Huffman v. Huffamn,* 50 Ill. App. 3d 217, 365 N.E. 2d 270 (1977); *Gall v. Gall,* 336 So. 2d 10 (Fla. Dist. Ct. App. 1976); *In re Leskovich,* 385 A. 2d 373, (Pa. Super. Ct. 1978); *Brand v. Brand,* 441 S.W. 2d 750 (Mo. Ct. App., 1969); *Loebenburg v. Loebenburg,* 85 R.I. 115, 127 A. 2d 500 (1956); *Gallagher v. Gallagher,* 60 Ill. App. 3d 26, 376 N.E. 2d 279 (1978); *Hare v. Porter,* 233 So. 2d 653 (Fla. Dist. Ct. App. 1970). *Asch v. Asch,* 164 N.J. Super. 499, 397 A. 2d 352 (1978); *Daniel v. Daniel,* 239 Ga. 466, 238 S.E. 2d 108 (1977).
295 Suprisingly few statistics are available on post-divorce litigation. It is reported that in Dane County, Wisconsin, 34.3% of cases in which there were an initial custody study return to court for further custody litigation within two years. Milne, *supra* note 85, at 5.
296 Hearings before the California Senate Committee on Judiciary, Conciliation Courts (Testimony of Christian E. Markey, Presiding Judge, Super. Ct. of Los Angeles Cty., Family Law Division) Dec. 6, 1978: "I believe quite frankly that there is no such thing as a "permanent" custody order. I think the law's fairly clear that when you're talking about the best interests of the minor, there really isn't a permanent custody order, thus, at any time. One must be prepared, it seems to me, to adjudicate the best interests of the child with respect to what's put properly before the court."
297 "Joint Custody," L.A. County Bar Family Law Section Newsletter, No. V, Winter, 1978, at 3.
298 Gaddis, *supra* note 3, at 19.
299 *Id.* at 20. Gaddis urges the following wording: In the event that the parents alone cannot resolve a conflict, they agree to seek appropriate, competent assistance. The matter shall be referred mediation (if that is not successful, for arbitration) to Family Court, a counselor, or to a lawyer or professional person skilled in the area of resolution of the problems of children and their families. This procedure shall be followed to its conclusion prior to either party seeking relief from the court.
300 *Id.*
301 The American Arbitration Assocition, in its pamphlet "Family Dispute Services (1978) suggests the following arbitration provision in separation agreements: "Any controversy arising out of or relating to this agreement or the breach thereof, shall be settled by arbitration in accordance with the Rules of the American Arbitration Association. Both parties agree to abide by the terms of the award rendered by the Arbitrator(s) and judgment upon the award may be entered in any Court having jurisdiction thereof." On the use and enforceability of arbitration clauses in separation agreements, see Holman & Noland, "Agreement and Arbitration: Relief to Over-Litigation in Domestic Relating Disputes in Washington," 12 Willamette L.J. 527 (1976).
302 Correspondence from Shirley J. Burgoyne, Esq., Ann Arbor, Mich. Oct. 20, 1976 (Shared Custody Agreement Form).
303 Gaddis, *supra* note 3, at 20.
304 See Elkin, "Postdivorce Counseling in a Conciliation Court," 1 J. of Divorce 55 (1977). S.B. 477, pending in California, would specifically encourage the use of conciliation courts "to resolve any controversy which has arisen in the implementation of a plan for joint custody previously approved by the court."
305 See *infra,* section IX, Criteria for Decree of Joint Custody.
306 See *Caroll v. Caroll,* 4 Fam. L. Rep. (BNA) 2768 (Ill. Ct. App. 1978).
307 *In re Brantner,* 67 Cal. App. 3d, 416, 422, 136 Cal. Rptr. 635, 638 (4th Dist. 1977).
308 See *e.g., Caroll v. Caroll,* 4 Fam. L. Rep. (BNA) 2768 (Ill. Ct. App. 1978).
309 See Gaddis, "Joint Custody of Children: A Divorce Decision-Making Alternative," Wash. St. Bar News, March 1978, at 17.
310 Private mediation as well as court connected services may be utilized for this purpose. See Coogler, *Structured Mediation in Divorce Settlement* 161 (1978). See also note 304,

supra for proposed California legislation on point.

311 See *e.g., Asch v. Asch,* 164 N.J. Super. 499, 397 A. 2d 352 (1978).

312 See *e.g., Burge v. City of San Francisco,* 41 Cal. 2d 608, 262 P. 2d 6 (1953).

313 See *e.g., Huffman v. Huffman,* 50 Ill. App. 3d 217, 365 N.E. 2d 270 (1977).

314 Where a father violated a joint custody order by asserting, without benefit of a "neutral determination by a court," that he would henceforth be sole custodian of the children, the appellate court directed the lower court to "... consider appellee's disrespect for the legal process and evaluate how it bears on his fitness to be awarded custody of the children." *In re Leskowich,* 385 A. 2d 373, 378 (Pa. Super. Ct. 1979).

315 Calif. SB 477, now pending, expressly allows a court to consider a parent's "failure to adhere to the plan for implementing the joint custody ..." See note 175 *supra.*

316 See Bodenheimer, "Progress Under the Uniform Child Custody Jurisdiction Act and Remaining Problems: Punitive Decrees, Joint Custody and Excessive Modifications" 65 Calif. L. Rev. 978, 1013 (1977).

317 *Id.* at 1004, 1006.

318 See discussion section VIII(D), *supra.*

319 Gaddis, *supra* note 3, where a form provision is suggested restricting removal from the jurisdiction without prior consent or court approval.

320 See Woolley, *supra* note 3.

321 See *e.g.* Bodenheimer, "Equal Rights, Visitation, and the Right to Move," 1 Fam. Advocate 19 (1978).

322 But see, Bodenheimer, *supra* note 316, at 1004.

323 Bodenheimer, *supra* note 316, at 1011.

324 Woolley, *supra* note 3, at 34.

325 *Braiman v. Braiman,* 44 N.Y. 2d 584, 586, 407 N.Y.S. 2d 449, 452, 378 N.E. 2d 1019, 1022 (1978). See also Foster & Freed, *supra* note 127.

326 5 Fam. L. Rep. (BNA) 2144 (1978).

327 As the anger diminished over time and parental roles are isolated from marital conflicts, joint custody might then be considered. Stating "it's rarely too late to work out a joint custody program, no matter how much time has elapsed since the divorce ...", Ware tells of a couple who battled destructively over their children for four years before deciding to try co-parenting. Both parents now strongly advocate joint custody. Ware, *supra* note 2, at 54-55.

328 See notes 112-13 and accompanying text, *supra.*

329 Roman & Haddad, *supra* note 3, at 173. In a strong dissent in a recent New Hampshire Supreme Court decision that awarded sole custody to the mother, Judge Douglas urged trial judges and attorneys to consider a presumption of joint custody. *Starkeson v. Starkeson,* 397 A. 2d 1043 (Sup. Ct. N.H. 1979). Massachusetts (HB 2394), and Oregon (HB 2538) have bills pending which would establish a statutory presumption for joint custody of children upon divorce. California Senate Bill 447 would create a presumption that joint custody is in the best interests of a minor child, but only if 3 factors are present: (1) parental agreement, (2) consideration of the child's wishes where appropriate, (3) submission of an acceptable joint custody plan. Absent these three factors the court could award joint custody as a matter of judicial discretion.

330 *Lumbra v. Lumbra,* 394 A. 2d 1139 (Sup. Ct. Vt. 1978).

331 See *e.g., Gall v. Gall,* 336 So. 2d 10 (Fla. Dist. Ct. App. 1976); *Ralston v. Ralston,* 396 S.W. 2d 775 (Ky. Ct. App. 1965).

332 See comments of Justice Felice Shea who feels presumptions in custody cases are *per se* inappropriate. 5 Fam. L. Rep. (BNA) 2144 (1978).

333 Foster and Freed oppose use of presumptions in custody disputes and call for "meticulous fact finding", Foster & Freed, *supra* note 127.

334 The "preference" for joint custody which would be established in California with the

enactment of AB 1480 now pending in the California legislature has been referred to as a "mandatory joint custody bill." See Bach, "Mandatory Joint Custody Bill — A Help or A Hindrance to Lawyers?" The Los Angeles Daily Journal, June 11, 1979, at 3, col. 1.

335   Language that would require acceptance of a stipulated parental agreement is contained in House Bill 2387 introduced in the 1979 Massachusetts Legislative Session: "Where the parents have reached an appropriate agreement providing for the joint legal custody and the shared or sole physical custody of the children, the Court shall enter an order accordingly unless specific findings are made by the Justice indicating that such an order would not be in the best interests of the children." California S.B. 477 is similar. See note 329 supra.

336   In Alameda County, California, joint custody proposals are referred to conciliation court counselors for an evaluation. Bodenheimer, supra note 288, at 1011.

337   In Lumbra v. Lumbra, 394 A. 2d 1139, 1142 (Sup. Ct. Vt. 1979), the court listed factors trial courts should consider in joint custody cases. Included, among other things, were "age of the child," "distance between houses of the parents," and "frequency of transfer and proportion of each parent's custodial time;" factors taken from divided custody cases. See also Mayer v. Mayer, 150 N.J. Super. 556, 376 A. 2d 214 (1977).

338   See note 296 and text accompanying, supra.

339   As Elkins, supra note 180, at vi stated: "It is well known that when we expect more of people and ask them to stretch for their potential, people rise to the occasion and meet expectations. When we encourage divorced parents to be involved in shared parenting, as in joint custody, we are addressing ourselves to the strengths in them rather than their weaknesses."

340   In commenting on the role of law, Professor Carol Bruch observed: "In general, law works in at least two ways. It sets standards for acceptable behavior and it resolves disputes . . . [r]easonable societal expectations that are included in a court's judgment will be obeyed by the majority of people." Bruch, supra note 31, at 22, 26.

341   An unofficial estimate indicates that between 80 and 90 percent of contested custody cases involve two perfectly fit parents, P. Woolley, The Custody Handbook (1979).

342   Professor Carol Bruch argues that both parents can be compelled to assume part of the burden of caring for their children by use of "dual parenting orders," short of joint custody. Bruch, supra note 31.

343   Stephen Gaddis in a letter to the authors dated March 28, 1979, points out that "A responsibility rests on the practicing bar members of the bench, and others involved in the legal process to assert ourselves in teaching our clients what all the alternatives are, and what is appropriate behavior."

344   Court-connected conciliation and counseling services are now available in at least 15 states. They all offer custody counseling and some offer custody mediation without charge. Report of Exec. Dir., Association of Family Conciliation Courts, Annual Meeting, Hartford, Conn., 1979.

345   When two women claimed to be the mother of the same child, King Solomon called for his sword and threatened to divide the child. He observed the women's reactions and reasoned that she who was willing to give up the child rather than see it split in two was the true mother: 1 Kings 3:16-27.

Part 2: Child Welfare

Child Abuse and the Interdisciplinary Team:
Panacea or Problem?*

*Michael Benjamin***

INTRODUCTION

In 1962, Henry Kempe and his colleagues published the paper in which they first coined the phrase "the battered baby syndrome". The world, at least the world of child protective services, has never been the same since; for it was this paper which first succeeded in calling public attention to the phenomenon of child abuse.

The result was the relatively rapid development of a new awareness of and an interest in atypical parental treatment of children. As this interest grew, it was expressed in various ways, including the generalized enactment of statutory changes aimed at child protection; the widespread implementation of central registries aimed at improving abuse detection and reporting; the rapid rise in the number of reports of suspected abuse; the creation of institutions specifically mandated to collect information on and support research in the area; and, the striking increase in the size of the research literature on the subject.

Despite these developments, by the early 1970's child protective services in both the United States and Canada were in disarray. Throughout this period, the majority of abuse cases were handled by a multiplicity of autonomous service agencies. Their efforts at service delivery, however, were clearly inadequate to the demand. In retrospect, this is not difficult to explain. Agencies with limited fiscal and manpower resources were faced with a huge and rapidly increasing caseload (Rosenfeld & Newberger, 1977). The results were predictable: workers were overburdened and underpaid (D'Agostino, 1975); workers, both

---

* I wish to thank Norman Bell and Howard Irving for their helpful comments on a draft of this paper.
** Family Sociologist, Department of Sociology, University of Toronto, Toronto, Ontario.

experienced and inexperienced, were poorly supervised and provided with insufficient support of all kinds (Kriendler, 1976); the rate of worker burnout soared (Pine & Maslach, 1978; Armstrong, 1979), with some agencies reporting staff turnover of better than 50% per year (Helfer, 1975); agencies experienced difficulty maintaining a sufficient supply of competent staff in order to man existing programs (Rolde, 1977); and, there was rapid deterioration in the methods used to screen cases (Rosenfeld & Newberger, 1977), with many agencies either referring cases elsewhere, turning cases away or closing cases prematurely (Garbarino & Stocking, 1980: viii), with child death the result in some cases (Kempe, 1978).

As if these difficulties were not enough, efforts to relieve some of these problems by means of interagency co-operation were unsuccessful. Such efforts were characterized (Brown, 1978; Carter, 1976) by: fragmentation; duplication of services; minimal contact between direct contact service personnel; absence of consensus concerning the criteria of child abuse; minimal sharing of information; absence of feedback concerning action(s) taken; conflict concerning diagnostic and treatment goals; discontinuity of service resulting from the lack of interagency co-operation; and, failure to combine specialized services.

Such experience made clear to all concerned that child abuse is a problem of much greater complexity, both theoretically and logistically, than had previously been supposed; that it necessarily required the involvement of a variety of disciplines and skills; and, most important of all, that the urgency of the problem demanded that some remedial action be taken.

Such action has typically been in the form of the development and widespread implementation of the interdisciplinary team. Such a team may be defined as a set of professionals from different disciplines, often representing different agencies, working together for well defined purposes, including coordination, diagnosis, reporting, treatment, education and prevention (Roth, 1978). It is widely regarded, in both the United States and Canada, as the best and most effective current response to the problem of child abuse (e.g. Kaufman & Neill, 1977; Fotherigham, 1977).

If correct, this belief would recommend the universal establishment of such teams wherever local demand for service warranted it. If incorrect, however, pouring time, money and effort into such an endeavour would, at best, divert attention from other, more effective approaches to the problem, or, at worst, represent a considerable setback for current efforts at child protection.

In light of the size and complexity of the task of establishing the universality of a team approach to child abuse, it seems only reasonable that such an undertaking first receive careful and critical evaluation. Such an evaluation is the aim of the present paper.

To that end, I will first compare the expectations and the results of interdisciplinary team efforts. This will reveal a considerable discrepancy between the two. Next, I will examine three overriding limitations to the operation of the team. Finally, I will conclude by exploring several means by which team functioning may be made more consistent with the aim of effective child protection than is presently the case.

THE TEAM APPROACH: EXPECTATIONS AND REALITY

The interdisciplinary team approach is widely regarded as the single most effective means of responding to the problem of child abuse. It follows that the expectations associated with team intervention are correspondingly high. Specifically, such intervention is believed to be the best way to enhance reporting, improve diagnostic accuracy and provide treatment (Fisher, 1976; Hebert & Hendrix, 1977). Such faith in the substantive and educational consequences of the team approach leads one to expect that increasing the number of teams in operation should be highly correlated with (1) an increase in the level of reporting; (2) a decrease in the proportion of unfounded reports of abuse[1]; and (3) an increase in the proportion of identified cases which are treated successfully. In addition, (4) each of these changes should be closely interrelated since change in one index (*e.g.* reporting) without a corresponding change in the other indices (*e.g.* treatment) would be potentially harmful.

In three out of four cases, however, these expectations are not supported by available data. With respect to reporting, a combination of team involvement, statutory changes and public education has produced nothing short of a spectacular increase in the number of reports of suspected child abuse. In the United States, for example, many states report more than a tenfold increase in reporting over the period 1964 to 1976:

State	Number	Year	Number	Year
New York[2]	211	1964	3224	1971
California[3]	4000	1968	40000	1972
Florida[4]	10	1968	30000	1972
Michigan[5]	721	1968	30000	1972
Texas[6]	4000	1973	35000	1975
Massachusetts[7]	700	1974	40000	1976

In Canada, the change in the number of reported cases has been in the same direction, if somewhat less dramatic. Ontario, for example, reports an increase from approximately 320 cases in 1966 to 1054 in 1977 (Silverman, 1978).

These data suggest that team efforts at increasing professional and public awareness of the problem of child abuse has been quite successful. With respect to diagnosis, however, these efforts have been sigularly unproductive. With few exceptions (*e.g.* Hamory & Jeffery, 1977), report after report notes disconfirmation rates of between 30% and 60%: Florida, 45% (Christensen & Fuerst, 1974); North Carolina, 40-60% (Hunter *et al.*, 1978); Texas, 40-52% (Wood, 1977); New York, 55% (Select Committee, 1972: 58); the Province of Quebec, 50% (Comité, 1977). These data suggest, first, an appalling waste of time, money and effort in an area in which each of these is in short supply; second, an apparent lack of consensus concerning the criteria of abuse; and, third, a high level of subjectivity in diagnostic decision-making.

While the high disconfirmation rate is unfortunate, it is at least explicable. At present, the majority of abuse cases involve a considerable degree of judgment, interpretation and selection among available data (Nagi, 1977: 109-110). Further, it may be argued that it is better that many cases be investigated and subsequently disconfirmed than that one genuine case of abuse fail to receive treatment. Arguments regarding reporting and/or diagnosis, then, resolve into the issue of the level of treatment efficacy.

In this context, the data are unequivocal: with rare exceptions (*e.g.* Tracy *et al.*, 1975), most studies report a relatively low proportion of treatment successes. Cohn (Cohn, 1979: Cohn & Miller, 1977), for example, examined 11 child abuse demonstration projects in the United States, many of them using a team approach. He found that no project, whatever its treatment method, reported that more than 42% of its clients exhibited a "reduced propensity" towards abuse. He reports too that of those projects using an interdisciplinary team, all were relatively expensive ($100-$300 per case) and highly inefficient (never more than one or two cases reviewed at any single team meeting). Similar outcome results have been reported in Great Britain (Jones, 1977).

In addition to treatment outcome, data concerning other aspects of treatment are equally discouraging. A significant proportion of abusive families in treatment (*i.e.* 30-50%): (1) re-injure their children while treatment is in progress (Baher *et al.*, 1976: Cohn, 1979); and, (2) show very little change in the hostile, rejecting, punitive style of parent-child interaction which characterized them prior to treatment onset (Martin & Beezley, 1976). Further, several authors openly acknowledge the limitations of current treatment methods by stating that, depending upon circumstances, anywhere from 20-50% of all abusive families are simply untreatable (Dunsted *et al.*, 1975; Lynch *et al.*, 1975; Blumberg, 1974).

Moreover, in what must be the height of irony in the present context, a number of authors note that present methods of treating abusive families are sometimes iatrogenic, that is, they serve to add to the family's already high level of distress rather than offering them the help they so desperately seek and/or need (Kempe, 1978; Martin, 1978; Rolde, 1977).

Finally, the three elements of reporting, diagnosis and treatment are clearly out of synch. What this means is that our efforts in these areas have produced a large and growing population of families identified for abuse. Only a relatively small proportion of them, however, will receive a substantial amount of help and some of them may actually be harmed.

Taken together, these data provide a rather sobering picture of the consequences of interdisciplinary team efforts. While the proponents of the team approach remain confident of its validity, the foregoing discussion makes clear that there is a substantial gap between the expectations associated with this approach to child protection and empirical reality. The results of this discrepancy, as noted above, are that while many are detected, few are helped and some are harmed. This is hardly a propitious basis upon which to recommend the widespread use of interdisciplinary teams.

THE INTERDISCIPLINARY TEAM: THE BASES OF DISCORD

The limited effectiveness of the team approach notwithstanding, the foregoing data are hardly an adequate basis upon which to decide whether such teams should be expanded, modified or eliminated; that decision depends upon the reasons why teams function as they do.

However, description of the reasons for their present level of functioning is not a simple matter. Interdisciplinary teams are organizationally complex. They involve not only the members themselves, but also the various agencies they represent, the various "hosts" to which they are linked (*e.g.* government ministries, municipal departments, voluntary associations, etc.) and the ideological and conceptual contexts in which they operate. Furthermore, as Bell (1980) notes, "Whenever work involves a large component of human judgment, is guided by inexact theories strongly influenced by beliefs, and is difficult to assess in terms of results, the organization of that work tends to be unstable and problematic."

Accordingly, rather than attempt a definitive assessment (assuming that this was possible), I will instead focus on three aspects of team functioning selected on the basis, in my judgment, of their extreme importance: mistrust, competition and divergent conceptions of child abuse.

(a) Divergent conceptions of child abuse

Associated with any discipline or profession are a set of beliefs, assumptions and suppositions which are seen by their members as self-evidently correct. These beliefs are further supported by their association with a specific set of practical techniques. Thus, as Garbarino and Stocking (1980: 1) observe, "If you see your problem as a nail, then the only tool you can use is a hammer" and "If the only tool you have is a hammer, then you tend to treat every problem as if it were a nail."[8] The result is that a particular combination of perceptual style and practical technique tend to be uniquely associated with each discipline, an approach not shared by members of other disciplines. Consequently, while the physical gap between colleagues working together on the same case may be small, the conceptual gap is frequently large; in some cases, unbridgeable, with confused communication as the result.

With respect to interdisciplinary teams, there are at least three conceptual dimensions upon which team members tend to diverge.

The first of these concerns the conceptualization of abuse itself. Two such conceptions may be distinguished: one medical and the other legal.

The medical or illness conception of abuse is employed by a range of professionals, including social workers, psychologists, psychiatrists, nurses and medical doctors. It is based on "a cohesive schema that follows the basic history/physical medical model" (Wilcox, 1979) which holds that abuse may fruitfully be regarded as a "disease" entity. This view is epitomized by Gordon (1979) who flatly states that "There are definite medical criteria which makes it possible to say 'this is (non-accidental injury)' just as one says 'this is meningitis.'" This conception assumes that (a) abuse represents a phenomenon of sufficient consistency, regularity and homogeneity that it may justifiably be referred to as a specific "syndrome"; and (b) one may distinguish between a perpetrator and a victim, with the accent on pathology. Of course, insofar as an illness is undesirable, it follows that some form of intervention is required. While the nature of the intervention and the type of agent who initiates it will presumably vary with the specific nature of the "illness" in a given case, to the extent that abuse involves a physical component, this conception confers substantial authority upon the medical doctor (cf. Pfohl, 1977). However, as Bell (1980) observes, while this conception may be humane and well-meaning, "the question can still be posed as to whether the (medical) conception fits reality as commonly perceived and ... whether the conception does not structure what will be looked at and what will be seen."

In contrast to the illness conception, the legal conception focuses on child abuse as a legal category of behavior, emphasizing the issue of legal responsibility. While problematic because of the fuzziness of the law in this area (Chisholm, 1980; DeFrancis & Lucht, 1974), this conception assumes that (a) there is a victim, someone who suffers from the actions of others, and there is a victimizer, someone who can be held responsible for the objectionable actions; (b) the intent and responsibility of the victimizer can be determined; and (c) once a victimizer has been detected, responsibility attributed and guilt determined, there are legal sanctions which may be applied to the guilty party. Thus, the legal conception tends to focus on the differentiation between legal categories, the attribution of guilt and the assumption of legal responsibility.

Corresponding to these divergent conceptions of abuse are two additional dimensions which involve conceptions of intervention. The first of these concerns the distinction between punishment as opposed to therapeutic intervention (Nagi, 1977: 24-25). In the former view, typically associated with a legal conception of abuse, the harsh and irresponsible behavior of the abuse parent warrants punishment for two reasons: it is a clear indication of the moral repugnance with which abusive acts are viewed and it is presumed to serve a deterrent function, preventing either the initiation or the repetition of abusive acts in the future. Further, from this perspective, the court is regarded as the main institutional vehicle for dealing with such offenders.

In contrast, the latter view, that of therapeutic intervention, is typically associated with an illness conception of abuse. Proponents of this perspective tend to emphasize various mental and emotional conditions presumed to be beyond the individual offender's control. They also pay much attention to environmental circumstances in the precipitation of abusive acts. Consequently, abusive parents tend to be seen not as willful offenders fully aware of the consequences of their acts, but rather as patients desperately in need of treatment.

In this context, a survey of the views of over 1000 persons affiliated with various service agencies in the United States revealed that the punishment versus therapy dimension continues to be important (Nagi, 1977: 24-25). While a substantial proportion of all respondents (76.2%) supported a therapeutic stance — with child protection workers highest (91.8%) and policemen lowest (44.7%) — a significant proportion (22.7% overall) supported a stance between the two extremes, with child protection workers lowest (8.2%), policemen highest (50.2%) and hospital medical personnel in between (20.5%).

The second treatment dimension concerns the distinction between family autonomy as opposed to coercive intervention (Newberger & Bourne, 1978). The former view, grounded in common law and most consistent with a legal conception of abuse, holds that (a) within limits, families should be free to raise their children as they see fit; (b) the state has neither the right nor the prerogative to set standards for the appropriate means by which parents should raise their children; and (c) it is only under the most extreme conditions, in light of a weight of reliable evidence, that the state is warranted to intervene in the relationship between parents and their children. This perspective would thus counsel the use of intervention techniques which favour, for example, persuasion, guidance and education.

In contrast, the latter view, that of coercive intervention, is typically associated with an illness conception of abuse. It holds that (a) the state via its many agents is ultimately responsible for the health and general well-being of all of its citizens; (b) protection of its citizens not only involve response to the fact of an offence, but also extends to prevention in terms of an apprehended threat of an offence; and (c) the state is compelled to react in the strongest possible terms whenever an offence or the threat of an offence is detected, and this especially with respect to that proportion of the population that is least able to protect itself, namely, the children. This perspective would thus counsel the use of intervention techniques that favour, for example, high risk screening, parental licensing and child/victim removal.

These divergent conceptions of abuse together with their associated views of intervention, help to explain the difficulty members of interdisciplinary teams experience in understanding, supporting and communicating with each other (Wallen et al., 1977). It is hardly surprising, therefore, that teams frequently take a long time to reach decisions (Cohn & Miller, 1977), experience difficulty in reaching a consensus (Nagi, 1977: 110-112) and frequently leave various team members dissatisfied with the results even after a decision has been reached (Wallen et al., 1977).

(b) Competition

The ideal picture of the relationship among team members is aptly captured by the definition of the team presented in the introduction: members of different disciplines working together toward some common goal. The picture, then, is one of co-operation, harmony and mutual support. This may very well be correct in many cases.

There are several factors, however, which tend to seriously undermine this image in practice: (1) team members are typically not only present as individuals, but also as representatives of autonomous agencies; (2) the demand for service delivery is geat in a context of extremely limited resources; and (3) agency "domains" — an "organization's right to do something, and its access to the resources it needs in order to do it" (Warren, 1972, cited in Nagi, 1977: 28) — while mutually exclusive in most contexts, may overlap in a team setting. The result is that the relationship among team members is more frequently characterized by competition than by co-operation (Newberger, 1975). This is so because "The relations among organizations and professions can be seen in large part as the management of domains and the articulation of boundaries" (Nagi, 1977: 28). Consequently, agencies tend to protect and attempt to expand their domains.

In the present context, several aspects of these domain processes seriously limit the effectiveness of team operation. First, insofar as agencies tend to jealously guard their "organizational turf" (Garbarino & Stocking, 1980: 11), team members tend to be wary of sharing information that would tend to compromise their agency's autonomy (Hamory & Jeffery, 1977). For example, member agencies may attempt to apply for the funding of demonstration projects in which "applicant organizations emphasized the creation of new services under their control, rather than further development of and closer working relations with agencies already offering these services ... The(se) attempts ... are not merely to expand domains, but to expand them in ways that would assure control over wider aspects of the 'task environment'" (Nagi, 1977: 28-29).

Second, teams tend to involve senior agency personnel (*e.g.* department heads, supervisors, etc.; Nagi, 1977: 120) and tend to be organized hierarchically. Since they are frequently established within a hospital setting, they are often headed by medical personnel.[9] The result tends to involve a great deal of intrateam friction concerning issues of prestige and conceptualization; a relatively rigid bureaucratic structure; and, a high level of commitment to the use of relatively traditional techniques and procedures, a trend consistent with the fact that senior personnel tend to have less contact with abusive clients compared to direct contact service personnel.

Third, competition among team members over prestige and domain control frequently results in confusion concerning (*a*) which personnel are to take management responsibility (*b*) with respect to which types of cases (*c*) involving which intervention methods (*d*) at which particular times (Newberger, 1975). These problems, moreover, are exacerbated by recent statutory changes, especially in the United States, which have had the effect of increasing the level of reporting, decreasing the clarity of either the definition of abuse and/or the mandated boundaries of the relevant service agencies, and increasing confusion concerning the mandated courses of action available to involved professionals (Rolde, 1977).

Fourth, the establishment of a team represents access to important new resources, both human and fiscal, and may also involve strategic gains in both agency prestige and/or political influence. It follows that competition for a seat on an interdisciplinary team may tend to favour those for whom such an appointment would enhance their organizational prestige, wealth and power (Wilson, 1977). On the one hand, this process tends to consolidate power in the hands of organizations which are already powerful and which tend to support a perspective on abuse which is ideologically conservative. On the other hand, it tends to foment resentment, suspicion and hostility among other team members whose organizations are not so favoured, who have comparatively less influence in the operation of the team and whose more liberal perspective on abuse is seldom translated into action.

Finally, team operation may be undermined by both intra- and extra-agency processes. Wallen *et al.* (1977) suggest that such things as agency reorganization, staff turnover (especially changes in key personnel (Hamory & Jeffery, 1977)), political conflict and the regressive influence of funding sources, can all take their toll in reduced team efficacy.

Acting in concert, the ultimate consequence of these various processes is that the larger goal of child protection frequently, if inadvertently, is superceded by parochial interests involving competition over the protection and/or the expansion of agency domains.

(c) Mistrust

The final issue concerns the level of trust and respect among professionals within and between disciplines. While both are typically present to a high degree in most areas of mutual endeavor, there is general agreement in the literature that they tend to be absent in the area of child abuse (U.S. Dept. H.E.W., 1975; Matthews, 1977). In essence, while everyone concerned with child protection agrees that the work is difficult and unrewarding, professionals in the field seem to be saying that, "I don't like it, but I don't want anyone else to do it" (Bell, 1980; Matthews, 1977).

There appear to be several bases for this lack of trust. Two of these have already been discussed above: divergent conceptions of abuse and conflict over domain control and expansion.

A third component concerns what Newberger (1975) has called "professional chauvanism". By this he means that different professional disciplines assert that their particular blend of skills, perceptions and perspectives are best suited to deal with the problem of child abuse. Nor does the complexity of the phenomenon discourage such claims. Abuse frequently involves physical injury to young children. Pediatric specialists can thus legitimately claim that this is their particular area of expertise. However, abuse also involves families in crisis. This is the province of the social worker and the family therapist. It may also involve various parental and/or child emotional problems, the reserve of the psychiatrist. And, finally, it may find the family involved in the legal system, the acknowledged domain of the lawyer. It appears, then, that while professions may mouth the principles of interdisciplinary co-operation, in reality they are more akin to a group of blind men each feeling a different part of the elephant; each loudly proclaims that *only* he or she knows what the elephant is *really* like, but none can legitimately claim an overview of the beast.

In addition, this state of affairs is exacerbated by the existing structure of legal statutes with respect to child abuse. An illustrative example concerns the province of Ontario. In an effort to encourage reporting, especially among doctors, a group known for their reluctance to become involved in cases of abuse (Helfer, 1975), mandatory reporting legislation was enacted. At the same time, recent changes to the Child Welfare Act designated the Children's Aid Society, staffed primarily by social workers, as the agency mandated to handle abuse cases in the province. Consequently, doctors wishing to report a suspected case of abuse must, in effect, refer them to the Children's Aid Society. This means that in the area of child abuse, doctors, always seen by themselves and (sometimes) by others as representatives of an elite profession, are now obliged to report to social workers, commonly perceived by doctors as representatives of a lower status profession. Understandably, this arrangement has done little to encourage rapport among members of these two disciplines.

A fourth element concerns the attitude of various professionals towards group versus individual action. Doctors, for example, are trained within the context of individual action, taught to be independent and self-reliant, and exposed to patients the overwhelming majority of whom have only the most rudimentary knowledge of modern medicine. It is little wonder, then, that such professionals experience some difficulty in adapting to the team approach and tend to be somewhat reluctant to share confidential information (Matthews, 1977). It also helps to explain why they might have less than the highest regard for other professionals many of whom do not share their academic background, their specialized knowledge and their long years of rigorous training.

A fifth factor concerns the cultural isolation of many professionals (Newberger, 1975). Having little direct contact with each other, operating from widely divergent conceptual and operational perspectives, the resulting high level of interdisciplinary ignorance can, quite naturally, give rise to harsh and distinctly perjorative stereotypes of professionals in other disciplines. Bard (1969), for example, notes that policemen tend to characterize psychologists and psychiatrists as eggheads, do-gooders and nuts. Conversely, psychologists and psychiatrists frequently characterize policemen as latent or actual sadists, paranoids and criminals. While these stereotypes are both destructive and wide of the mark, the lack of mutual contact tends to leave them intact, unassailed by any contradictory empirical data. Consequently, it is only logical that when such professionals first come in direct contact within a team setting, their relations should frequently be coloured by suspicion and mistrust.

A sixth element concerns the ambiguities inherent in the role of helper in the area of child abuse. Detected child abuse signals three levels of crisis: crisis prior to the act, crisis attendant upon the abuse itself and crisis associated with detection for abuse. Crisis at all three levels is related to intense distress on the part of the families in question. In this context, the main function of helpers across disciplines is to provide various forms of support. Exercise of this function, however, is complicated by the fact that it occurs within the context of a control system, with members of various disciplines in the guise of agents of control. Thus, the professional is not only helper, but also gatekeeper, informant, crown witness and, from the client's perspective, "child snatcher". Since these divergent roles will vary at different times and in different contexts, both between and within disciplines, it is not uncommon for members of different disciplines working on the same case to accuse each other of acting in ways that do not serve the best interest of their client (Rolde, 1977).

A case in point concerns a relative new role for lawyers, that of child advocate. From a legal perspective, this essentially involves protecting the child's rights and privileges before the law, just as it would if the client were an adult. From a treatment perspective, however, protection of a child's rights may not be synonymous with protecting the child's best interests. The logic of these respective positions frequently leads to a curious paradox: optimal performance of their respective roles may lead professionals, typically a lawyer and a social worker, to diametrically opposed views with respect to the same case. Neither can be accused of doing anything but their very best for their client, but the course of action recomended by only one of them can be implemented. Moreover, the social worker's recommendations may be implemented in one case while the lawyer's may be enacted in the next case. The inevitable short-term results are mutual hostility and frequently dissatisfaction with the outcome of the cases in which they are mutual participants. The probable long-term consequences of such experience are intense mutual mistrust and the development of mutually perjorative professional stereotypes.

Nor is this the only source of conflict connected with the ambiguities of the role of helper. For associated with a supportive as opposed to a control stance are quite different conceptions of the natural history of abuse. From the perspective of a control agent, the helper operates within a legal framework. This requires that abuse be perceived as an incident actionable before the law; either child abuse has occurred or it has not. From the perspective of the supportive worker, however, abuse tends to be seen not as an event, but rather as a pattern of complex and interdependent processes. Thus, abuse does not involve merely an injured child and a guilty parent; it also includes the relational and circumstancial contexts in which the injury occurred, the institutional and the treatment histories of the family in question, the motivational and case history accounts of the participants, and so on. Consequently, depending upon which "side" of a given case they happen to be on, members of different disciplines can experience great difficulty in comunicating with — and thus trusting — each other. This is not because one or the other is less skilful or dedicated, but rather because they literally "see" the case from fundamentally different perspectives.

Finally, a seventh factor concerns the relations between professionals and non-professionals. Lay groups, such as Parents Anonymous (see Lieber & Baker, 1977), have their own conception of child abuse and their own notions of the best ways of dealing with it. Consequently, they see professionals as having no monopoly on expertise and frequently hold views "which are at some point in conflict with the views, or at least (the) practices, of legal and medical authorities" (Bell, 1980). Conversely, professionals are frequently unwilling to share information with non-professionals and tend to see them as unskilled and unhelpful (Garbarino & Stocking, 1980: viii).

Interestingly, in this context, Cohn's (1979) evaluation of eleven child abuse demonstration projects in the United States revealed that any treatment method used in conjunction with lay services yielded better outcome results than the same treatments used without them. It appears that professional disdain of non-professionals in the area of child abuse merits re-evaluation.

These data suggest that at least part of the basis of interdisciplinary team inefficiency may be traced to a lack of mutual respect and trust between professionals, and that such mistrust is frequently grounded in ignorance, misinformation and fear.

The foregoing discussion highlights three main points: (1) the ineffective operation of interdisciplinary teams may be traced to a high level of interprofessional discord; (2) such discord may in turn be explained by a combination of divergent views, competition over domains and a lack of mutual trust; and (3) only a reduction in this level of discord will ensure the future viability of child protective service in general and the interdisciplinary team in particular. Indeed, as a recent Ontario Government report correctly observed, "models (of child abuse intervention) are numerous but most of them experience fundamental problems in establishing sound, workable and continuing collaboration between and among professionals and non-professionals. Unless and until these relationships can be made productive, service will probably continue to flounder" (Ministry of Community and Social Services, 1976: 25, cited in Bell, 1980).

THE FUTURE OF THE INTERDISCIPLINARY TEAM: SOME TENTATIVE SUGGESTIONS

The future of the team approach to child abuse seems uncertain. The problems besetting it are serious and their definitive solution far from clear. What *is* clear is that the problem of child abuse is more urgent now than ever before and that its solution requires the involvement of professionals from a range of disciplines. It appears, then, that the team approach is defensible in theory, if only it can be made to work in practice.

How might this be achieved? Clearly, some modifications are required. At least four interrelated types of change seem likely to yield beneficial results.

First, the integration of professionals and non-professionals within a team context seems indicated. Lay services have a proven track record and have a somewhat different relationship with their clients than do professionals. Professionals can benefit from both. Similarly, professionals have a fund of knowledge and experience which non-professionals should see as an invaluable resource.

However, lest the relationship between professionals and non-professionals become yet another source of team conflict, two further innovations are required. The first of these involves increased efforts at interdisciplinary education, at the very least with respect to child abuse, preferably in a wide range of areas. The ignorance and the disdain that divides professionals is sustained by a lack of regular contact. While the term itself may provide one context for such contact — frequently with beneficial results (Wallen *et al.*, 1977) — the evidence presented above suggests that it is both too little and too late. The real place to initiate such contact is before professional socialization is complete and hardens into a shell that thereafter constricts the professional's view of his or her colleagues in other disciplines.

The second innovation concerns the proliferation not of inter-disciplinary teams, but rather of interdisciplinary research. It is unfortunate that many professionals in the field seem to have come to the conclusion that our understanding of the phenomenon of child abuse is now more than adequate; what is required, they suggest, is not more research, but rather the implementation of remedial programs. I can only categorize such a view as misguided. This is made only too clear by the fact that, despite our best efforts, we are neither able to stem the rising tide of abuse nor offer effective help to families detected for abuse. This state of affairs may be laid squarely at the feet of disciplinary parochialism; each professional, highly sensitive to the findings and the insights of his or her intradisciplinary colleagues, frequently seem unaware of the findings and insights of any other discipline. Interdisciplinary research efforts are one way to reverse this process, while contributing to increased understanding between professionals in varying disciplines and yielding superior insight into the fundamental processes underlying the phenomenon of child abuse.

Finally, in the same context, existing conceptions of abuse and its treatment tend to be too narrow to be generally applicable across disciplines. The solution is the selection of a conceptualization that both incorporates existing models of abuse and goes beyond them. Such a model may be drawn from general system theory (Benjamin, 1980). From this perspective, the family system becomes the unit of special concern, with individual behaviour seen as symptomatic of family functioning. Consequently, the victim-victimizer dichotomy is abandoned; rather, it is suggested that "all abusive family members actively contribute to the dysfunctional interactional process in which they are trapped and from which they all suffer accordingly" (Benjamin, 1980). Moreover, individual behaviours, feelings and motives are not ignored, but merely placed within their appropriate transactional context. Such a perspective, by focusing on the linkages both within family systems and between family systems and other institutional systems, would provide a common context and a common language within which interdisciplinary communication could occur.

REFERENCES

Armstrong, K.L. "How to avoid burnout: A study of the relationship between burnout and worker, organizational and management characteristics in eleven child abuse and neglect projects", CA & Neg. 1979, 3, 145-149.

Baher, E., Hyman, C., Jones, C., Jones, R., Kerr, A., Mitchell, R. *At Risk: An Account of the Work of the Battered Child Research Department,* NSPCC. London: Routledge & Kegan Paul, 1976.

Bard, M. "Family intervention police team as a community mental health resource", J. Crim. Law Crim. Pol. Sci. 1969, 60, 247-250.

Bell, N.W. "Metatheories of child abuse", in R. Volpe, M. Breton, J. Mitton (eds.) *The Maltreatment of the School-Aged Child.* Toronto: Lexington, 1980.

Benjamin, M. "Abused as a child, abusive as a parent: Practitioners beware", in R. Volpe, M. Breton, J. Mitton (eds.) *The Maltreatment of the School-Aged Child.* Toronto: Lexington, 1980.

Blumberg, M.L. "Psychopathology of the abusing parent", Am. J. Psychother. 1974, 28, 21-29.

Brown, H.F. "Organizational and research strategies for families of abused and neglected children in large cities", in M.L. Lauderdale, R.N. Anderson, S.E. Cramer (eds.) *Child Abuse and Neglect: Issues on Innovation and Implementation.* Proceedings of the Second Annual National Conference on Child Abuse and Neglect, April 17-20, 1977. Vol. 3. Washington, D.C.: U.S. Dept. H.E.W., 1978.

Carter, J. "Co-ordination and planning of services", in J. Carter (ed.) *The Maltreated Child,* Westport, Conn.: Technomic, 1976.

Chisholm, B.A. "Child abuse — some social aspects (a Canadian perspective)", in R. Volpe, M. Breton, J. Mitton (eds.) *The Maltreatment of the School-Aged Child,* Toronto: Lexington, 1980.

Christensen, D.L. & Fuerst, J.R. *Child abuse: Alternatives and You,* St. Paul, Minn.: SEP Consultants, 1974.

Cohn, A.H. "Essential elements of successful child abuse and neglect treatment", CA & Neg. 1979, 3, 491-496.

Cohn, A.H. & Miller, M.K. "Evaluating new modes of treatment for child abusers and neglectors: The experience of federally funded demonstration projects in the U.S.A.", CA & Neg. 1977, 1, 453-458.

Comite pour la Protection de la Jeunesse   First Progress Report, Quebec City, Que.: Ministere de la Justice, Gouvernement du Quebec, 1977.

D'Agostino, P. "Strains and stresses in protective services", in N.B. Ebeling & D.A. Hill (eds.) *Child Abuse: Intervention and Treatment,* Acton, Mass.: Pub. Sci. Group, 1975.

DeFrancis, V. & Lucht, C.L. *Child Abuse Legislation in the 1970's.* Rev. Ed. Denver, Colo.: Am. Humane Assoc., Child Div., 1974.

Fisher, G.D. "Interdisciplinary management of child abuse and neglect," Ped. Ann. 1976, 5, 114-128.

Fotheringham, B.J. "Interdisciplinary approaches to child abuse and neglect in South Australia," CA & Neg. 1977, 1, 241-244.

Garbarino, J. & Stocking, S.H. In J. Garbarino, S.H. Stocking with Associates (eds.) *Protecting Children from Abuse and Neglect: Developing and Maintaining Effective Support Systems for Families,* San Francisco: Jossey-Bass, 1980.

Gordon, R.R. "An attempt to reduce the incidence of N.A.I.", CA & Neg. 1979, 3, 795-801.

Hamory, J. & Jeffery, M. "Flexibility and innovation in multi-disciplinary management of child abuse in Western Australia", CA & Neg. 1977, 1, 217-239.

Hebert, L.J. & Hendrix, J. "Louisiana's statewide interdisciplinary approach to the diagnosis, protective and treatment services to abused and neglected children and their families," CA & Neg. 1977, 1, 347-358.

Helfer, R.E. "Why most physicians don't get involved in child abuse cases and what to do about it", Child Today 1975, 4(#3), 28-32.

Hunter, R.S., Kilstrom, N., Kraybill, E.N., Loda, F. "Antecedents of child abuse and neglect in premature infants: A prospective study in a newborn intensive care unit", Ped. 1978, 61, 629-635.

Jones, C.O. "A critical evaluation of the work of the NSPCC's battered child research unit", CA & Neg. 1977, 1, 111-118.

Kaufman, C. & Neill, K. "The hospitalized abused child: An interdisciplinary approach", CA & Neg. 1977, 1, 179-186.

Kempe, C.H. "Child protective services: Where have we been? Where are we now? Where are we going?" in M.L. Lauderdale, R.N. Anderson, S.E. Cramer (eds.) *Child Abuse and Neglect: Issues on Innovation and Implementation.* Proceedings of the Second Annual National Conference on Child Abuse and Neglect, April 17-20, 1977. Vol. 1. Washington, D.C.: U.S. Dept. H.E.W., 1978.

Kempe, C.H., Silverman, F.N., Steele, B.F., Droegemueller, W., Silver, H.K. "The battered-child syndrome", J.A.M.A. 1962, 181 (No. 1), 17-24.

Kempe, R.S. & Kempe, C.H. *Child Abuse,* Cambridge, Mass.: Harvard Univ. Press, 1978.

Kriendler, S. "Psychiatric treatment for the abusing parent and the abused child", Canad. Psychiat. Assoc. J. 1976, 21, 275-280.

Lieber, L.L. & Baker, J.M. "Parents anonymous — self-help treatment for child abusing parents: A review and an evaluation", CA & Neg. 1977, 1, 133-148.

Lynch, M., Steinberg, D., Ounsted, C. "Family unit in a children's psychiatric hospital", Brit. Med. J. 1975, 2, 127-129.

Martin, H.P. "A child-oriented approach to the prevention of abuse", in A.W. Franklin (ed.) *Child Abuse: Prediction, Prevention and Follow Up,* London: Churchill Livingstone, 1978.

Martin, H.P. & Beezley, P. "Therapy for abusive parents: Its effect on the child", in H.P. Martin (ed.) *The Abused Child,* Cambridge, Mass.: Balinger, 1976.

Matthews, P. "A multidisciplinary urban response to child abuse and neglect", CA & Neg. 1977, 1, 245-254.

Nagi, S.Z. *Child Maltreatment in the United States: A Challenge to Social Institutions,* N.Y.: Columbia Univ. Press, 1977.

Newberger, E.H. "A physician's perspective on the interdisciplinary management of child abuse", in N.B. Ebeling & D.A. Hill (eds.) *Child Abuse: Intervention and Treatment,* Acton, Mass.: Pub. Sci Group, 1975.

Newberger, E.H. & Bourne, P. "The medicalization and legalization on child abuse", Am. J. Orthopsychiat. 1978, 48, 593-607.

Ounsted, C., Oppenheimer, R., Lindsay, J. "The psychopathology and psychotherapy of the families of battered children: Aspects of bonding failure," in A.W. Franklin (ed.) *Concerning Child Abuse,* London: Churchill Livingstone, 1975.

Pfohl, S.J. "The 'discovery' of child abuse", Soc. Probl. 1977, 24, 310-323.

Pines, A. & Maslach, C. "Burn-out in mental health professionals", in M.L. Lauderdale, R.N. Anderson, S.E. Cramer (Eds.) *Child Abuse and Neglect: Issues on Innovation and Implementation.* Proceedings of the Second Annual National Conference on Child Abuse and Neglect, April 17-20, 1977. Vol. 2. Washington, D.C.: U.S. Dept. H.E.W., 1978.

Rolde, E.J. "Negative effect of child abuse legislation", CA & Neg. 1977, 1, 167-171.

Rosenfeld, A.A. & Newberger, E.H. "Compassion vs. Control: Conceptual and practical pitfalls in the broadened definition of child abuse", J.A.M.A. 1977, 237, 2086-2088.

Roth, R.A. Multidisciplinary Teams in Child Abuse and Neglect Programs: A Special Report from the National Center on Child Abuse and Neglect. Washington, D.C.: National Center on Child Abuse and Neglect, 1978.

Select Committee on Child Abuse   Report of the (New York) Select Committee on Child Abuse. N.Y., April, 1972.

Silerman, P. *Who Speaks for the Chldren?* Don Mills, Ont.: Musson, 1978.

Tracy, J.J., Ballard, C.M., Clark, E.H. "Child Abuse Project: A follow-up", Soc. Wk. 1975, 20, 398-399.

U.S. Department of Health, Education and Welfare   Child Abuse and Neglect: The Problem and its Management, Vol. 1. An Overview of the Problem. Washington, D.C.: U.S. Dept. H.E.W., publication number 75-30073, 1975.

Wallen, G., Pierce, S., Koch, M.F., Venters, H.D. "The interdisciplinary team approach to child abuse services: Strengths and limitations", CA & Neg. 1977, 1, 359-364.

Wilcox, K. "Child abuse: An approach to early diagnosis", J. Family Practice 1979, 9(#5), 801-806.

Wilson, E.P. "An interdisciplinary approach to family diagnosis and treatment: The S.C.A.N. center", CA & Neg. 1977, 1, 375-379.

Wood, D.A. "International aspects of child abuse in the military and the arm's new role as 'child advocate'", CA & Neg. 1977, 1, 427-434.

---

1   Cases in which a report of child abuse is found, upon investigation, to be false are referred to as either "unfounded" or "disconfirmed".
2   Select Committee, 1972.
3   Kempe & Kempe, 1978: 8.
4   *Ibid.*
5   *Ibid.*
6   Wood, 1977.
7   Rolde, 1977.

8   While these quotations are taken from Garbarino and Stocking (1980: 1), they are originally attributed to Abraham Maslow (Newberger, 1975).

9   This is noteworthy insofar as Pfohl (1977) argues that child abuse was "discovered" by medical personnel in order to serve their own interests, that is, expand their domain.

Court Avoidance In Child Neglect Cases

David A. Cruickshank*

I wonder why we call them "Family Courts". They separate children from their parents and parents from each other. They are certainly not there on behalf of families. They are courts of law but few lawyers enter them. The lawyers who do attend these courts may know some law, but they rarely have the knowledge of those who work with families. Perhaps these courts protect families from the state, but the state rarely loses a case.

As a legal institution, it may be convenient shorthand for us to call them Family Courts. As a social institution the more appropriate title is: "A Legally Authorized Body Regulating the Futures of Family Members." Fortunately for their place in history, no master plan was drawn to give us the family courts that now adjudicate child neglect and abuse cases. Indeed, no plan could have designed an institution to be so completely inept at directing the future of a family involved in a child neglect proceeding.

Professionals working in the Family Court forum must bear some of the responsibility for this development. When child care workers bring the clearest case of physical abuse to the Court, they claim that the lawyers' use of evidence and technicalities prevent a finding of neglect. Lawyers hearing their clients' stories of long-term removals of children without review are

* David A. Cruickshank, B.A., LL.B. (Western Ontario), LL.M. (Harvard), Professor, Faculty of Law, University of Calgary.

rushing to the dusty precedents to revive parental rights doctrines. The judge is reviewing the evidence of parent-state conflict, but he or she may have a more subtle conflict to mediate — the tension between the professional goals of the lawyer and the child-care worker. This interstitial professional conflict produces many results which damage the public reputation of the Family Court as a competent arbiter of child neglect cases. In my view, this perceived incompetence is a product of some serious misunderstandings about the utility of the court and some equally serious misallocations of legislative power in child care matters. It is my thesis that in Canada we are on the threshold of developing legislative mechanisms to avoid court proceedings in the great majority of neglect and abuse cases and that this development is to be welcomed.

Court avoidance is a praiseworthy objective for lawyers, child care workers, children and parents. In fact, two expressions of that objective have practically become cliches for the professionals involved. First of all, we go to court "as a last resort". Secondly, the goal of intervention, before or after court proceedings, is "family re-unification". Considered against the outcome of hundreds of cases, these aims have been myths.[1] Court is not the light at the end of a long tunnel; it is more often the destructive explosion at the end of a short fuse.

This is not to say that Family Courts have no place in child neglect cases. They are charged with the application of compulsory state intervention in family matters and they take an important position in child welfare services. But that place should no longer be a central location, draining the main energies of child care professionals. The court should retreat to one end of a wide spectrum of child care services. A range of services exists now, but many are not recognized as formal methods of family intervention. No province has yet collected and legislated the spectrum of alternatives available in child care practice in Canada. Until this happens, I suggest that the courts will, by force of history, predominate in the handling of many child neglect cases which should never come before the bench.

In the province of British Columbia, a Royal Commission on Family and Children's Law has reported on the range of alternatives that could be implemented in child neglect cases. Their 1975 report on "Children and the Law" recommended legislated rights of children as part of a comprehensive code of children's law.[2] In the Part concerning protection of children, the possibilities for avoiding judicial intervention were outlined: the offer of services by the government, custody by agreement, voluntary surrender of guardianship, the child care conference, and short-term custody.[3] These legislative devices are now contained in a draft Children's Act, 1976[4] which awaits action by the government of British Columbia.

EXISTING LEGISLATION AND NEW DIRECTIONS

The child welfare legislation in Canadian provinces reveals the operative child care systems only to those who can read between the lines. In most provinces, an antique statute has been patched and expanded to cover immediate crises. In Saskatchewan[5] and Manitoba,[6] there is evidence of a comprehensive revision and a change of philosophy in the statutes, but the diehard premises of state intervention remain the same. The familiar trademarks of quasi-criminal procedures, language derived from the Poor Laws,[7] broad administrative discretion, and an obsession with financial matters still characterize child welfare statutes. And yet, behind the legislation, there are some dynamic efforts being made in Canada to strengthen troubled families without judicial intervention.

Some case examples will illustrate the operation of existing statutes at their worst. In British Columbia, when the capable parents of a physically handicapped child cannot afford the therapy and mechanical devices necessary for rehabilitation, they go to the Department of Human Resources. The child care worker will inform them that only children in care may receive such financial assistance,[8] and, to obtain this, if the parents are not on social assistance themselves, they must submit to the indignity of a court proceeding in which they admit to being "unfit, unable, or unwilling to care properly" for the child.[9] The child is then declared "in need of protection" and returned to the parents under a supervision order.[10]

This is a bureaucratic conspiracy between the federal Canada Assistance Plan and the provincial child welfare authorities. In order to keep tidy, manageable categories for financial assistance, legislation forces the family through a costly, inappropriate court hearing. At a minimum, British Columbia might adopt the voluntary relinquishment sections of some provincial legislation.[11] In those procedures, no court hearing is required, but the child comes into care by agreement and can receive financial aid. But the root assumption — that state custody and supervision must always accompany financial assistance — should be challenged. Otherwise, this misdirected use of legislative authority and court proceedings will continue to alienate parents and swell the child care caseloads.

In the *Mugford* case, the Child Welfare Act of Ontario was found wanting when the natural mother sought return of her child after an adoption placement.[12] But the *ad hoc* response of the legislative amendments in 1969[13] have re-routed cases through legal hoops that are not designed to serve children as much as they are calculated to facilitate a smooth-running adoption system. Briefly, the mother in this case wanted her child back after consenting to Crown wardship. The Children's Aid

Society resisted because the child had been placed for adoption. The mother's circumstances had changed to the degree that she was clearly ready and able to care for her child. Nevertheless, the parties embarked upon two years of litigation before it was decided (in the Supreme Court of Canada) that: 1) a natural mother could apply under the Child Welfare Act to terminate a Crown wardship;[14] and 2) the mother, on the merits of the application, was entitled to custody of her child.[15]

The Legislature of Ontario responded to the decision by granting time-limited rights of appeal to parents who seek termination of Crown wardship. The limits work in two ways. First, the parents may appeal from the original decision within 30 days.[16] Failing that step, they may apply for termination of wardship at any time before an adoption placement. However, once the adoptive parents have executed a notice of intention to adopt, the Crown wardship cannot be terminated and the parental rights to guardianship are extinguished.[17]

For the immediate crisis, the solution seems to be sound. Parental rights are recognized, and the integrity of an uninterrupted adoption system is preserved. But the costs of this patching job may be greater than its short-term benefits. A startling number of Ontario adoptions, instead of being authorized by the adoption consents that have always been available to achieve the same end under a different Part of the Child Welfare Act, are now being processed as neglect (*i.e.* "wardship") cases.[18] The natural parents are subjected to a legal process which reinforces the guilt associated with abandonment of their child. The child too can suffer; if an adoption placement breaks down, only the Crown, through the Director of Child Welfare or a Children's Aid Society, has a legal relationship to the child. A series of damaging placements may lie ahead and the natural parents are at this point legal strangers in the eyes of the agency. Finally, there is little evidence to suggest that adoptive parents will become an extinct species if the authorities use conventional adoption consents which avoid court hearings for the natural parents.[19]

In the *Mugford* case, the Legislature failed to project the consequences of their one-shot answer. In so doing, they have allowed the courts to become an instrument of the child care agencies for the wrong purposes and at the wrong time. I suggest that in many cases of uncontested adoption placements, the intervention of the courts at this stage is serving neither the parents or the children involved. Neglect proceedings should be confined to actual facts related to neglect or abuse. In the alternative, the neglect and adoption provisions of the Child Welfare Act should be completely re-cast to allow for termination hearings in which parental rights can be tested against any placement proposed by the agency. Surely the courts cannot be blamed for this legislative misallocation and agency exploitation of judicial power.

A third illustration from the Alberta Child Welfare Act[20] highlights a frequent problem in Canada concerning the delays in child neglect proceedings. When a child is apprehended or taken into care under the Alberta Act, a hearing does not have to be held until twenty days from the date of apprehension.[21] Even at that first presentation of the case, the child does not have to be present or be represented by counsel.[22] The judge can, and often does, adjourn the hearing on neglect for "such further period" as he "may direct".[23] Accused persons under the Criminal Code get far better attention to their fundamental freedoms.[24]

Child welfare organizations will complain that it takes time to notify parents of the hearing and to prepare the agency's case. In many cases, one parent is out of the jurisdiction or the legal requirements of serving notice cannot be met within the necessary ten days preceding the hearing.[25] But child welfare authorities must also acknowledge the extent of their unfettered power during the twenty day period. They have sole discretion to determine whether the child should be detained in custody, placed in a temporary home, or returned to the parents.[26] Also, the maximum period has become the standard rule for processing apprehensions, not the outside limit; as a result, an unsupported apprehension canot be challenged for at least three weeks. Finally, the practice of "withdrawing" an apprehension just before the court appearance has the effect of shielding the authorities from any judicial scrutiny of their original intervention and subsequent twenty days of work with the family.

In adult criminal matters, an abuse of the arrest power by a common practice of "withdrawing" would lead to civil actions against the police for false arrest. The parents in a child welfare apprehension would have difficulty proving a similar charge on behalf of their child. The apprehension may not even be like an arrest because it is undertaken to protect the child. The broad grounds for apprehension exclude any notion of a "reasonable cause" criterion. Finally, the release of the parents from court proceedings is no doubt sufficient to dampen their wishes for vindication in the courts.

This example of delay mandated by legislation raises many serious questions of civil rights for parents and their children. But more importantly, it points to a legislative failure to give individual attention to different types of cases. A documented case of repeated child abuse may well require a twenty-day period of preparation. However, leaving a child unattended in a parked car for an hour may call for only a one-day period preceding minimal judicial intervention. The sweep of present legislation fails to separate legitimate, short-term extra-judicial intervention from cases which require the full protections of a court hearing.

The courts have a dual role to play in child neglect cases directed to them by legislation. Their existing role calls primarily for the legitimation of the child welfare authority's activities prior to a hearing. This is done explicitly by confirming agency actions with a disposition that matches agency expectations. It is done implicitly by a failure to examine closely the work of the authority during the pre-hearing delay. The second role, as watchdogs over the child welfare authorities, is not encouraged by Canadian legislation. In my view, it is proper for the courts to hold the administrative agencies accountable for compulsory intervention in family lives. Our legislation needs to make this mandate precise without returning to the shackles of "parental rights over best interests".

The malfunctions of existing legislation must be faced with a comprehensive response. The *Mugford* case leaves behind the dangers of streaming cases through the courts that don't belong there until the day of a final adoption order. The handicapped child in British Columbia becomes a court statistic in order to receive financial aid. The delays built into Alberta child neglect apprehensions apply to all children, regardless of their individual needs. Advocates of law reform must, therefore, meet demands for individualized, non-adversarial child care; but they must also find the fulcrum between court avoidance as an aid to therapy and court intervention as an accountability feature of child care systems. The British Columbia Royal Commission proposals must be tested with these goals in mind.

THE OFFER OF SERVICES

The most basic duty of child welfare authorities — to provide supportive services to families — is rarely reflected in Canadian legislation. The British Columbia Commission saw this duty as the starting point for a new group of legislative options. The Commission recommended that the government and its child care agencies should be obligated by legislation to offer child care services to families who cannot meet the needs and rights of their children and that this offer of services should be accompanied by legislative protections for the persons who are carrying out the services.[27]

This recommendation has been carried out to some degree in Saskatchewan, where the Minister of Social Services "may, in order to enable a parent to maintain a child in his home and in order to prevent the child from becoming a child in need of protection, assist the parent by providing such welfare services as the minister considers necessary and advisable."[28] The goal of preventive services is laudable, but the Saskatchewan legislation has not left the direction in the hands of the people who actually deliver child care services. Ministerial discretion is subject to political restraints and tends to be reserved for special cases. The motive behind ministerial control is undoubtedly the need for budgetary restrictions. However, an annual budget for preventive services could be established without imposing ministerial discretion on its day-to-day application. The drafting of a statutory service always carries financial implications,[29] but these should be balanced with the opportunity to re-formulate the whole doctrine of *parens patriae* through an "offer of services" clause.

The practising doctrine of "the state as parent" centres around the need to substitute legally the state as a parent. The rationale for intervention is to protect the child because of the state's interest in future generations. Wherever compulsory intervention seems necessary, the courts are relied upon to give a fair hearing and attendant legal rights for those objecting to the state's interference. Yet, at an earlier stage, before courts even become entitled to hear a case for intervention, there should be statutory protections which reflect a new doctrine of *parens patriae*.

The developing doctrine could be termed the "family support" theory of state intervention. It holds that no compulsory intervention by the courts should be permitted unless the family has first been offered supportive services in the home. Furthermore, in the event that services are refused or would clearly be late and inadequate, the neglect finding of the court should always be tested against the available dispositions and resources. If the child cannot get a proper placement through the child care agency, the finding of neglect should be vacated and the child returned to the parents. It has also been suggested that the judicial finding should be one of "family intervention," not "neglect," in order to remind child care workers of the family re-unification goal.[30]

This "family support" theory cannot be found in Canadian legal literature. Social workers and other child care professionals have been negligent in their failure to educate lawyers, judges and legislators about the trends in their practice which keeps families together and away from courtrooms. Lawyers are unlikely to learn from their colleagues about child abuse programmes involving lay therapists, parents' anonymous groups, crisis nurseries and homemakers.[31] Law schools which take a multidisciplinary approach to their family law courses are beginning to remedy this situation for future lawyers. In the meantime, it is submitted that an evolutionary doctrine of *parens patriae* could be founded by new legislation that requires attempts at supportive services to precede judicial intervention.

In the United States, the "family support" doctrine has received attention as a "right to remedial services," which in turn can be traced to the "right to treatment" cases.[32] The emerging right is derived in part from the intention clauses of the state child care statutes; in terms of federal policy, there is increased financial backing for those agencies which can demonstrate better community prevention services and well-organized service delivery.[33] The contribution of the "right to treatment" cases to the "right to remedial services" has been described by one writer as follows: "The basic premise of the theory is that, since noncriminal confinement can be justified only by the provision of treatment, where adequate treatment is not provided the authority for state intervention is vitiated and the state may not restrain the individual."[34]

Although the theory stated here has only been applied to American cases involving institutional settings, it has attractions as a legislative device for court avoidance. If the British Columbia recommendation is to be adequately implemented, the "offer of services" legislation will have to contain a number of guarantees which are consistent with the "family support" theory. First, the statutory conditions leading to a finding of neglect need to be revised. The broad net of the existing standards has been criticized in many quarters.[35] The Family and Children's Law Commission recommended more narrow grounds for neglect which could be called "emergency neglect."[36] Perhaps the best general statement of the proper reform goals was made by Sullivan in 1968:

"In summary, the court should find neglect only when parental action or condition has or is likely to have an effect on the child which conflicts with the self-perpetuating interest of the state and which effect the child is not likely to overcome without the protection of the state."[37]

By restricting the gateway to court intervention, an increasing number of cases will have to be handled in a rehabilitative service environment which cannot deny parental participation. At the same time, it would be unwise to make supportive services a necessary prerequisite for all apprehensions or findings of neglect. There will always be some serious cases of abandonment or continuing abuse, which have come to the attention of the agency for the first time, and which require agency-supervised placement following a court order.

However, the "family support" theory need not be abandoned on the courthouse steps. A second guarantee of prevention can be drafted in the disposition sections of new legislation. When a judge is prepared to order supervision or guardianship, he should order that care and control "which the child is unlikely to receive unless the court makes an order."[38] This legislative phrase would require the court to review the efforts previously made by child care workers, and to examine the less coercive measures that could be made available before the court orders some form of guardianship. This proposed change in the disposition powers and the re-writing of grounds for apprehension again point to the need for a comprehensive approach to legislation. Preventive measures cannot be isolated from court powers.

A third safeguard attached to the "offer of services" should be a "right of refusal" by parents or guardians.[39] If child care services proceed on the basis of consulting the community which is served, workers should have little difficulty in accepting the right of parents to turn down an offer of service. The approach to the family is a voluntary one and should carry no threat of compulsory intervention. Therefore, a legislative guarantee of a parental right to refuse should not only be found in the books, but also in the information passed by child care workers to their clientele. In the event of a refusal of services, the crucial thrust of child care practice should be toward revised methods of prevention, not an immediate leap to legal proceedings.

From the child-care worker's viewpoint, another guarantee should attach to the "offer of services". The worker needs legal protections from certain actions in tort when working in the home. In recent amendments to Canadian legislation this concern has been reflected in the protections for homemaker services.[40] The homemaker may enter the home in the absence of the parents and immunity from liability has, therefore, been granted in matters such as trespass and the exercise of "reasonable control and discipline" over children.[41] The specific mention of homemaker services allows these protections to be advanced, but it also dampens flexibility in preventive services. The homemaker provisions only apply where the parents are absent from the home; the continuation of services depends upon a judicial order, not a voluntary compact between the parents and the child care worker.[42] The Saskatchewan legislation seems to be more flexible in the provision of homemaker services where it stipulates that "... the officer or person may in lieu of removing the child take such steps as he considers necessary to provide for the safety or welfare of the child."[43] If this pattern is followed, the legal protections for child care workers will have to be drafted in a similarly flexible vein.

In summary, we must go back to the starting point of child welfare services — the duty to provide supportive and preventive child care services. This must be a legal duty, prescribed by statute and resting on the shoulders of government generally, not in the discretion of one minister. The existing statements of intention in child welfare legislation have produced no significant legal results because they have no force in the daily processing of cases. If an "offer of services" becomes a prerequisite to judicial intervention, except in serious emergencies, new legislation will contain the roots of a new "family support" doctrine of *parens patriae*.

CUSTODY BY AGREEMENT

Custody by agreement, or non-ward care, is becoming an established legislative device for court avoidance in many Canadian provinces.[44] Even those jurisdictions which do not authorize non-ward care agreements by statute have been using them for years.[45] This absence of legislative authority in British Columbia prompted the Family and Children's Law Commission to make the following recommendation:

"New legislation should provide for custody by agreement between parents and the Superintendent of Child Welfare. The maximum period for custody by agreement should be fifteen months."[46]

The fundamental aims of custody by agreement are sometimes expressed in legislation; but more often Canadian legislation has lost sight of those goals and is presently in danger of undermining the trust that resides at the centre of this device for court avoidance. Custody by agreement aims at agency child care for a temporary period, during which time the parents are expected to work with the agency toward re-unification of the family. Normally, there should be no evidence of continuing, wilful neglect or abandonment of the child. The parents should have a positive attitude toward their future responsibilities and should be willing and equal participants in child care decisions during the period. For these goals to be fulfilled, the parent must remain in close contract with the child and the agency must encourage that contact through geographic proximity in their placement of the child. In British Columbia, the self-imposed question of child care workers sums up many of these objectives: "What can we offer a child committed to care by the Court that we cannot by non-ward care?"[47]

The serious omissions of existing legislation offer little comfort to those who advance custody by agreement as a short-term means of family re-unification. Some statutes have no limit on the term of the agreement.[48] A more common technique is to allow one-year agreements which are renewable for an indefinite number of terms.[49] Although the parents and the child welfare authorities are supposedly equal partners in the agreement, some statutes only allow the director of child welfare to terminate an agreement.[50] Furthermore, the termination by the director in Alberta or New Brunswick is deemed to be an apprehension of the child.[51] In other words, the parents are asked to relinquish custody on a basis of a mutual trust which can be unilaterally violated at any time by child care authorities.

The Manitoba statute contains some progressive elements of custody by agreement,[52] but no Canadian legislation has met all the key issues of this form of child care. First of all, there should be an initial term of three months for the agreement. This term, renewable for six months, would meet the convincing argument raised in *Beyond the Best Interests of the Child* — that a child's sense of time should govern placement decisions.[53] For a pre-school child, three months' absence from parents can feel like the adult equivalent of two years. The law should take account of the child's perceptions and demand that child care practice accommodate the child, not the convenience of workers.

Moreover, if the parent-agency agreement is truly being used to facilitate a family reunion, there should also be a maximum term which prevents automatic renewals for an indefinite period. The Manitoba legislation stipulates eighteen months,[54] in Ontario, a twenty-four month aggregate term is the upper limit.[55] In British Columbia, a fifteen month term has been recommended.[56]

The fifteen month limit, composed of a three month initial term and two potential renewals of six months each, would be sensible as part of a broader spectrum of child care options. In the existing legislative milieu, where nothing but judicial intervention can supplant an agreement, it is easy to see how non-ward care has expanded to a medium and long-term child care method. The "circumstances of a temporary nature"[57] which initiate an agreement, are not being applied to the actual length of many non-ward care agreements.[58] The fifteen month maximum would return custody by agreement to its original short-term goals. Furthermore, the frequent renewals within that term would serve as a regular measure of accountability for both the parents and the agency.

Accountability is the second main issue to be faced in non-ward care agreements. Because the courts are not involved in monitoring these agreements, the balance between the parents and the agency must be fair and equal. A minimum requirement should be an equal right to terminate the agreement. This is possible in Ontario and Manitoba, where the parents are allowed to give notice in writing, to terminate the agreement, and to regain custody of the child.[59] Even in provinces where the parental right to terminate is not clear, it is difficult to see how an agency could resist a writ of *habeas corpus* for the return of the child.[60] The agency must, therefore, satisfy the parents that the services for the child are in fact directed toward returning the child. Policies such as strictly limited parental visits cannot survive where parents have a right to regain custody that is easily exercisable.

The equal partnership concept can be empty unless the parents are confident that their past incapacities will not be used against them. The legislation in Ontario, Alberta and New Brunswick allows a child to be brought before a judge as a child in need of protection immediately upon termination of custody by agreement.[61] In most of these situations, the evidence justifying apprehension and protection relates to a time preceding the original agreement. As a result, the agency holds a Damocles' sword over the parents. Even a legitimate case for termination of the agreement by the parents could be upset by the agency going immediately to court. In order to maintain parental confidence in custody by agreement, the threat of apprehension should be removed from the non-ward care sections of legislation. If the child is truly in present danger by returning to the parents, the clauses reserved for all cases of neglect will be sufficient to bring about protective measures.

The third major issue surrounding non-ward care is the provision of services to children with special needs. Custody by agreement should be a device for the accommodation of the needs of someone like the handicapped child in British Columbia. The parents are not forced into the courtroom and yet they can receive shared federal-provincial funds for their child.

Some provinces have properly distinguished the "provision of services" agreement from the ordinary case of non-ward care.[62] This distinction should be made within the general framework of custody by agreement because the degree of agency supervision and control should be significantly reduced in cases of services for the child with special needs. Ideally, the mentally or physically handicapped child should reside at home and be a recipient of the "offer of services" proposed earlier in this paper. However, recognizing the existing fiscal structures and the need for agency custody in some programmes, legislation should contain the alternative of a "special needs agreement", as one option within custody by agreement.

VOLUNTARY SURRENDER OF GUARDIANSHIP

The technique of court avoidance that is probably most open to administrative abuse is the voluntary surrender of guardianship. The complete absence of a means to surrender permanent guardianship without a fault-oriented court proceeding was noted by the British Columbia Family and Children's Law Commission when they made the following recommendation:

"New legislation should provide for the voluntary surrender of guardian-ship, without the necessity of a court appearance. This administrative process should be reviewable by a Provincial Court judge within thirty days of the surrender."[63]

This recommendation was made in contemplation that adoption consent procedures would remain in child care legislation. As the *Mugford* case illustrated, the purposes of wardship and adoption proceedings are often confused. Where permanent guardianship orders become a routine step in an adoption process, that confusion reaches an apex. Voluntary surrender of guardianship is susceptible to this same kind of abuse, and it must receive careful attention from the legislative draftsman.

At the outset, adoption consents need to be kept distinct from voluntary surrender of guardianship, although both can have the same purpose of giving legal rights of guardianship to the Crown.[64] Because of case law developments, the adoption consent is thought to be a "weaker" means of terminating parental rights. In some provinces, the parent can apply to revoke a consent until the day of the adoption order.[65] There must be a serious effort made to obtain the consent of a known father of an illegitimate child or an Ontario Crown wardship order may be ineffective as a basis for an adoption order.[66] Child welfare authorities have complained that adoption placements can be disrupted by the uncertain legal position of the natural parents. Consequently, the use of judicial permanent guardianship proceedings seems to be the "safe" way to shut the door on the claims of natural parents, even when they agree to an adoption placement.

The next step toward court avoidance would be to substitute court proceedings for permanent guardianship with a voluntary, administrative means of surrendering guardianship. This step would respond to critics who say that it is unfair to subject the parents to a fault-finding judicial hearing. Canadian Legislatures to date have answered in two ways: (1) they retain a court hearing, but remove the fault orientation by allowing the parents to submit to the court's orders without an admission of fault,[67] or (2) they allow permanent guardianship to be surrendered by agreement or by an instrument of surrender which does not have to be reviewed by the court.[68] Some legislation covers both bases of voluntary relinquishment.[69] The British Columbia Commission recommended that the second avenue be included in new legislation.[70]

However, existing legislation has not reserved the voluntary surrender of guardianship for legitimate cases of continuing Crown wardship. A "legitimate case", in my view, is one which does *not* have an adoption placement secured at the time the voluntary surrender is executed. This could involve a handicapped child, an adolescent, or any child who is not in high demand for adoption. Child welfare authorities need to make an early placement in an environment where the child can learn to feel secure. Such a placement could mean a permanent foster home or a residential treatment program. The concept of shared guardianship between psychological parents and the Crown can also serve these children.[71] In all of these cases, no future involvement or rehabilitation of the natural parents would be contemplated. Otherwise, custody by agreement would serve the purposes of the agency. The agency must, therefore, be satisfied that the parents are fully informed of their abdication of parental rights and that they have no opposition or hesitancy in using non-judicial procedures to terminate parental rights. Indeed, a child care worker should be looking for positive benefits to be gained by court avoidance before recommending voluntary surrender.

Insistence on separate streams for adoption consents and the voluntary surrender of guardianship should not cut the child off from adoption if he is made a Crown ward. In a permanent foster home, for example, the parents may be prepared to adopt the child if assisted by a subsidized adoption programme. But it is important to remember that this plan for the child may not emerge until years after the initial placement. When it does emerge, the agency is unfettered by the rights of natural parents. In the British Columbia proposal, only inheritance rights would remain between the child and the natural parents until the day of the adoption order.[72]

Nevertheless, the parents would have a time-limited opportunity to reconsider a hasty decision about voluntary surrender. Within thirty days, they could go to the Provincial Court for a review of the administrative process in the voluntary surrender. Grounds for review will have to be developed, but it should be noted that unlike adoption, this would not be a parental request to revoke the surrender on the basis of the child's best interests.[73] Instead, it is an opportunity for a judge to determine that the parents fully understood the process, and gave their informed consent to the termination of parental rights. Beyond the Provincial Court, an appeal would lie to the Supreme Court within sixty days of the first judicial decision.[74]

At the present time, no Canadian statute contains all these proposed requirements of a voluntary surrender of guardianship. Only Manitoba, Saskatchewan and Alberta allow voluntary surrender to take place outside the courtroom.[75] The Alberta and Saskatchewan provisions seem tied to an adoption placement and do not have the flexibility advocated here for Crown wardship through a surrender.[76] The Manitoba Act has not linked voluntary surrender to adoptions, but that statute, along with the Alberta Act, omits any reference to judicial review. It is submitted that this latter omission could be fatal to the success of any voluntary surrender provision because the normal legal rights to judicial review of administrative action will be available to any parent wishing to get a voluntary surrender re-examined by a court.[77] New legislation in those provinces which do not have voluntary surrender provisions should establish this new form of wardship as one that has legal protections within a reviewable administrative framework.

Two parallel reform efforts should be made. First, adoption consents should be given a legal status that terminates parental rights at a fixed time well before the adoption order is finalized.[78] The present use of neglect proceedings to smooth the adoption process would be unnecessary if parental rights were terminated by adoption consents well before the final order. After a reasonable period for the revocation of consents and an appeal period following an unsuccessful revocation attempt by the natural parents, full guardianship of the child should vest in the Crown. Secondly, child care authorities should develop understandable administrative procedures to accept a voluntary surrender of guardianship. The "indenture" used in Alberta for this purpose is a fine example of what should be avoided.[79] The technical eighteenth-century language of the indenture is more unwieldy than a land deed. Child care workers who deal with these cases should be experienced and educated in the legal significance of the procedures. Above all, they should appreciate when a case needs to be referred to a lawyer or converted into a voluntary appearance before a judge.

In summary, voluntary surrender of permanent guardianship should be enacted as an administrative child neglect proceeding. There are appropriate cases for this type of court avoidance; they cannot be handled by adoption consents because the child is difficult to place in an adoptive home. Voluntary surrender also presents a challenge to child care workers, who must develop fair administrative procedures, and accept the need for judicial review in some cases.

SHORT-TERM CUSTODY

In many child abuse and neglect cases, there may not be the time or co-operation necessary to engage the parent in a voluntary programme designed to protect the child. For example, absent parents cannot be consulted when a young child is lost and apparently forgotten at the local fairground. In the "bad old days" of child protection, such a child might be apprehended as one "found wandering about at late hours"[80] and made a ward of the Crown. That apprehension, as we noted in Alberta, can lead to a twenty day separation from the parents. In more enlightened child care practices, the worker who finds the parents shortly after an apprehension often withdraws the apprehension and the child is quickly returned. No Canadian legislation addresses itself adequately to the withdrawal of apprehensions or the accountability of child care workers in this practice.

This situation, along with a legislative idea from the Yukon, motivated the British Columbia Commission to recommend that:
"Under new legislation, designated child care workers should be empowered to take custody of a child in emergency circumstances for a single period of forty-eight hours. The workers should be guided by specific grounds for use of this short-term custody and they should be accountable to the Family Court."[81]

In the Yukon, where weather conditions and travelling distances often overrule the finer legalities of a child neglect case, the forty-eight hour period was introduced as a pragmatic means of reducing the judicial caseload that would result from a literal application of the Child Welfare Ordinance.[82] The section outlining this technique of court avoidance reads:
"16(4) Where a child is apprehended pursuant to sub-section (1), the person who apprehends the child is not required to bring the child before a justice if the child is returned within forty-eight hours of the apprehension to his parents or the person having the actual care and custody of the child at the time of the apprehension."[83]

The Ontario Child Welfare Act bears some resemblance to this provision where it instructs workers to either go before a judge or return the child to the parents "as soon as is practicable and within five days of detaining a child in a place of safety."[84] This "hurry-up" direction for all apprehensions stands in sharp contrast to the much-abused twenty day delay in the Alberta statute.

In a spectrum of child welfare legislative reforms, short-term custody has an important role. However, if it is to be freed from a court hearing, some strict limitations must be placed on its application so that it does not become a powerful form of child arrest. Specific cases which justify short-term custody have therefore been proposed in the British Columbia Draft Children's Act, 1976 as follows:

"(a) a dependent child has left his home and no adult person appears to be exercising necessary care and control over him,

(b) the child appears to be in physical danger or represents a potential physical danger to himself or others,

(c) a child under 12 years of age is apparently unattended, and

(d) a child incapable of giving his own consent for medical treatment must, for his own protection, in the opinion of the person apprehending the child, be taken immediately to a medical facility for assessment and diagnosis of his condition, and no parent or other person is willing or able to take alternative remedial action."[85]

It is also clear from the draft legislation that a worker must have a short custody period in mind, not a regular apprehension followed by court proceedings.[86] Short-term custody should not become a regular "pre-apprehension" step which gives the agency a new period of contemplation. This suggestion is not to discourage the normal reflection and change of circumstances that often lead an agency to withdraw an ordinary apprehension. But the proposed forty-eight hour custody term may well divert cases from the court-oriented conveyor belt and reduce the incidence of withdrawn apprehensions.

Two themes emerge once again from this recommendation:

(1) if adversarial proceedings can be held off in certain cases, preventive and remedial work can be immediately substituted before the child care agency is perceived as "the enemy";[87] and

(2) without accountability features, legislative power which has a compulsory element can be misallocated and abused.

This latter theme was of such concern to the British Columbia Commission that they introduced several checks on short-term custody.[88] First, the workers entitled to exercise this power would have to be specially designated by the Director of Child Care. Presumably they would be properly trained for these cases and would be familiar with temporary custody facilities that are completely divorced from juvenile delinquency resources. Secondly, the repeated use of short-term custody would be discouraged. Each time a child was detained on this basis, a written report would have to be filed with the Family Court in the locality. Those reports could then be reviewed by a judge as part of a child's case history; repeated inaction by child care workers, following previous uses of short-term custody, would be scrutinized by the court. Finally, if the period extends beyond forty-eight hours, the designated workers must either return the child to a parent or make an apprehension and go before a judge within seven days. If the apprehension is to be withdrawn, the worker will have to explain that step in person to the judge on the day the case is called.

In conclusion, the short-term custody device could be a valuable, though dangerous, piece of legislation. It carries the benefit of fast intervention without being committed to the one-way street that so often begins with the first court appearance of the family. On the other hand, particularly in the area of controlling potential criminal activity by young persons, the power could be irresponsibly used. Careful evaluation of the uses and effects of short-term custody should accompany the already cautious legislative drafting of this power.

THE CHILD CARE CONFERENCE

A stroke of the legislative pen can sometimes convert the "obvious" or "commonplace" solution into the "bold, unprecedented" measure. The conversion can occur without political chicanery and noisy announcements because the "new" idea has always been right before our eyes. With regard to the child care conference idea, the British Columbia Family and Children's Law Commission was well aware that it was re-discovering the case conference used commonly by social workers. The Commission recommended:

"New legislation should introduce the child care conference as a voluntary means of resolving child care cases. The conference should be chaired by a mediator who can assist the parties in reaching a child care agreement. The discussions in the conference should be confidential and informally structured."[89]

The proposal of an informal method of dispute resolution is not revolutionary among child care professionals. Lawyers, too, negotiate the outcome of a child neglect case before they enter the courtroom. But the child care conference invites a middle alternative to both the child welfare and legal processes. The cases most amenable to such a solution will be those where family re-unification is possible and the parents have a strong concern for the protection of their interest in the child. When preventive measures have been exhausted and the removal of a child by non-ward care is not desirable, the existing notion of a case conference often requires a consideration of only the judicial orders available. If the exclusive professionalism of these conferences was broken down and the court alternatives were momentarily set aside, there would be new hope for a resolution, evidenced by a formal agreement in writing, that could satisfy both the parents and the child care authorities.

The legislator will immediately face the question of how formalized the conference should become under legislation as opposed to unwritten guidelines. Who should initiate and control the conference? Who should attend? Will the conference have a professional orientation, a community base, or a family-centred composition? What will be the legal significance of discussions and agreements arising from the conference? There is very little precedent for legislation on these issues, and it may take considerable amendment in future years to accommodate new developments in this concept of negotiation.

The province of Quebec has taken a parallel initiative in the establishment of their "Comité pour la protection de la jeunesse."[90] Although this committee is not limited to negotiation and it has some powers of compulsion, the goal of court avoidance by assiduous use of child welfare professionals is the same. The ten person committee of professionals has broad powers to under-take preventive programs, investigations, and the disposition of some cases of reported child abuse.[91] Insofar as the Quebec committee diverts cases from court, the function is similar to the child care conference. However, the institutional character of the committee and its power to refer cases directly to court set it apart from the British Columbia proposal.[92]

The only regular and continuous participant in a child care conference would be the mediator.[93] He or she must be a person with adept communication skills and experience in negotiations. The mediator should be independent of the child care system, but must respond to the system's request for a child care conference. Independence is preserved by the fact that the parents would also have the right to ask that a conference be convened. Furthermore, the parents could control the invitations of professionals who should attend the conference. Once assembled, the mediator would aim to facilitate discussion of the common ground between the parents and the various professionals interested in the child's future — the teacher, the public health nurse, the homemaker, the social worker and others called to assist.

A significant departure from the present case conference would be the active participation of the parents in the child care conference. This method of court avoidance would not compel their attendance. They would speak for themselves; the involvement of lawyers would be discouraged. Supportive friends and relatives would be invited to assist the parents in working toward the child care agreement. If the child in question is sufficiently mature, his or her views should also be heard. In this consultative process, the mediator's most difficult job will be to keep the family's views afloat and credible in order to balance the tendency of the professionals to overwhelm the parents with mounds of articulated and written evidence.

The parties should, at the conclusion of the conference, seek to record their areas of mutual agreement. Although the discussions in the conference would be held in total confidence, it is recommended that the written agreement should be admissible in any subsequent court proceedings. A breach of the agreement by either the parents or the agency would be helpful to the court upon disposition of a case.

There would only be one means of compelling parents to participate in a child care conference. The British Columbia Commission recommended that among the court disposition powers, the judge should be able to refer the parents to a child care conference for a mediated solution.[94] It must be remembered that the case would come to court in the ordinary way — where a child is "in need of care". Obviously this disposition would be fruitless if a child care conference had failed previously. However, where the parental attitude has changed and there is a willingness to negotiate, rather than oppose, some form of agency intervention, the judge should be able to direct the convening of a child care conference.

Finally, the child care conference must be immunized from the criticism most often levelled at the courts — the delay in processing cases. The proposal calls for the conference to take place within four weeks of the date it is initiated. The mediator would also limit the time for the session; it would be the rare case that consumed more than half a day.

Lawyers may find the concept of the child care conference unpalatable. The parents are fully exposed and without a champion for their rights. The agreement may prove to be lop-sided in favour of the agency. While the agreement is admissible in a later court hearing, it is not enforceable by judicial proceedings. The final card is held by the agency, which can apprehend a child if a child care agreement breaks down and the child is in jeopardy. Despite these potential objections, it is submitted that lawyers would be wiser to join the movement toward negotiated child neglect matters. In my view, the child care conference is the future setting for a majority of child neglect cases. Lawyers have negotiation skills and should be welcome to apply them in this forum, as long as their adversarial robes are left in the corridor.

CONCLUSION

My original militant stance against Family Courts has mellowed. I have made no attempt to advocate an alternative which fully removes the functions of the Family Court. Nor has the term "court avoidance" been used to suggest that the court is to be approached like a tank full of piranhas. In considering alternatives to the judicial process, the argument is simply this: we must have a broader range of legislative alternatives to handle the unique features of each child neglect case; the Family Court is but one alternative reserved for contested matters or cases of abandonment, where parental rights must be removed or diminished. The techniques should be legislative, in order to promote uniformly high standards within a provincial child care system and to guarantee that child care administration will be accountable to families and to the public interest. Furthermore, alternatives like those recommended by the Family and Children's Law Commission have some precedent in Canadian legislation or child care practice. The collection and refinement of these techniques is a logical development that child welfare systems and provincial governments should be prepared to accept in the near future.

Law reform efforts directed at the unification or demolition of the Family Courts we know today are not in conflict with the proposals made here. In British Columbia, an experimental panel system, consisting of a judge and two lay persons for child neglect cases was attempted at the same time that the Commission worked out its recommendations for court avoidance.[95] But the courts now represent too much of the core of existing child welfare systems, and wholesale reform of judicial institutions is notoriously long in coming. Therefore, we should be looking at the "front end" of child neglect problems, where a spectrum of alternatives could be developed more quickly and where successes could produce a demonstrable reduction in judicial caseloads.

Finally, the issue of tension between lawyers and child care professionals deserves comment. The repeated argument for accountability is directed to this problem. Lawyers must be ready to accept a greater movement into the administrative realm in child neglect matters. However, they will insist on the protection of parental and children's rights even within that administrative process. Child care workers, in response to this demand, need not become "legal beagles". However, they should be willing to articulate procedures and policies which make their actions open to parental scrutiny and, in some cases, open to judicial review. Furthermore, these policies, guided by new founding legislation, will only be successful if they are anticipatory. Too often, child care professionals meet situations like the *Mugford* case which make them revile lawyers for another decade. But when the parents of a child have had no recourse within the administrative system they can hardly be blamed for going to the courts. An understanding of the need for court avoidance and the parallel need for accountability may help both professional fields to unfold a broader concept of teamwork in cases of abuse and neglect.

1 A 1974 study in the District of Columbia revealed that out of a random sample of 100 child abuse or neglect complaints, 89 complaints were followed by petitions for court action. In 82 of the 89 cases, the children were removed from their homes for the period of time prior to the court hearing. Burt, *The System for Neglected and Abused Children in the District of Columbia* 10, quoted in Areen, "Intervention Between Parent and Child: A Reappraisal of the State's Role in Child Neglect and Abuse Cases" (1975) 63 Geo. L.J. 887.

2 The Fifth Report of the Royal Commission on Family and Children's Law, "Children and the Law", Queen's Printer, Victoria, B.C. (1975) contains seven parts: I. The Legislative Framework II. The Status of Children Born Outside of Marriage III. Children's Rights IV. The Special Needs of Special Children V. The Protection of Children (Child Care) VI. Custody, Access, and Guardianship VII. Adoption.

3 The Fifth Report of the Royal Commission on Family and Children's Law, "Part V, Protection of Children (Child Care)", (1975) at 10-25.

4 This draft was completed by Cruickshank and Adamson in December 1975, and is a supplement to the Commission's Fifth Report.

5 The Family Services Act, 1973 (Sask.), c. 38: *e.g.* s. 5(1) — "Subject to the approval of the Lieutenant Governor in Council, the minister may do such things as he considers advisable to promote the growth and development of community services and resources designed to support families in the proper care of their children and to prevent circumstances that lead to family breakdown."

6 Child Welfare Act, 1974 (Man.), c. C-30.

7 Fraser, "Children in Need of Protection" in *Studies in Canadian Family Law,* (1972 ed. Mendes da Costa) Vol. 1, Butterworths, Toronto, 1972, at 72-73. The frequent use of the term "ward" to describe children before the courts first appeared in the time of Henry VIII, when he established a Court of Wards to sell the guardianship of children and (more importantly) their estates to the highest bidder. The clinging attitude toward children as chattels and objects of financial concern remains a reality in our present use of the term. See: Areen, "Intervention Between Parent and Child: A Reappraisal of the State's Role" (1975) 63 Geo. L.J. 887-937.

8 "Services Policy and Procedures Manual", Department of Human Resources, (1976) at 8:01.

9 Protection of Children Act, R.S.B.C. 1960, c.303, s. 7(k) [re-en 1968, c. 41, s. 3].

10 *Ibid.* ss. 7, 8(9)(*a*)(i) [re-en. 1968, c. 41, s. 4].

11 *E.g.* Child Welfare Act, R.S.O. 1970, c. 64, s. 23*a* [am. 1975, c. 1, s. 15]:
"(2) Subject to the approval of the children's aid society having jurisdiction in the area where the parent resides, or the Minister, a parent,
(*a*) who through circumstances of a temporary nature is unable to make adequate provision for his child; or
(*b*) who is unable to provide the services required by his child because of the special needs of the child, may voluntarily place the child into the care, custody or under the supervision of the society or of the Crown, as the case may be."

12 *Mugford v. Children's Aid Society of Ottawa* [1969] S.C.R. 641, 4 D.L.R. (3d) 274; reversing [1968] 2 O.R. 866. *Re Mugford* [1970] 1 O.R. 601, 9 D.L.R. (3d) 113. Affirmed [1970] S.C.R. 261 (*Sub nom. Children's Aid Society of Ottawa v. Mugford*), [1970] 1 O.R. at 610n, 9 D.L.R. (3d) at 123n. See Green, "Re: Mugford — A Case Study of the Interaction of Child-Care Agency, Court and Legislature" (1971) 1 R.F.L. 1; Baxter, Law and Domestic Relations, (1973) 51 Can. Bar Rev. 137 at 145.

13 Child Welfare Amendment Act, 1968-69 (Ont.). c.9[now Child Welfare Act, R.S.O. 1970, c. 64, ss. 32, 36].

14 *Mugford v. C.A.S. of Ottawa, supra* note 12.

15 *Re Mugford, supra* note 12.

16 Child Welfare Act, R.S.O. 1970, c. 64, s. 36.

17 *Ibid.* s. 32.

18 Because of a change in reporting methods, only the years 1969-72 give a statistical picture of the number of Crown wards who were discharged from care via adoption. The following statistics are relevant:

Year	Crown Wards Adopted	All C.A.S. Handled Adoptions
April/69 - Mar/70	4,192	5,947
April/70 - Mar/71	3,986	5,877
April/71 - Mar/72	3,273	5,265

Source: Annual Reports of the Ontario Department of Social and Family Services, Queen's Printer, Toronto, 1969-72.

19 *E.g.* in British Columbia, where parental rights are never foreclosed until the day of the adoption order, the normal adoption route is attractive enough to have a waiting list of hundreds. See Fifth Report of the Royal Commission on Family and Children's Law, Part V, at 42-44 and Part VII, at 2-6.

20 R.S.A. 1970, c. 45.

21 *Ibid.,* s. 18(1).

22 *Ibid.,* s. 18 requires no attendance of the child and counsel is only appointed at the request of the Director of Child Welfare.

23 *Ibid.,* s. 18(1).

24 Criminal Code (Can.), 1976, s. 454(1) requires an accused to be brought before a justice within twenty-four hours of the arrest in most cases; s.465(1)(b) requires that no remand can be longer than eight clear days without the consent of the accused and the prosecutor.

25 Child Welfare Act, R.S.A. 1970, c. 45, s. 19(1).

26 *Ibid.,* s. 16(1) [am. 1972, c. 18, s. 4].

27 See notes 2, 13.

28 Family Services Act, ss. 1973, c. 38, s. 6.

29 The usual objection to preventive services is their expense. There is no demonstrable return and they are often cut from government budgets. However, some recent cases in the U.S. have brought to light the greater expense of foster care and institutional care as opposed to state-supported home care for children. See Thomas, "Child Neglect Proceedings — A New Focus" (1974) 50 Ind. L.J. 60 at 60-63.

30 Areen, "Intervention Between Parent and Child: A Re-Appraisal of the State's Role" (1975) 63 Geo. L.J. 887 at 934.

31 One of the few articles directed to lawyers concerning non-legal alternatives in child abuse cases was written by a lawyer: Fraser, "A Pragmatic Alternative to Current Legislative Approaches to Child Abuse" (1974) 12 Am. Crim. L. Rev. 103 at 122-124.

32 Thomas, see note 29, at 71-78. See also "The Relationship Between Promise and Performance in State Intervention in Family Life" (1972-73) 9 Columbia Journal of Law and Social Problems 28; Levine, "Caveat Parens: A Demystification of the Child Protection System" (1973), 35 U. Pitt. L. Rev. 1 at 36-37.

33 Thomas, see note 29 at 72-76 (table of state statutes).

34 Thomas, see note 29, at 77. The author cites the "mutual compact" theory enunciated by Judge Ketcham, in which the absence of promised governmental care breaks the agreement between parents and state, resulting in the loss of legal or moral justification for asserting state control over the child. See Ketcham, "The Unfulfilled Promise of the American Juvenile Court" (1962) Justice for the Child 22 at 25-27.

35 *E.g.* Foster and Freed, "Unequal Protection: Poverty and Family Law" (1967) 42 Ind. L.J. 192; Katz, "Foster Parents Versus Agencies: A Case Study in the Judicial Application of the Best Interests of the Child Doctrine" (1966) 65 Mich. L. Rev. 145; Sullivan, "Child Neglect: The Environmental Aspects" (1968) 29 Ohio St. L. J. 85; Note "The Custody Question and Child Neglect Rehearings" (1968) 35 U. Chi. L. Rev. 478 at 480-84.

36 Fifth Report of the Family and Children's Law Commission, *Part V: Protection of Children (Child Care),* (1975) at 29-32. See also Draft Children's Act, 1976, Queen's Printer, Victoria, B.C., Part V, s. 1.

37 Sullivan, "Child Neglect: The Environmental Aspects" (1968) 29 Ohio St. L. J. 85 at 93.
38 This phrase is close to that used by Sullivan, see note 37, at 9. It has also been used in the Family and Children's Law Commission Report, see note 36, in the definition of "emotional neglect" (p. 27 of Report).
39 Fifth Report, see note 36 at 13-14:
    "4. Recommendation: Parents or guardians who are offered child care services on a voluntary basis should have the absolute right to refuse the services offered."
40 *E.g.* The Child Welfare Act, S.M. 1974, c.C-30, s.12; The Child Welfare Amendment Act, S.O. 1975, c.1, s.15.
41 The Child Welfare Amendment Act, 1975 (Ont.), c.1, s.15 [enacting s.22a(3)].
42 *Ibid.,* s.22a(7).
43 The Family Services Act, 1973 (Sask.), c. 38, s. 17.
44 *E.g.* Child Welfare Act, R.S.O. 1970, c. 64, s. 23a [am. 1975, c. 1, s. 15]; Child Welfare Act, R.S.A. 1970, c. 45, s. 35, [am. 1973, c. 15, s. 7]; Child Welfare Act, R.S.N.B. 1973, c. C-4, s. 16; Child Welfare Act, 1974 (Man.), c. C-30, s. 13; Family Services Act, 1973 (Sask.), c. 38, ss. 8, 10.
45 British Columbia has used non-ward care agreements for over eight years; most children discharged from care in the first six months are in non-ward care: Fifth Report, see note 36, at 6-7 (App. III).
46 Fifth Report, see note 36, at 15.
47 "Non-Ward Care: Policies and Procedures," Vancouver Resource Board, November 1974.
48 *E.g.* Alberta, Saskatchewan, New Brunswick, see note 44.
49 *E.g.* New Brunswick, Saskatchewan, see note 44.
50 *E.g.* Alberta, New Brunswick, see note 44.
51 Alberta, New Brunswick, see note 44.
52 Manitoba, see note 44: the legislation has an eighteen month maximum term, termination rights for parents, and no automatic tie to apprehension if the agreement breaks down.
53 Goldstein, Freud and Solnit, *Beyond the Best Interests of the Child* (1973) at 40.
54 See note 44.
55 See note 44.
56 See note 46.
57 Child Welfare Amendment Act, 1975 (Ont.), c. 1, s. 15 [enacting s.23a(2)(a)].
58 The wording of all Canadian legislation and policy directives seems to indicate the temporary nature of non-ward care. However, as a British Columbia study pointed out, 14% of children in non-ward care remained in care after two years: Fifth Report, see note 36, App. III, 7.
59 Ontario, Manitoba, see note 44.
60 None of the legislative provisions for custody by agreement allow the parents to relinquish fully their rights to custody. Unless the agency has obtained a voluntary surrender of guardianship or a court order, they would have to return the child to the persons having the primary legal right to custody.
61 Ontario, Alberta, New Brunswick, see note 44.
62 *E.g.* Child Welfare Amendment Act, 1975 (Ont.), c. 1, s. 15 adding s.23a(2), see note 11. Saskatchewan has a similar bilateral agreement in s.8 of the Family Services Act ss. 1973, c. 38, but in s. 7 they also allow for the unsupervised unilateral provision of services by the minister:
    "7. The minister may make such payments as he considers necessary to or for the benefit of a parent, child or other person where special services or moneys are considered by the minister essential to enable the parent to care for the child."
63 Fifth Report, see note 36, at 18. The Commission recommendation for the voluntary surrender of guardianship on a temporary basis is not discussed, because of the similarity to non-ward care.
64 *E.g.* Family Services Act, 1973 (Sask.), c. 38, s. 11(8) (voluntary surrender) provides for complete termination of parent rights:

"Except as provided in this section and section 12, a committal of a child made under this section is irrevocable and the parent is not thereafter entitled to the guardianship or custody of the child or to any control or authority over, or any right with respect to, the child."

However, adoption consents, before the adoption order, give less explicit rights of guardianship. This can be seen from s. 56(4) of the Act, which provides that adoptive parents who have not made a timely application to adopt must return the child to the director of the social services department.

65   *E.g.* Adoption Act, R.S.B.C. 1960, c. 4, s. 8(5). See also Child Welfare Act, R.S.O. 1970, c. 64, s. 73(1).

66   Children's Aid Society of Metro. Toronto v. Lyttle, [1973] S.C.R. 568, 10 R.F.L. 131, 34 D.L.R. (3d) 127. See also Cruickshank, "Forgotten Fathers: The Rights of the Putative Father in Canada" (1972) 7 R.F.L. 1, 41.

67   *E.g.* Child Welfare Act, R.S.O. 1970, c. 64, s. 20(1)(*b*)(i).

68   Child Welfare Act, R.S.A. 1970, c. 45, s. 30; Family Services Act, 1973 (Sask.), c. 38, s. 11; Child Welfare Act, 1974 (Man.), c. 30, s. 15.

69   Child Welfare Act, R.S.A. 1970, c. 45, ss. 14(*e*)(xv), 30; Family Services Act, 1973 (Sask.), c. 38, ss. 11, 13; Child Welfare Act, 1974 (Man.), c. 30, ss. 15, 16(a)(ii).

70   See note 63.

71   Fifth Report, see note 36, at 55-57.

72   Fifth Report, see note 36, at 17.

73   *E.g.* Adoption Act, R.S.B.C. 1960, c. 4, s.8(5). The case law on revocations indicates that a best interests test will prevail over "parental rights": *Re Wells* (1962) 33 D.L.R. (2d) 243, 37 W.W.R. 564 (B.C.C.A.). In practice, very few revocation attempts by a natural mother are successful; in British Columbia, one application out of ten was successful in the period 1970-74: Fifth Report of the Family and Children's Law Commission, Part VII, Adoption, Appendix A, Table III.

74   Fifth Report, see note 36, at 17.

75   See note 68.

76   Child Welfare Act, R.S.A. 1970, c. 45, s. 30(1):
   "Where a parent, by instrument of surrender . . . surrenders custody of a child to the Director *for the purpose of adoption* . . . ." (emphasis added).

See also: Family Services Act, 1973 (Sask.), c. 38, s. 11(3) (return of child after one year limited to child placed for adoption).

77   Although no reported case has tested the voluntary surrender sections on administrative law grounds there is some support for bringing the prerogative writs in analagous areas: *M.T. v. Family and Children's Services of Lunenburg County* (1975) N.S.R. (2d) 348 (C.A.) (mandamus to compel Director to reveal time and place of adoption hearing to natural parents); *Kociuba v. Children's Aid Society of Halton* (1971) 18 R.F.L. 286 (Ont.) (habeas corpus to compel delivery of child to father, who had no notice of Child Welfare Act proceedings); *Re Child Welfare Act; Worlds v. Director of Child Welfare* (1967) 61 W.W.R. 513, [1968] 2 C.C.C. 88, 65 D.L.R. (2d) 252 (Alta.) (habeas corpus with certiorari in aid to examine permanent committal order and court record). In a voluntary surrender, the availability of judicial review depends on whether the function of the administrative procedures is classified as "administrative" or "quasi-judicial". If the latter classification prevails, remedies such as certiorari will be available to review the procedures. Under a voluntary surrender clause, a key problem may be the doctrine of waiver, which holds that a person's conduct in consenting to certain procedures may result in the forfeit of rights to a later hearing. See Reid, *Administrative Law and Practice,* (1971) at 111 *et seq.,* 159-161, 214.

78   This was recommended by the British Columbia Family and Children's Law Commission: Fifth Report, Part VI, Adoption, at 13-15. The Commission cited the survey of the English Houghton Report which stated that 84% of mothers giving up their children wanted their consents to be irrevocable.

79   Alberta Department of Social Services and Community Health, Child Welfare Branch, Edmonton, Form H.S.D.33A:

"*e.g.* Now Therefore this Indenture Witnesseth that the Party of the First Part doth voluntarily commit and make over the said child to the care and guardianship of the Party of the Second Part, and doth resign all claim to the custody or any control or authority over or any right to interfere with the said child."

80   Protection of Children Act, R.S.B.C. 1960, c. 303, s. 7(1)(*h*).

81   Fifth Report, see note 36, at 25.

82   Child Welfare Ordinance, c.C-3, Rev. Ord. of N.W.T. 1974, s. 16(1), (2).

83   *Ibid.*, s. 16(4).

84   Child Welfare Amendment Act, S.O. 1975, c. 1, s. 16.

85   Draft Children's Act, 1976, Part V, s. 21 (Supplement to Fifth Report, B.C. Family and Children's Law Commission).

86   *Ibid.*, s. 21(3): (3) Notwithstanding subsection (2), no person must apprehend a child under this section where, prior to apprehension, that person has concluded that it will be necessary to proceed for an order under section 37 (children found in need of care).

87   *Ibid.*, s. 21(5): (5) Subject to subsection (4), a person acting under this section *must assist the parent or other person to remedy the situation which gave rise to the apprehension* and must return the child to that parent or other person within 48 hours of apprehension (emphasis added).

88   All the checks discussed herein are mentioned at pp. 22-25, Fifth Report, see note 36.

89   Fifth Report, see note 36, at 22.

90   Youth Protection Act, R.S.Q. 1964, c. 220, as amended by Bill 78, 2nd sess., 30th Legislature, National Assembly of Quebec, 1974.

91   Bill 78, see note 90, ss. 14b, 14c, 14g, 14n.

92   *Ibid.*, s. 14n.

93   The main features of the child care conference discussed herein are outlined in the Fifth Report, see note 36, at 18-22, and Appendix V.

94   Fifth Report, see note 36, at 54-55.

95   The Use of Lay Panels in the Unified Family Court, Third Report of the British Columbia Family and Children's Law Commission, (1974). See Also: The Family, The Courts, and the Community, Fourth Report of the British Columbia Family and Children's Law Commission, (1975) 92-98.

Therapeutic and Legal Formulations of Child Abuse*

*Arthur W. Frank, III.***

That the "facts" of a situation are never neutral is an important truism, and often a neglected one. However true they may be, "facts" are only understood when placed in a certain context which provides for their integration and interpretation. The context for interpretation represents the perspective of a particular observer: what he chooses to see, and how he sees it. To be what society calls a "professional" is to have, among other things, a certain way of integrating and interpreting facts. Professionals learn methods for ascertaining and assessing facts about certain kinds of situations, and these methods differ among professional groups. Thus the "facts" for one group of professionals may be quite differently understood by another group.

The kind of professionals who work in the child abuse intervention agency discussed in this paper will be characterized as "therapists". Certainly "therapeutic" orientations differ among the physicians, nurses, psychologists, and social workers in the agency, but there seems to be a commonality in their methods for ascertaining and assessing facts. This paper is about the way in which "therapist" professionals assemble the "facts" of one of their cases.

The agency's primary mandate is to treat abusing parents; their work, however, is not exclusively therapeutic. Although the agency has no direct legal mandate, its work takes place in a thoroughly legal context. Many parents suspected of abuse must be coerced into accepting "client" status and attending therapy sessions. Such coercion usually takes a legal or quasi-legal form, including intervention by the provincial government child welfare worker who does have the legal mandate to remove children from their homes. When therapeutic efforts seem to fail, agency members may provide expert testimony leading to the apprehension of children. This

---

* My thanks to Catherine E. Foote, Howard Irving, and Lynn McDonald for their comments on an earlier draft of this paper.
** Associate Professor, Department of Sociology, University of Calgary, Calgary, Alberta.

apprehension normally implies temporary removal of the children from their homes; in rare cases removal may be permanent. Agency members' testimony in criminal proceedings against parents is rarer still, but such cases receive considerable attention when they do occur, and this occurrence constitutes an important aspect of the agency's self-conception of its activities.

The issue which this paper addresses is why the "therapist" professionals working in the intervention agency have trouble presenting what they know as "facts" to another professional group, the "legal" professionals in the court system. That they *do* have troubles is clear from extensive observations within the agency, and some observations within the court system. Although these troubles are a frequent topic of complaints and informal comment, their extent is difficult to document. Percentages of court cases won and lost hardly tell us much, since for therapists, cases which should have been prosecuted and, on legal advice, were never brought to court may be most important in their understanding of how responsive and effective the courts are. Among those cases which do get to court, even one child being returned to parents whom therapists "know" as abusive can be a traumatic trouble. So as long as there is anything less than perfect congruence between therapeutic recommendations and court dispositions, there is a trouble which deserves attention.

My thesis is that this trouble arises, at least in part, because therapeutic and legal professionals assemble facts in different ways, or, to put the matter more strongly, they have a different sense of what the facts are, in a given situation. The implication of this thesis is that therapeutic and legal professionals will continue to have troubles together until each realizes that the other, having assembled different facts, sees a different situation. Because the present research has been in therapeutic settings, the paper is about therapists' assembly and interpretation of facts. Understanding how therapists under the "facts" of a case has two practical implications. For therapists themselves, it allows greater self-reflection of their activity; for lawyers and judges, it allows more effective coordination with therapists. But mutual understanding, however important, probably will not be enough to eliminate the troubles between the therapeutic and legal systems, and this issue also is considered below.

SOCIAL INTERVENTION AND "FORMULATION"

A number of verbs are used above to describe how professionals put together facts into an interpretation: assemble, assess, ascertain, integrate, and interpret are some. I would like to summarize the activity which is described in part by each of these verbs as that of *formulation*. To formulate something is to make it knowable; formulation is the activity of coming to know something as ..., where the elipsis represents what the thing in question is known as. Before presenting data on how intervention agency members formulate a case of child abuse, three general observations must be made about formulation.

First, social intervention work, whether concerned with child abuse or something else, is necessarily an on-going process of formulation: the interveners must understand the situation as having a particular "form," because it is that form which legitimates and requires their intervention. To formulate a situation as one of child abuse is to understand that situation as having an intervenable form. Those who do social intervention work in child abuse must perform at least two acts of formulation: they must formulate the child as an abuse *victim*, and they must formulate a parent(s) as an *abuser*(s).[1] The formulations are the subject of this paper, and are discussed in the two sections below, but some additional comments on formulation should help in reading these sections.

Formulation means something more than "definition," because the latter implies that whatever is being defined is already there and lacks only a name, or at most lacks clearly "defined" boundaries. Formulation means something less than "creation," because to create implies to bring into existence something which was not there before, in any but the most latent sense. Something being formulated is already there for those doing the formulation, but they must do more than define it. In order for them to talk about it, and eventually act upon it, they must give it a particular cognitive shape and sensible reality. By a "sensible" reality I mean a reality which makes sense to a certain group, in terms of their background knowledge, predispositions for action, and interests in the social world. Confronted by something in the world, a group must formulate what "it" is for their purposes. The problem, as has been suggested above, is that different groups have different purposes, and they may formulate the same thing quite differently.

The problem of these different formulations is compounded by the second observation. Formulations come to be regarded by a group not as something which they themselves have done — the products of their own formulating activities — but rather as taken-for-granted "facts" of unquestioned and unquestionable status. I suggested above that being a professional consists in part in knowing a certain way of formulating; the thesis of the paper can now be restated as being that therapists and lawyers formulate differently, and each tends to take its formulations for granted as what the situation "is".

Professionals, certainly therapeutic professionals, usually understand intellectually that their work involves formulations of others and situations, and that these formulations are only one version of what is "really" there. This understanding, however, tends to get lost when daily activities become subject to certain pressures. The data which are presented below illustrate what this getting-lost looks like, in agency practice. Based on certain instances of agency practice, I will argue that much of the trouble which social intervention workers experience in legal spheres stems from therapists having lost the capacity, or at least the inclination, to reflect on their own formulating activity in a case. Instead of continually remembering that their understanding of a case is the product of their formulations, agency members often talk and act as if their formulations *are* the case. When others formulate differently, the capacity to mediate different versions is no longer there, and troubles must follow.

The third observation is that reflection on doing formulation does not get lost as a result of overwork or poor concentration. Instead, reflection on the activity of formulating seems to get lost when those with therapeutic training are required by their work to adapt a quasi-legal orientation. As suggested above, child abuse interveners constantly work with attentiveness to the impending or potential development of court cases: apprehensions, wardships, and so forth. When a therapeutic case becomes a court case, formulations which therapists could take for granted among themselves must now be treated as problematic: those legally trained require different verifications before they will accept the therapeutic formulation of the situation. But this conflict of formulative styles is not the full extent of the problem. I hope to show that matters are more complex: in anticipating court processes and adapting a quasi-legal formulative style, therapists seem to confuse their own therapeutic formulations, and end by doing neither good law nor good therapy. Because of this further confusion, a solution of mutual understanding between therapists and lawyers is insufficient. Instead, therapeutic practice in social intervention seems to require modification. Before developing this idea, it is necessary to present some data on how therapeutic formulations are done.

FORMULATING THE CHILD AS ABUSE VICTIM

The data presented below are verbatim transcriptions (only place and personal names have been changed) of a clinical conference in the child abuse intervention agency. My formulations of this transcription are based on the observation of many such conferences, the recording and transcription of several, and participant observation within the agency over a period of several years.[2]

The agency uses a multi-disciplinary "team" approach, employing a physician as medical director, a nurse, several social workers, a psychologist, and students in social work and nursing. The agency is administered by a large hospital, but the team is fairly autonomous in its daily clinical operations. Liaison with the provincial child protection department is frequent, although a protection worker did not attend the particular conference presented below. Referrals to the agency come from a variety of sources; hospital emergency rooms are a major source. The confidentiality of the referral process makes data on these referrals difficult to report: we do not have data on how many referrals are not accepted, or why, or how many preliminary investigations led to dropping cases immediately. Our impression is that few if any cases which are referred are dropped without extensive intervention.

For a case to remain a "case," *i.e.,* a proper subject of agency investigation and intervention, the child must be formulated as a victim of either abuse or neglect. This formulation involves treating the actions and physical body of the child as an object for investigation by agency members. The child may be investigated indirectly, through the media of x-rays or psychological tests, or directly, through physical examination and diagnostic interaction. These investigations produce the "facts" of the case: broken bones, a failure to smile at appropriate moments, or an inappropriate attentiveness to the moods of others all may be understood as "documents" of abuse or neglect. These documents then support the formulation of the child-as-victim, but it must be remembered that this same formulation was the initial auspice of the investigation. The formulation of the child-as-victim requires the investigation in the first place, and then it emerges as that which is required *by* the investigation. This circularity will be evident throughout the data below: the conference is ostensibly a formulation of child and parent, but it has already been necessary to formulate both, in order to bring them to the conference in the first place.

When the documents of abuse/neglect are sufficient, they become the basis of the agency's claim that others, significantly courts, should share the agency's formulation of the child. If this claim is contested, usually by parents, the agency formulation will be contrasted with an alternative formulation, based on other documents, or other formulations of the same documents. Thus, for example, the child-as-victim-of-abuse formulation may be contrasted by the child-as-victim-of-bad-luck, natural accident, inherent disease or disorder, and so forth. As suggested above, agency trouble is the court's acceptance of one of these formulations rather than its own.

Cases are discussed in conference when there is some impass in therapy, *e.g.,* the client is not keeping appointments, and/or the case is at a particular juncture, such as the imminence of court action. In the conference, the validity of the formulations already arrived at is taken for granted, for *therapeutic* purposes. What is to be discussed by the team is whether the formulations are acceptable in terms of what team members understand as appropriate *legal* criteria. As will eventually be shown, team action frequently modifies therapeutic practice in order to meet what they anticipate as legal requirements.

In the case to be discussed below, the initial document of abuse was a severe burn on the child's face. The problem with the burn as a document on which the formulation of the child as abuse victim could be based is that the burn could also document other possible formulated identities, such as victim-of-accident. The child's mother claimed that the burn resulted when the child's bottle tipped over in the crib and came to rest against the child's face. This alternative formulation was regarded by team members as implausible, but sufficient to undercut the legal value of the document. The impass in the case is the need for other documents having sufficient legal force to assert the team's formulation of the child.

The conference discussion of the case begins with a statement by the team nurse, orienting team members to the state of the case. In the transcription of the conference each utterance is numbered sequentially, so in this quotation and those below the initial number represents the sequence of utterances:

22 Brenda: so the purpose of the conference is because the baby's weight is starting to fall back cause Nancy has a lot of concerns about ah developmental delays and lack of stimulation and and uh [voice drops] some of the things that are going on in thuh home and we thought maybe we should sort it out and just see [pause] what more we can do with her.

In this and in transcriptions below, our spelling has been modified to conform to the speaker's intonation and punctuation has been used to attempt to represent the pace and inflection of speech, rather than to reconstruct grammatical intent.

The significance of Brenda's statement is its demonstration that the formulation of the child has already been accomplished. As subsequent talk will make even more obvious, the purpose of the conference is not to determine *if* the weight has dropped or *if* there have been developmental delays; these "facts" are taken for granted. The issue is whether these documents have legal force.

The child's apparent weight loss is considered first. A sufficient weight loss, well documented, could support an acceptable legal formulation of neglect; the problem is whether the measurements have been accurate. Two different, but equally "official," weights have been recorded within an eight day period. The first, recorded by a team member, is low enough to constitute a "significant" (for legal purposes) weight loss, or to be a valid document of neglect. The second however, recorded in a hospital clinic, is "normal," or, fails to contrast sufficiently with the expected weight of a child of that age. In the discussion of the discrepancy of weights, the validity of the hospital weight is impugned, but the documentary value of the team-recorded weight is recognized as weak. The summary of the discussion is an exchange between the medical director of the team, "Jim," and the public health nursed assigned to the case, "Pam". Utterance 49 illustrates particularly clearly the team's attention to legal formulation:

47   Jim: [has been discussing standard weight measures] and uh she drops off from the twenty-fifth, isn't it? above, a little bit above the twenty-fifth percentile to well below the third percentile if public health's scales are accurate now we've had — don't misinterpret this — ah we've had difficulty with weights ah from hospital wards ...

48   Pam: yeah

49   Jim: in our own control weights as well as weights elsewhere and so we wanted to make it possible as sure as we could that there was a significant weight drop ah if this ever gets into a legal situation, we'd be in quite a bind

50   Pam: un hum.

The team continues to accept the weight loss as a document of neglect for its own purposes, but the value of this document in a legal formulation is understood to be undercut by the hospital weight. In a "legal situation," this document could not be asserted as an unambiguous formulation of the child.

The failure of weight loss as a usable document is suggested soon after the topic is raised. The topic of developmental delay is managed quite differently, suggesting more clearly the intent of team conferences. The topic is introduced in utterance #59, in which Pam (the public health nurse) states: "there's also concerns, Nancy [a nursing student] did a developmental test on [the baby] about ... three weeks ago?" Since developmental delay has been mentioned by Brenda as one reason for having the conference (utterance 22, quoted above) and is now described as a concern, team members would be expected to assume that Nancy has test results documenting such a delay. There are repeated requests for the exact results, but these are not mentioned until utterance #98. Between utterances #59 and #98 then, the conference proceeds under the assumption that delays are documented. During this time, team members describe experiences with the child, formulating these experiences on the assumption of interacting with a child who is slow to develop. The problem is that when the test results are finally stated, they prove nothing: no significant delay has been established.

Team members' management of the talk about developmental delay raises at least two questions. First, why was there such a delay between the introduction of the topic and the statement of the test results? Second, why was the topic raised at all?

One answer to both questions is that the topic provides the team members with the possibility of a "fishing expedition" in which each recounts an interaction with the child, based on the assumption that the child is "slow" to develop. Possibly one of these experiences will provide the missing document, which the test results are assumed to provide but do not. As suggested above, the understanding of "facts" depends on a certain interpretive context; the statement of developmental delay as a documented "concern" provides such a context, in which "facts" may emerge. If it had been stated from the beginning that the test scores failed to show any developmental delay, then team members would not have formulated their interactions with the child as documenting delay, and no further documents could have been forthcoming.

If such an explanation seems implausibly cynical, the following exchange illustrates a clear case of such a fishing expedition. The two main candidates for documentary status having failed, the team leaders see if any other documents are available:

129 Jim: Brenda wasn't there a ... I'm remembering here what — well wasn't there some other event in the past in terms of trauma as well?

110 Pam: yeah

131 Brenda: um, I don't think so, don't know of any other injury, do you? [whispering, laughter in background]

132 Pam: there was ah, something that was mentioned to me and ah, I wouldn't want to say it officially because I I just heard it from someone I can't remember who told me but apparently up in Smalltown they had been followed by some agency up there because they'd left the baby in the apartment in the car unattended or something.

Utterance 131 illustrates the conference's purpose: to gather documents which may be used to formulate a legal case. That legality is the issue is suggested by Pam's qualifier, "I wouldn't want to say it officially. ..."

What is significant is that the failure of the legal status of documents does nothing to undercut the formulation of the child as victim of neglect. What is startling is that the very documents which have been systematically undercut still retain full "factual" force for team members. Near the end of the conference this force is articulated in a social worker's statement that even though no legal formulation has emerged, there is still a need for continuing intervention:

306 Helen: ... talking about weight loss and developmental delay and inadequate personality [attributed to the mother and considered below]; it certainly sounds like a set-up for this child in a lot of ways. . . . I'm not sure that maybe we're not leaving that baby in a bad position.

307 Jim: Well, I must say I'm assuming that we're going to find that this child hasn't thrived and it will be taken up from there and brought in.

This exchange is perhaps the most singular display of the agency's practices of formulation. First, those documents which have been undercut are cited again as having a factual status: for team purposes, the baby is losing weight and is suffering developmental delay, whatever the inaccuracies of scales and the results of test scores. Second, the conference is governed by the assumption, assumed at the beginning and unchanged throughout, that neglect is taking place — "failure to thrive" being a legal category of neglect — and there will be an eventual apprehension of the child.

The child-as-victim has been formulated before the conference begins, and, it seems, before any investigation (testing, weighing, etc.) begins. The agency does not gather documents to produce a formulation which is initially uncertain. Instead they begin with a certain formulation and then search for documents to support it, for legal, not team/therapeutic, purposes. When documents fail, the initial formulation is not called into question; the failure is only for "official" purposes. The conference is about documenting a formulation which remains unquestionable.

In the final sections of this paper, I will argue that agency practice does not represent perversity, but rather is an attempt — which I believe is misguided — to adapt to a legal model of formulation. The result seems, unfortunately often, to be poor therapy and poor law. Before arguing this, the agency's second formulation must be considered, that of the "inadequate personality." the parent-as-abuser.

FORMULATING THE PARENT AS ABUSER

The team must anticipate a possible refutation of their formulation of the child, which is that the child is not a victim of abuse or neglect, but only of natural circumstances. In order to establish their case that the parent has, in some active sense, abused or neglected the child, the team must formulate the moral identity of the parent as an abusive or neglectful person. This formulation of the parent is only somewhat secondary to the formulation of the child, because there is a circularity in the two formulations. In the formulation of the child as victim, the formulation of the parent as abusive stands as taken-for-granted background, though as yet unestablished. The formulation of the parent then has as its background the knowledge that the chld is a victim.

As in the formulation of the child, the team does not seek information to determine an identity, but rather seeks only to document a known identity. The following exchange illustrates how potentially neutral documents of the parent's life are understood as part of a formulation of the parent as neglectful:

138 Jim: I guess I'm just thinking of the whole family, a chaotic sort of, un, different life styles

139 Pam: apparently Dr. Smith said that they lived in a sort of hotel up there; it was like [a] motor cycle gang, and they lived in a way out sort of thing, and she came from that situation; I don't know.

*****

144 Brenda: yeah, I think he expressed a lot of concerns about mother's life style and about her own uncleanliness and mother's own ill health. For instance mother has a hearing problem she's known for, before she left Eastern Province over two years ago that she was to have had some ear surgery and she left there without having it done ...

Nothing which is said is, necesarily and by itself, a document of an abusing or even a neglectful parent. Many people live in hotels, associate with motorcyclists, and fail to conform to physicians' and nurses' standards of cleanliness. The "failure" to have had ear surgery is perhaps most interesting in its documentary status.

One might elect not to have surgery for a number of reasons: lack of funds, feeling that the problem was not sufficient to warrant the discomfort of surgery, lack of time for recuperation, or lack of confidence in one's physician. Brenda does not consider any of these possibilities; apparently for her, none would qualify as a "good" reason. By excluding these possible reasons, Brenda presents the non-surgery as documenting the parent's "ill health" as a *motivated* condition: she is not unhealthy as a result of bad luck in her genetic constitution, poverty, or any other "natural" condition; rather she is unhealthy as a result of her conscious failure to attend to her health. This failure is documented by her knowing that she needed surgery and having "left there without having it done." There are two obvious implications, for the team formulation of the parent. First, because the parent has no ability to maintain her own health, she cannot be expected to care for the health of her child. Second, her failures are motivated failures; she is not simply unfortunate, instead, she is culpable. As she is culpable for her own ill health, so she is culpable for her child's troubles.

This same formulation procedure — using the already known identity to make sense of the document, which in turn validates the initial identity attribution — is illustrated again, soon after the ear surgery comment. Again a potentially neutral incident is reported, but it is taken as unquestionable that the parent was culpable. The only variation from the talk in #138-144 is that "Nancy," a nursing student, fails initially to share the team's sense of what is unquestionable and requires some brief socialization into team thinking:

165 Brenda: She said she had an appointment for herself [with a physician] on the 20th and she would take the baby along, but instead she apparently broke the appointment.

166 Nancy: She did go one day and he wasn't there or something.

167 Brenda: Yeah, well the office told me that she broke the appointment.

168 Nancy: She told me that ... oh ... so

169 Brenda: hahaha [laughter from others]

170 Jim: Yeah, it's pretty, you know, ah, manipulative here.

Again, no evidence is presented to decide the issue one way or the other, either as the physician's failure, his secretary's, the parent's, or a misunderstanding without "fault". Instead it is taken for granted that the physician's office is efficient and correct, and that the parent is being manipulative. If Nancy had questioned Brenda further, she probably would have been referred back to the ear surgery incident as evidence of the parent's motivated ill health; thus each incident supports the interpretation of the other, and together they formulate the parent.

The formulation of the parent is given a summary statement near the end of the conference by the team psychologist; it is his phrase which is repeated by the social worker quoted above (#306):

284 Keith: ... sounds more like an inadequate kind of personality; I think ... she's [either] in an area of diminished capacity or she's inadequate to care for the child ...

This formulation of "inadequate personality" has not been arrived at; it was the initial basis for understanding the documents of the parent's life as they were presented: knowing her to be inadequate, then it was necessarily her fault when the appointment with the physician was missed. The missed appointment then becomes a document of her inadequacy.

The full circularity of the formulations of parent and child can now be understood, remembering how Helen (utterance #306) included the "inadequate personality" attribution along with the weight loss and developmental delay as documents of the child's status as neglected. Because the child was known as neglected, the parent is formulated as neglectful. This formulation of the parent is then used to validate the initial formulation of the child. The mother's actions are interpreted in a certain light ("uncleanliness" and "manipulative"), and then the parent's "inadequate personality" is presented as a basis for understanding the child as being "in a bad position".

*****

This presentation of the agency's formulation practices — child-as-victim and parent-as-abuser — has not been made to denegate the agency, but rather to demonstrate how self-consciousness of doing formulation gets lost in practice. What is remarkable is that no one questions, ever, that there is serious neglect in the situation; no one ever refutes the documentary status of weight loss and developmental delay. Having formulated the case as one of neglect, this formulation is rendered unquestionable. The formulation is only a problem insofar as legalities are concerned. A large part of Helen's frustration, expressed in #306, "leaving that baby in a bad position," is with the inadequacy of the legal system. The courts fail to recognize what the team members already know, that neglect is going on.

As suggested in the beginning of this paper, the agency's legal problems have to do with their methods of formulation, though not only the circularity of their formulations of child and parent, and the further circularities within these formulations. The deeper problem seems to be that therapeutic and legal formulations are different, and the agency is confusing the two. In the final sections, I will provide a model of this difference and suggest reasons for the confusion; I will then suggest certain changes in agency practice which could reduce the confusions somewhat.

LEGAL AND THERAPEUTIC FORMULATIONS

The argument advanced below makes reference to obvious aspects of the situation, but these aspects are reorganized in a way which may be less than obvious. As at the beginning of this paper, there are three major points.

First, most therapy is not social intervention. Whether medical, psychiatric, or social relational, most therapy involves a self-identified client. Such a client seeks out a therapist, claims to have some trouble (a bad back, a bad marriage, and so forth), and asks for help. In such a situation, the therapist is perfectly justified in accepting at least the essence of the client's self-formulation: it is not only possible but morally obligatory to believe that the client is a troubled person. The therapist may or may not accept the client's explanation for this trouble or the client's plan (if he has one) for curing it, but he will accept that the client is troubled. In seeking to help the client, the therapist may legitimately search the client's life to find documents of the trouble. The important point about such a search is this: since the client has been legitimately formulated as troubled, it is equally legitimate to formulate documents as documents of that trouble, and to treat them that way. Thus in a *voluntary* model of therapy, formulating documents based on a taken-for-granted state of trouble is the approved procedure.

Second, the legal intervention model is quite different. The kind of law which social intervention cases fall into is not properly civil or criminal. An apprehension or wardship case might rather be called accusatory law, since the basis for the action is that someone, usually a parent, is being accused, although neither criminal nor civil proceedings will be involved, usually. The client, as accused, typically refutes the formulation of him/herself as troubled, *i.e.,* abusive. Lawyers defending and prosecuting the accused/client may initially assume a formulation of troubled or not troubled and gather evidential documents based on this prior formulation, but then the difference enters in. When these documents are presented in court, the formulation must follow *from* the evidence/document, not *vice versa.* The justice of due process in accusatory law demands that the initial formulation of the accused be neutral — innocent until proven troubled — and that the documents of the trouble must speak for themselves. The evidence must formulate the identity of the accused; it must not be the case that the evidence itself becomes understandable only on the basis of prior knowledge of the accused's guilty identity. Rules of admissibility of evidence exist to ensure that the sequence of formulation, at least as it takes place inside the court, proceeds from documents to identity.

Family courts may depart from strict rules of evidence, but for present purposes these courts also can be considered to function on a legal model. If the evidence does not support the formulated identity of the accused as a culpable perpetrator, that is the end of it. Clearly courts do not always function according to their own ideal principles, but at minimum the legal model does have a mechanism for dropping cases. As suggested above, intervention agencies rarely, if ever, seem to drop cases.

Third, social intervention work is not like most therapy, but rather is based on an *involuntary* model. The term "client" is quite euphemistic with reference to most of the persons who are the agency's cases. They are not contracting with the agency to remedy some trouble which they themselves have identified. Instead the agency typically intervenes in their lives, telling them they have some trouble, and demanding the continuation of the intervention until that trouble is remedied to the agency's, not the "client's" satisfaction.

Involuntary therapy is a confusion of both the voluntary therapeutic and the legal models. In the legal model, the lawyer, as advocate, speaks for or against the accused, and the accused knows which. In the involuntary model, the "therapist" speaks *both* for and against the client. On the one hand, team members claim to do for the client what voluntary therapists do, and they expect the client to treat them as a voluntary client would treat his chosen therapist. Clients are expected to be trusting, motivated to co-operate, and so forth. On the other hand, the intervention agency is constantly preparing a case against the client, and so what the client says or does in therapy may later be used against him/her in court. As "Pam," the public health nurse, says about the client in the above case, "I think she suspected all along that we were watching her to make sure she was looking at her baby" (#225). The team expects the client to accept their legal monitoring role, but also to be "motivated" to work with their therapeutic efforts.

The involuntary model confuses everyone. Clients are confused when they are expected to act as volunteers for therapy but are confronted with a potential legal opposition. Team members themselves are confused when their therapeutic formulations, which they know to be true, fail to meet standards of legal evidence. They are also confused when their clients refuse to present themselves as motivated. This dual uncooperation, from courts and clients should hardly be surprising; it should instead suggest the confused nature of involuntary therapy, which totally muddles its own advocacy.

The formulation practices of intervention agencies would be quite reasonable, *if* these formulations were made in a context of voluntary therapy. If a parent claimed some trouble on behalf of his/her child, the team members would be entirely justified to treat the child as troubled and to conduct "fishing expeditions" to seek further documents of that trouble. The problem comes when the client is not voluntary. By seeking to do both therapy *for* the client and para-legal investigation *of* the client, the team puts itself in an irremedial position of conflict of interest. Neither good therapy nor good legal investigation will result.

The ideal conclusion to this paper is that intervention agencies delimit their activities to either therapy on behalf of voluntary clients or investigation as a specialized branch of the family courts. Theoretically the latter function is the role of government child protection departments, but the activity of private agencies in this area suggests that these departments are at least thought of as incapable of doing the job which is required. Unfortunately this ideal conclusion will not be realized: varieties of involuntary therapy seem on a constant increase. A weaker though more practical conclusion is that intervention workers develop a greater self-awareness of their own formulation practices, and particularly the ends which their formulations serve.

AGENCY POLICY RECOMMENDATIONS

Self-awareness is rarely the result of good intentions alone; some structural modification is usually required. A basic modification is that agencies keep, and constantly review, statistics on the proportion of cases dropped, and at what stage of the intervention process they were dropped, *i.e.*, on hearing the initial referral, after preliminary investigation, after a certain number of interviews, and so forth. Obviously there is no magic proportion of cases which should be dropped, but if no cases are being dropped, that should raise questions. These questions should raise the following general issue as a constant point of self-reflection for agency therapists: does the fact that a case is "a case" predispose me to formulate the child as victim and the parent as abuser, and then understand other aspects of their lives as documenting these identities? Having statistics on cases dropped may encourage therapists not to assume they can always answer this question in the negative.

A second suggestion is that when a case is being discussed in conference, an agency member not directly involved be appointed "client advocate". Such a role would involve asking questions which challenge agency presuppositions concerning clients; *e.g.*, is this child really losing weight? are there not good reasons for avoiding ear surgery? and so forth. Having such a role institutionalized would not only lead to interesting questions being raised in conferences, but it would also sensitize agency members who act as client advocates to what possible alternative formulations are.

Third, if agencies must continue to perform both a therapeutic and a para-legal role, teams should seek to clarify, at the beginning of a conference, how the case is being treated. It seems doubtful whether the team can perform both roles on the same case at the same time, but perhaps they can work sequentially. While working on a therapeutic level, the potential development of a legal case would be excluded from discussion. When therapeutic means are judged to have failed, then a lawyer should be brought to the conference as a consultant, and the advocacy role accepted unequivocally.

Finally, a less practical but perhaps more important suggestion is that agency members consider the limits to which intervention therapy ought to protect, since protection also involves intrusion. Because of their experiences, intervention therapists can become so sensitive to the need for protection that they fail to see the real risks of legally mandated intrusion, and an intervention from one perspective is always an intrusion from another. The reality of an abused child compels us to action so forcefully that it seems pedantic to speak of that reality as the observer's formulation. The problems which abuse intervention agencies have, both in courts and with clients in therapy, indicate, however, that no phenomenon is self-evident in the same way to all. Self-reflection on the formulation process — realizing that all realities are formulations — may help therapists clarify their own intervention activity. Understanding how therapists formulate should help those working with them to clarify and question their formulations.

---

1   A third formulation is also involved, in which the agency must formulate itself as the legitimate agent of public response to the abuse situation. Agency members self-formulation is considered in Arthur Frank, "The Language of Social Intervention: Formulating 'Competence.'" Presented at the Annual Meeting of the American Sociological Association, New York City, August 1980.

2   Data was collected between 1977 and 1979 by myself and Catherine E. Foote, who also collaborated in the transcriptions and continues to edit reports on the research.

Children in the Courts:
A Selected Empirical Review

*Katherine Catton**

This article reviews the small body of empirical research relevant to five central issues concerning children in the court system. These consist of discretion in the court system, the child as participant in the hearing, legal representation, the use of expert social evaluation reports and alternative forms of processing. The author concludes that there is a visible need for and yet a regrettable lack of empirical data on the effects and effectiveness of processing children through the court.

INTRODUCTION

One central focus of both law and social science is human behaviour. Implicit predictions about how a given legal policy or reform will alter human behaviour usually underlie any decision for change. Yet such decisions are usually made without adequate knowledge about the effects of present policy and legislation or the probable consequences of adopting a different approach. Much jurisprudence is amenable to scientific analysis. However, little relevant empirical research has been conducted and therefore little relevant data exist to enlighten the choices made. The body of this paper examines several issues respecting children in delinquency, child protection and custody proceedings noting where social science research, if undertaken, could help clarify or focus concerns, or point out probable solutions to the many difficult questions confronting legislators and policymakers when they make decisions aimed at furthering the child's "best interests" in the court process. In the end, there emerges a clear picture of the need for and yet regrettable lack of scientifically-based factual information to assist in the decisionmaking process.

In Canada in 1975, over 50,000 marriages ended in divorce, an

* Katherine Catton, M.A., LL.B., of the Ontario Bar, is Legal Research Coordinator at the *Child in the City Programme,* University of Toronto. This interdisciplinary research project, sponsored by the Hospital for Sick Children Foundation, is studying the problems of urban children.

increase of 12.4 percent over 1974.[1] While the legal system has rules regulating this process, no one knows how, or even how many, children under eighteen are affected by these divorces. Many children live with a parent who is separated. Even less is known about how the separation process itself or the resulting long-term living arrangements alter the lives of these children.

In 1976 in Ontario, more than 20,000 cases of children "in need of protection" came into the legal system.[2] In these instances, the judge has to determine whether the custodian has failed to provide the child with a minimum standard of care. If the court so decides, it can permit social agencies to intervene coercively to protect the child "at risk". Yet how effectively these agencies enhance the well-being of the children involved, if at all, remains unknown at this time, although suspicion exists that their potential for harm at least equals their potential for good.

An even greater number of children are brought into the legal system as delinquents. Approximately 140,000 children were dealt with by the police in 1976 in Canada and, in 43 percent of these cases, charges either were recommended to be laid or were laid, but beyond this, basic delinquency data are collected only sporadically[3] and little is known of the effects or effectiveness of this process.

In each of these three types of proceedings, the legal system seeks to promote the child's "best interests". Yet the absence of comprehensive, systematic and continuous data collection leaves us with only the vaguest notions, based mainly on surmise and supposition, of what actually happens to children involved in such court proceedings. Policy decisions are, therefore, set in a vacuum. An accurate data-based picture of the process and its consequences is an essential first step in elucidating the problems[4] and reforming the process.

In this paper, five key issues affecting children in the courts will be examined, noting the results found in the small body of existing empirical research and emphasising those areas where further systematic research is needed to provide the requisite information on the effects and effectiveness of the legal process in delinquency, child protection and custody proceedings. The issues to be canvassed are (1) discretion in the court system; (2) the child as participant in the hearing; (3) legal representation; (4) the use of expert social evaluation reports; and (5) alternative forms of processing. The review will focus on the need to document and understand what *actually happens* as children are processed through the courts, rather than merely on what the pertinent legislation or case law envisages should happen, for it is well known that "living law is different from the law on the books".[5]

DISCRETION IN THE COURT SYSTEM

The first issue to be explored is the wide discretion in decisionmaking which occurs at all levels of processing in the juvenile justice system, that is, prior to, at, and following the court hearing. This discretion cannot be considered true legal discretion, for legal discretion requires effective guidelines,[6] and vaguely drawn substantive laws with indefinite standards provide little guidance for decisionmakers. Law is meant to provide the principal framework to inform and constrain official action.[7] But the "best interests" standard prevalent in children's law is not really a standard at all. Rather, it serves as the decisionmaker's rationalisation to justify his judgments about a child's future. By offering no guidelines for the exercise of this power, the law has left uncontrolled the perceptions and prejudices of the decisionmaker.[8] Unfettered discretion leads to individualised judgments. Yet individualised decisions offend the basic precept of our common law system tht requires that similar cases be treated similarly. Thus, the best interests test serves little purpose for two reasons: it furnishes the decisionmaker with little meaningful guidance in making his decisions and it requires him to make impossible predictions about the contingencies of life.

(a) Discretion in the delinquency system

The present Canadian approach to delinquency grew out of the wider 19th century child saving movement.[9] This approach, in one American scholar's view, is characterised by broad, intolerant, morality-based legislation, tempered by administrative discretion on the part of police, court-intake workers, judges and ordinary citizens. The result is virtually unlimited scope and "benevolent" discretion in this area of law.[10] Sociologist Paul Tappan has observed that the vast majority, if not all, normal children indulge in forms of behaviour which come within the purview of the delinquency laws.[11] Whether a child ends up being officially processed, however, depends upon the discretion of the officials with whom he comes into contact; upon their subjective interpretation of his behaviour.

The Canadian juvenile justice system, like its American counterpart, has confusing, even contradictory, objectives. Along with the rhetoric of treatment and rehabilitation,[12] which ostensibly justifies the broad discretionary intervention powers, there exists considerable sentiment for punishment and social protection.[13] Principles of punishment, however, must be governed by the rule of law, not individual discretion. Laws based on coercive sanction should be defined with specificity, certainty and uniformity, so that the individual may thereby know exactly what conduct is proscribed.[14] An increased emphasis on these punishment and social control elements in Canada's delinquency process should lead to a shift away from the rehabilitative rhetoric towards greater incorporation of criminal law jurisprudence and, as such, should lead to a decrease in discretion and a greater emphasis on due process.[15] The proposed new Canadian delinquency legislation, which encompasses only Federal offences, represents precisely this type of philosophical shift. But whether this proposed reform, if enacted, will actually decrease the discretion exercised can only be determined empirically.

(i)   Diversion prior to the delinquency hearing — the problems with diversion

The concept of diversion[16] encompasses a variety of activities, including police, social agency, and pre-trial screening to channel offending juveniles back to the family or social agency, or into a pre-trial settlement procedure, rather than on to court.[17] Most juvenile infractions are minor offences which do not reliably indicate future delinquency or adult maladjustment. Hence, diversion is considered by many to be desirable in terms of both time and cost. Indeed, the smooth operation of the juvenile justice system may require diversion; these courts could grind to a halt if virtually all children were brought before them.

Presently in Canada, however, there is no formal diversion policy or structure. Since no formal guidelines define the diversion process, officials must rely on their own discretion. Hence, irrelevant factors and personal bias frequently may come into play. In studying the extent to which factors *not* related to the alleged offence affected the probability of a juvenile being referred for a formal court hearing, American research indicated that extra-legal as well as legal criteria played major roles, including age (*i.e.,* older children were referred to court more often), family instability (referred more often), co-defendants (referred more often), and race (blacks referred more often).[18] Moreover, other studies have shown that, overall, diversion has tended to *increase* the number of children in official or semi-official hands.[19] That is, there is little diversion *from* the system; rather, it occurs mainly within the system. Thus, as the number of diversion programmes has grown, so has the total number of children brought within the juvenile justice system.[20] Hence, diversion, in practice, appears to accomplish exactly the opposite to what diversion theory seeks to accomplish.

To develop systematic and effective diversion programmes, effective guidelines are needed to help structure and control the diversion process. Those agencies performing diversion activities must be monitored and held accountable for their performance. In Canada, diversity in local attitudes and resources, which variably affects opportunities for diversion, provides a unique opportunity for experimentation and comparison.[21] To understand how such discretionary decisionmaking works and to know its role and function in the delinquency system requires basic empirical research. Only then might this discretion be managed more effectively.[22]

(ii) Discretion at the delinquency hearing

Again at the hearing itself, few guidelines exist to structure the judge's broad threefold discretion. Firstly, judges decide *what* behaviour to process further, for in the omnibus clauses in delinquency legislation, judicial authorities find the discretion to impose upon youth whatever standards of behaviour they deem appropriate.[23] The judge, as statutory *parens patriae*, acts for the state in the role of a benevolent parent to "aid, encourage, help and assist" a "misdirected and misguided" child.[24] Yet the behaviour one judge considers "misguided and misdirected" at one time, he may another time choose to ignore. Even if the individual judge is consistent in his approach, the behaviour he proscribes may differ radically from the behaviour proscribed by another judge. For example, one judge may go to great lengths to declare a child delinquent if it appears that the child needs help. Another will rely only on the behaviour which brought the child to court in determining delinquency. Hence, the process of defining delinquent behaviour is based on wide judicial discretion.

Secondly, the judge, to a large extent, is able to decide *how* the proceedings are conducted. hearings are informal.[25] Research has shown that, in practice, due process protections are often set aside despite the fact that the case law now enumerates a range of due process protections. In his work on civil liberties, the former Chief Justice of the Ontario High Court, James C. McRuer, had argued that:[26]

> Strict adherence to the procedure of the ordinary Courts might well work to the detriment of the child. The function of the Judge is not so much to determine guilt as to find out the underlying causes which have brought the child before the Court, and, when these have been determined, to prescribe treatment.

In his view, while "some basic" legal protections require recognition, the function of the judge as:[27]

> ... a social physician charged with diagnosing the care and issuing the prescription ... cannot be properly performed if he is surrounded by too many legalistic trappings.

Further, because Canadian legislation limits appeals to cases where there exists a gross abuse of process and because the proceedings are not open to public scrutiny, there is limited review to check procedural abuse. In consequence, one juvenile court may be conducted in a highly legalistic manner while another totally disregards due process procedures.

Thirdly, judges decide *what penalty* to set. Since there is no specific fine, penalty or treatment for any given offence, the judge may invoke any one or combination of the dispositions set out in section 20 of the *Juvenile Delinquents Act,* ranging from an adjournment *sine die* to an indefinite training school committal. In sum, it is apparent that all major decisions at the delinquency hearing are, to some extent, discretionary. And while both consistency and predictability are central to any system of law, there can be no consistency in a system which relies on discretion at every level.

The proposed new Federal delinquency legislation, which limits the court's jurisdiction to children who violate federal laws and which circumscribes procedural discretion, reflects the prevailing dissatisfaction with this system of discretionary justice for juvenile offenders, even though little reliable data exists about the actual effects or effectiveness of the complex network of inter-related components making up our delinquency system. While the confusing and even contradictory goals in our present system make meaningful evaluation of its effectiveness difficult, presently, even the most basic descriptive research remains to be undertaken. Attempts should be made to develop a solid data-based description of the effectiveness of the present delinquency laws. Otherwise, there will exist no basis for comparing the new Federal proposals when they are implemented and without such comparisons, it will be impossible to measure the effectiveness of these statutory reforms.

(b) Discretion in the child protection system

The fundamental fault with child protection laws, claims law professor Robert Mnookin, is the wide discretion which they permit.[28]

(i) *Discretion prior to the protection hearing*

Prior to bringing on a child protection application, the child protection agency usually works with the family in an attempt to resolve their problems. This, suggests one American commentator, should be a prerequisite to intervention;[29] only after the State has been unsuccessful in ameliorating neglect by providing services to the child and family should other forms of intrusion be permitted.

As an alternative to protection proceedings, the legislation of several provinces permits parents to agree to place their children into the care of child protection authorities voluntarily when they are temporarily unable to care for the child or when the child has special needs beyond the resources of the parents.[30] Yet, relatively little is known about how, when, why or how often these "non-ward care agreements" are employed. Their use appears to be entirely at the individual social worker's discretion. Because these agreements are private contracts requiring no judicial scrutiny, the agency may use these in place of care proceedings. Moreover, no external checks exist to prevent the threat of formal proceedings from being used to coerce a family into entering non-ward agreements. Nor is there any monitoring or evaluation to see how successful such agreements are in comparison with other forms of intervention.

In a narrow range of circumstances, the legislation of Manitoba and Ontario gives children's aid societies the power to place a homemaker temporarily in premises where a child has been left without proper care.[31] This option is limited to providing temporary care only and is not available as a broader family problem-solving technique. In theory, though, homemaker services have the potential for ameliorating a wide range of family problems which might otherwise lead to protection applications. Homemakers could be used to alleviate crisis situations, teach parenting, help families get to other needed services, protect children and perform a wide variety of other roles. Yet no study of their present or potential utility has been undertaken. The exposed goal of child welfare agencies is to rehabilitate families rather than remove children. Innovative experimentation with and evaluation of homemaker services and other forms of child care may help transform this policy into reality.

Finally, little is known about the process leading up to a protection hearing or about the exercise of worker discretion prior to the case reaching court. Is there a series of predictable stages through which each case must pass? Are there formal guidelines to delimit and standardise decision-making? If so, do they work? Especially important are the variables which enter into the decision to commence the hearing itself. For example, one Ontario study indicated that, both within individual agencies and between different agencies, no common definition of what constituted child abuse could be obtained.[32] Thus, the need for understanding and controlling discretion prior to the hearing is apparent. Research which monitors standardisation and effectiveness is one possible technique which may facilitate the achievement of this end.

(ii) Discretion at the child protection hearing

Current criteria for declaring children in need of protection are couched in broad, vague statutory language. Yet because aiding children through coercive intervention has not been proven to be a success, American law professor Michael Wald believes that over-intervention into family life is a greater problem than under-intervention. Neglect is often defined in terms of parental conduct or home conditions, rarely requiring a showing of actual harm to the child.[33] In Wald's view, vague concepts such as parental fault or moral neglect should be abandoned in favour of statutory standards based on specific types of damage which justify intervention.

In theory, there are two stages with two different standards in child protection hearings. The court should first find whether the child is in need of protection and, if this is so, the judge must then consider which disposition would serve the child's best interests. But, in practice, the two separate stages, and separate standards overlap and individualised adjudications result. Yet, as noted, because the individual judges are forced to rely on their own personal biases, such discretionary determinations are frequently not consistent and often not fair. In a simulation study of judicial decisionmaking in child welfare hearings, a group of researchers for the Child Welfare League of America[34] found that every Judge operated on his own unique personal value system, different factors being important to different Judges.

Like Wald, Mnookin also insisted that the judge's discretion to remove a child from his home should be circumscribed. He suggested that objective measures be defined and that written judicial decisions, containing both the reasons for removal and an explanation of why proposed less drastic measures were found unsatisfactory, be required.[35] Whether some form of written decision could, in fact, check judicial discretion, and perhaps agency discretion too, is an empirical question. This and other possible techniques for controlling discretion merit further exploration.

In protection hearings, in Saskatchewan for example, a judge is faced with four alternatives: he can dismiss the case, leave the child in the home under agency supervision, remove the child from the home temporarily, or take steps to remove him permanently by declaring him a permanent ward.[36] If the child is found in need of protection, the present legislative standard for disposition — the best interest test — does not equip a judge to compare the probable consequences of the child's remaining in the home with the probable consequences of his removal.[37] The judge may not readily see the risks of foster care placement, since only the risks of the child remaining in the home are placed before him.[38] This results in a substantial bias in favour of removal. More basic still little is known about the consequences of placing the child under home supervision as compared with removal, for example.[39] But even if removal were to prove the better alternative, the benefits may not be sufficient to justify the substantial financial cost. The possible harmful effects of compelling unwilling clients to accept services must be investigated too, for this may have significant repercussions for the child.[40] Thus, the full range of innovative prevention measures should be evaluated and compared. One especially promising alternative, the "no-question-asked drop-off centre" where parents may deposit their children for a specified period of time is now being implemented in a number of locations.[41] Approaches such as this merit serious assessment.

In conclusion, indeterminate, discretionary standards fail to force social welfare bureaucracies to plan adequately for the children. In the plans they do make, the convenience of the social welfare system rather than the best interests of the child is often suspected to be the overriding factor.[42] Monitoring and evaluation, forcing accountability, could help overcome abuses. Systematic empirical research on the effects of removal and foster care can define and document problem areas. Such research can not only provide an effective tool in lobbying for legislative standards limiting discretion, but it may also indicate innovative avenues of reform.

(c) Discretion in processing custody issues

Custody and access questions are essentially matters of private law. The state will perform a dispute-settling function only if the question is brought to court.

(i) Discretion prior to the custody hearing

The majority of custody disputes are resolved before reaching court. A recent study of divorce-related custody dispositions in England indicated that custody was still in dispute by the time that the divorce reached the judicial hearing in only 2.1 percent of the cases in the sample. Most custody dispositions were found to be *pro forma* judicial confirmations of private arrangements made between the spouses prior to court.[43] And when the parties settle the custody matter out-of-court, this decisionmaking process is virtually free from judicial review.

Indeed, formal procedures are being created to encourage private settlement. In Ontario, for example, the Provincial Courts (Family Division), the Unified Family Court and the Family Law Division of the Supreme Court have established informal "pre-trials" between a judge and the disputing spouses.[44] These pre-trials seek to encourage the litigants to reach accord privately on as many issues as possible, including custody, prior to their formal divorce hearing.[45] Yet, without empirical research, one cannot know if these innovations actually effect satisfactory and lasting custody settlements.

(ii) Discretion at the custody hearing

While disputed custody matters are usually settled out of court, litigated cases often make important contributions to the relevant law. Most custody legislation directs the court to make that order which is consistent with the "best interests" of the child[46] but fails to elucidate the criteria on which this "best interests" decision is to be made.[47] Hence, the judge must resort to the case law for guidelines. Yet the precedents often provide little assistance either because their rules are either too vague or too flexible to be unequivocal or because they involve different facts with different people while the "best interests" test requires individualised decisionmaking.[48] Thus, the trial judge is left with substantial discretion in making his decision.

As a principle of law, Mnookin argues, the "best interests" test is so wide that one cannot know when a judge has used it improperly.[49] Hence, aside from appeals, there are no effective limits on judicial discretion in these proceedings.[50] Because no clear societal consensus exists on the best mode of child-rearing[51] and because the test itself is indeterminate, the judge is forced to rely on his own value choices, or, alternatively, to depend on the reports of social workers or psychiatrists who make questionable claim to special knowledge and predictive ability.[52] In consequence, the decisions of one court may appear inconsistent with those of another and the fundamental principle that like cases should be decided alike may be violated, or appear to be violated in the eyes of the parties.[53] One Canadian study on judicial discretion in contested custody matters concluded that no universal principles exist in this area of law.[54] And on an individual basis, because the vagueness of this standard makes the outcome of litigation hard to predict, an increased number of cases are taken to court.[55]

To counter this broad judicial discretion, many have proposed that substantive guidelines or presumptions supplement the best interests rule.[56] Such presumptions may, by directing the court to consider a number of matters relevant to the issue, limit discretion. While guidelines such as these should be developed out of rigorous scientific study, the necessary research has yet to be undertaken. The need for increased knowledge of the long-term consequences of alternative custody arrangements, the central question in any custody matter, is apparent. Yet little relevant data presently exist.[57] Before guidelines can be formulated, it is necessary to know how and under what circumstances custody arrangements cause emotional injuries to children and how various familial factors exacerbate or mitigate these effects.[58] Questions related to changes in mother-figures,[59] the effects of psychological ties, the need for continuity of relationships, the benefits of access and the like are all empirical questions which require research to provide the much needed information on which to base guidelines aimed at structuring and defining discretion in the custody decisionmaking process. Then the effects and effectiveness of the guidelines themselves must be assessed.

THE CHILD AS PARTICIPANT IN THE HEARING

Regardless of the type of hearing, serious questions exist about the child's participation based on a variety of considerations. These include the child's status in the hearing, his ability to understand both the nature and purpose of the hearing and the manner in which it is conducted, his perceptions of the fairness of the procedure and the justness of the outcome, and his capacity to know and express his own views, either through a lawyer or directly to the court.

(a) The child's status in the hearing

The word "party has a precise meaning in legal parlance. It is that person by or against whom legal action is brought or who otherwise has a legally recognised interest in the proceeding, and who, therefore, has a right fully to participate in the proceedings.

In delinquency proceedings, the child clearly has party status.[60] In child protection and custody matters, however, his status is less clear. In Manitoba and Quebec, the child is specifically granted a statutory right to participate through legal counsel in a protection hearing.[61] In other parts of the Dominion, the child's status as a party is doubtful. A recent decision of the Ontario High Court[62] seems to confirm this doubt. Nevertheless, Ontario's child welfare statute has a unique provision allowing the judge, if he so chooses, to hear any person on behalf of the child;[63] presumedly, "any person" might include the child himself. Newfoundland offers a distinctly similar provision, permitting a judge "to consult the wishes of a child" in respect of the order to be made.[64]

With respect to custody matters, Alberta seems to be the only jurisdiction in Canada specifically allowing the child to make application for his own custody.[65] Generally speaking, however, superior courts of record appear to be agreeable to the idea of independent representation for children in custody disputes, even in the absence of any special legislation.[66]

To possess party status in legal proceedings where one's rights are being affected is a fundamental tenet of the Canadian legal system. Without such status, a person cannot compel the court to hear his views on the matters being adjudicated, even though his rights may thereby be affected. That children still lack party status in some proceedings where their lives are affected may be viewed as an historical anachronism, a holdover from times when children were virtually legal non-entities. The trend today, however, is toward recognising children as full citizens in our society. Yet as long as such anomalies in our legal system survive, they must be acknowledged and children's status determined accordingly.

(b) The child's capacity to understand the proceedings

Delinquency charges cannot be brought against a child under seven years of age.[67] Custody and protection matters, on the other hand, often involve very young children incapable of directly participating in the hearing even if accorded party status. British barrister and lecturer, Dr. Olive Stone recently noted that:[68]

... the medical profession seems generally convinced that children aged six or seven years, even if below normal intelligence, may have decided . . . ideas and should be heard.

Yet no research has been undertaken to establish in a scientific manner the age below which most children are unable to understand the nature and consequences of legal proceedings and are thus incapable of meaningful participation. Therefore, no meaningful age line can presently be drawn below which children should be presumed incapable of participating.

The small body of empirical data which exists notes that prior to a delinquency hearing, most children have no clear understanding of what to expect at the hearing.[69] Moreover, once the proceeding is over, the research indicates that they have little understanding of what actually happened in court.[70] This lack of comprehension obtained equally for those with a long history of court appearances as for those appearing for the first time. The research also suggests that most parents did not understand what had occurred in the hearing either.[71]

These misunderstandings can be attributed to a variety of factors. Most legislation dealing with children is vague, broad in scope and based on individualised "best interests" determinations. And what actually occurs in these hearings often belies this espoused legislative goal. Parents and children have little factual knowledge of what should happen in court. The procedure may be unnecessarily confusing or complex. The informal nature of the proceedings may well contribute to the confusion for there are few clear and predictable steps in the process. Moreover, recent American research suggests that children learn much of what they know about law from television.[72] If this finding holds true in Canada, children would, on this basis, expect strict (probably American) criminal law due process in court. If the child's parents equally do not grasp what is happening in court and if the lawyer (when present) does not have or take the time to explain the process, then confusion on the child's part is an understandable consequence of a delinquency hearing. Bewilderment and perhaps dismay on the child's part may be normal reactions connoting real insight into the nature of children's legal proceedings and, as such, are indicative of capacity rather than incapacity in this context.

The comprehensibility of the informal procedures in delinquency and child protection hearings should be subject to further research. The child's lack of understanding may stem mainly from poorly defined procedures or from insufficient knowledge of what to expect rather than from inherent deficiencies in his capacity to appreciate the legal process. Because custody hearings are more formal, a comparison between children's comprehension in these proceedings and in the more informal delinquency and child protection hearings may help clarify matters. Because no efforts are made to apprise the child of the functions of the various participants in the proceeding — the judge, the lawyer, social worker, "prosecutor" — he may understand little about their respective roles in the hearing. But it is important to realise that children, like adults, act and react on the basis of their expectations. Research indicates that disappointed expectations, even though inaccurate, may lead to very negative attitudes towards the law.[73] On the basis of ignorance and misinformation, the child may react to his exposure to the legal system with a "profound sense of injustice".[74]

(c) The child's capacity to present his view to the court

There is little point in giving the child the right to participate in proceedings affecting him if he is unable to ascertain or express his own views. Research on children's perceptions of delinquency hearings indicates that they frequently feel that they do not "get their say" in court. They feel that they are treated in a routine and superficial manner.[75] These same feelings may also occur where the judge, in a custody matter, interviews the child in chambers, although no research has been undertaken on this point. To improve this situation, children are being provided with their own legal counsel. The ramifications of this will now be explored more fully.

LEGAL REPRESENTATION

In examining the lawyer-child relationship, one must review three central concepts: access — how and when do children retain counsel; capacity — when are children able to instruct counsel; and finally, quality — how effective is the representation provided?

American lawyer Andrew Kleinfeld maintained that, for adults, the right to counsel is premised upon the incompetence of the ordinary lawman to cope with the technicalities of legal proceedings. In his view, this logic compels an even broader right to counsel for infants because of their presumably even greater incompetence.[76] In delinquency proceedings, children, as parties, have the right to retain and to instruct counsel.[77] In custody disputes, the superior courts of record of several provinces have had occasion to appoint a person such as an "Official Guardian" to represent children, often with full powers to act as if the children were parties to the proceedings.[78] In respect of child protection matters, however, particularly in those provinces whose statutes are silent on representation for the child,[79] judicial appointment of independent counsel may be virtually impossible.[80]

The potential benefits of representation are numerous. Children, like adults, need assistance in understanding the proceedings. They need representation to ensure that their rights are upheld, to ensure procedural regularity, to protect them from potential abuse endemic in a system based on broad discretionary justice, to present impartially and articulately their views to the court and to help make new law by appealing cases. Child advocates may also form an effective lobby for statutory changes.[81]

Judicial and legislative activity in this area has reflected the general up-surge in concern over legal representation for children. Hence, the issue today is not so much whether to provide children with legal representation but rather how to ensure that children obtain representation which is both timely and effective. Central to this issue is the child's capacity to instruct counsel and, in the obverse, the role the lawyer should assume. Should he act in his traditional adversary role as an advocate for the child's view, assuming he can determine what the child's views are? Should he modify his role to that of an *amicus curiae*,[82] assisting the court by bringing to its attention matters that might otherwise be overlooked? Or should he act as the child's guardian, advocating the decision he sees as being in the child's best interests?

Both the child's ability to instruct counsel and the philosophy and procedural structure of the court in which the lawyer acts may affect his final role definition. Based on their studies in the Ontario Provincial Courts (Family Division), a group of researchers reported that lawyers representing children in delinquency hearings were under pressure to perform diametrically opposing roles in court.[83] These researchers found that the lawyer's training as an advocate conflicted with the informal, social service orientation of the juvenile court. This conflict created pressure on counsel to assume a less adversarial stance. The judges and social workers were also found to have contradictory expectations about the function the lawyer should fulfill.[84] Some judges and social workers indicated that he should act in a highly legalistic manner; others insisted that he should do whatever is "best" for the child. Similar results were obtained in an American study, where it was also observed that lawyers themselves varied in their preferred orientation toward representing juveniles.[85] Further, the role which counsel was able to assume depended, to a large extent, on whether the court itself was legalistic or informal in its orientation. Finally, this data indicated that, while the adversarial approach was highly successful in obtaining discharges in a "legalistic" court, in an informal, "family model" court, the adversarial approach led to an increase in conviction rates.[86]

In custody hearings, which are formal, adversarial due process proceedings, the lawyer is expected to, and therefore does, perform a much different role than in informal "family model" delinquency or protection hearings. Thus, the exact role which a lawyer finally adopts in any given proceeding is influenced by a number of variables, including the philosophy of the court, the model underlying the procedure, the lawyer's own preferred orientation toward the proceeding, the role that other participants in the hearing expect the lawyer to perform, and the lawyer's assessment of the child's capacity to instruct him. Each of these variables merits further research to determine what effects it has on the lawyer's role, the child and the hearing itself.

Whether the lawyer looks to the child for direction depends on his opinion of the child's capacity to instruct him. While a child as young as seven may have decided views and be a proper source of information, most children involved in protection proceedings and many in custody disputes are even younger than this.[87] The lawyer may, therefore, be required to make an independent assessment of the child's best interests in this situation.

The psychological literature generally endorses the notion that children over six have, to a degree at least, the capacity to make choices and convey information to direct a lawyer and by about age 13 should be able to instruct counsel specifically. Yet no empirical research has been directed specifically to this question. Since children are being represented with increasing frequency, the effects and effectiveness of legal representation should be explored more fully. In fact, the whole area of representation abounds with questions which can only be answered through empirical research. For example, at what point in the process must a lawyer be provided to be effective? What role should the lawyer perform? Should his role differ, depending on the nature of the hearing? What training does the lawyer need to help him communicate with and understand children? Conversely, what training do children need to help them deal with, speak to and understand lawyers? Can procedures be modified to make lawyers more effective in representing children? If so, how? Does having legal representation really make any difference in the nature and outcome of the proceeding? If so, is it for the better? Should there be a full-time representative providing legal services to all children? Or should the judge have the discretion to appoint counsel as he sees fit? These and many other questions are ripe for empirical investigation.

In several provinces, an "Official Guardian" or a similar official provides a limited range of legal services for minors.[88] He may provide the court with social reports on all children involved in divorce proceedings, covering therein matters related to their care, maintenance, custody and access; in Ontario for the year 1976, this alone involved the Official Guardian of that province in some 14,900 cases.[89] The court may also request that he provide a report in a non-divorce custody proceeding. And in a growing number of cases the Official Guardian is being asked to act as counsel for children in contested custody and child protection matters. An analysis of the Official Guardian's role could be a useful first step in examining issues relating to legal representation for children.

Many provinces offer duty counsel through a legal aid plan to represent children involved in undefended delinquency prosecutions.[90]

This system, too, should be evaluated. Preliminary research results[91] indicated duty counsel-child communication was so poor that some children did not even realise duty counsel was a lawyer present to represent them. Moreover, duty counsel was observed to make few attempts to advocate actively on the child's behalf in court.

When a child contests a delinquency charge, he may be able to retain a private lawyer through legal aid to represent him. Despite the unique opportunity for comparative research which these two modes of delivering legal services to children provide, no evaluation has yet been undertaken. In 1977, however, the Ontario Attorney General's Committee on the Representation of Children[92] recommended that a series of pilot projects be established to assess the quality of present modes of delivering legal representation to children and to determine ways of improving this service. Preliminary work is now underway.[93]

THE USE OF SOCIAL EVALUATION REPORTS IN COURT

Social evaluation reports usually come before the court in two ways. Either the court itself orders a social investigation[94] or one of the parties retains the assistance of an expert, such as a psychiatrist or psychologist, to prepare a report or present evidence in support of that party's claims.

Social investigation reports are designed to assist the court in deciding the case before it by expeditiously bringing to the judge's attention matters which he would not learn of otherwise. The scope of the report may depend on the judge's directions. Usually though, it encompasses the complete personal and economic backgrounds of all parties before the court, the rationale being that almost any variable could be relevant in determining the "best interests" of the child in question. In the words of one American commentator:[95]

> Experienced and disinterested workers make an unbiased examination of the qualifications of each party and of the circumstances surrounding the child.

The predictive inadequacy of present judicial guidelines accounts for the interest in behavioural science opinion as a source of decisionmaking assistance.[96] Traditional adversary procedures in custody matters seldom produce the kind of information which a judge needs to determine the child's best interests. In protection and delinquency hearings, the justification for using such reports stems from the court's ostensible need to have a complete picture before it can act in the child's best interests.

Yet it is important to note that these reports are based on opinion rather than on scientifically based fact, for the research necessary to produce such knowledge remains undone. American law professor Sheila

Okpaku argues that the current use of such reports is premised upon the mistaken belief that the behavioural sciences are sufficiently advanced to supply answers to individual questions such as "which long-term custody placement is best for this child?" In its present unverified state, she claims, psychological theory can, at best, only suggest such questions as areas where research is needed. It offers no panacea to the decisionmaking dilemmas faced by the judiciary, because the data upon which to base such knowledge remain to be gathered.

The use of clinical psychiatric and psychological insight to inform judicial decisionmaking has been subject to much criticism. Virtually any conduct, Okpaku asserts, can be taken as symptomatic of a psychiatric disorder. Even without regard to bias, psychiatric judgments involve a high risk of error. That psychiatric and psychological judgments are highly unreliable is well documented.[97] Okpaku concludes that clinical judgments of doubtful validity presently serve as the basis for predictions about the long-range effects of a particular placement or treatment on the child; well-intentioned clinicians, convinced of the accuracy of their unsystematic observations, can find in their over-broad descriptions of childhood needs and harms support for virtually any opinion.

In Ontario, for example, social investigations are mandatory in all custody matters and divorce actions involving children.[98] Freelance social workers investigate and prepare these reports in Toronto; in smaller centres, the child welfare agency is used.[99] In protection matters, court affiliated assessment clinics, where they exist, prepare such reports; otherwise, the local agency is used despite the conflict of interest between its role as the party commencing the protection application and its role as impartial investigator preparing an unbiased evaluation of the family situation. In delinquency proceedings, court clinics or court appointed personnel prepare these evaluations on the judge's request.

Although many participants in court hearings rely heavily on the reliability and validity of these social reports, little is known about when judges request them, how they are used, or how accurately they portray the family situation. Kraus[100] reported in 1975 that, despite its importance, he could find no empirical research on how presentence reports were used in juvenile court decisionmaking. His research into judicial use of these reports in the Australian Children's Courts indicated that the most significant factor in judicial decisionmaking was not the report *per se* but rather its actual recommendations. These recommendations carried more weight in judicial decisionmaking than any other factor he analysed. In the deliberations of Scottish Children's Panels, discussion focussed mainly on the contents of the social report.[101] Thus, the courts appear to rely on such reports to a considerable extent. Moreover, while it has been noted that judges express a strong desire for this type of expert assistance,[102] little empirical research on the function and utility of expert social reports in children's hearings has been conducted.

The need for further data-based research is readily apparent, especially in view of the steady increase in the number of requests for these reports which occurs each year[103] and the heavy judicial reliance on their recommendations. Empirical research can further our understanding of the present use of social reports and help establish directions for future policy.

ALTERNATIVE FORMS OF COURT

John Spencer, a leading Scottish researcher, had stated that systems of justice, above all in relation to children, cannot be divorced from the structure of social services responsible for the assessment and care of the child and of his family.[104] But concern has been expressed about the effects and effectiveness of transferring decisionmaking away from either the legal process or the family where it formerly resided and into the hands of social service agencies. Some would contend that the social service system, while lacking the formal checks and restraints found in the legal process, has come to function as a quasi-legal system. This section of the paper, therefore, explores the need for data on the use and utility of some of the wide variety of social services relevant to delinquency, child protection and custody matters.

In commenting upon the establishment of the National Youth Services Bureau in the United States, American sociologist Frederick Howlett suggested that this agency would only broaden the umbrella of ineffective services for children while further transferring the problems and responsibilities of the family away from the home, school and community where they belonged and into the public domain.[105] This agency, in his view, would divert from the legal system only those who should not be there anyway. Victor Streib, an American professor of forensic studies, suggested that, as the formal delinquency system in the United States found its discretionary powers circumscribed by the due process requirements of their Supreme Court, an informal system developed, composed of a college of service agencies, which now parallels and competes with the formal system.[106] Thus, discretion and procedural abuse have not disappeared. They simply re-emerged in another form. This informal service system performs exactly the same functions as the legal process but without the judge, without strict legal procedures and without formal hearings. Its sanctioning mechanism is the threat of court. Yet rather than simply abolishing this informal system, which may provide a viable and less costly alternative to judicial processing, Streib said that it was necessary to learn more about how it operates and to evaluate its effectiveness.

Courts exert little effective control or supervision over the decision-making of service agencies. In consequence, these agencies exercise virtually unbridled discretion. Because the variety of services surrounding the legal processing of children often have unclear or inconsistent goals and operating procedures, meaningful comparisons are difficult to undertake. But unless both supervision and evaluation are undertaken, service agencies may tend to serve their clients according to the agency's function rather than the client's needs.[107] Yet if these service agencies prove no less effective than courts in controlling antisocial behaviour and achieve their results more simply, efficiently, humanely or cheaply, then this option deserves further consideration. If, however, as Howlett predicted, research demonstrates that more children are netted by ineffective services, then other alternatives must be sought.

The movement away from legal processing toward service processing as the preferred way of dealing with children's legal problems mirrors the dissatisfaction with the present system. In custody and protection proceedings, and to a lesser degree in delinquency matters, dissatisfaction focuses on the adversary system. Because it tends to entrench acrimony and further polarise those involved, the adversary system is often ineffective in achieving amicable and lasting dispute settlement. Those who advocate alternative approaches to solving family problems hope that informal procedures, fostering conciliatory attitudes and encouraging the parties themselves to participate in the dispute resolution, will lead to permanent, effective solutions. Dissatisfaction with the present system also centres in the trauma of court hearings, on overloaded court schedules leading to repeated delays, and on the time and dollars involved in litigating issues which might be settled more efficaciously by other means.

The alternatives, either proposed or operative, fall into three broad conceptual categories. Firstly, there are procedures established prior to court which seek to settle as many issues as possible or to channel the case out of the legal system entirely. Examples of this are formal and informal delinquency diversion programmes and the conciliations, arbitrations or pre-trials often used in matrimonial matters. Secondly, some systems eliminate judicial processing entirely. In its place, service hearings are substituted. The Scottish lay panel system is an example which has been empirically evaluated to some extent. Thirdly, some jurisdictions have attempted to unify the existing judicial and service elements of the family law process. The movement in Canada toward a system of Unified Family Courts illustrates this approach. As stated, these three categories are conceptual only. Any of these service aproaches, in combination or permutation, may be employed in seeking solutions to the deficiencies in the present system. The small amount of empirical research relevant to these three categories will now be examined.

(a) Pre-court services

Diversion within the delinquency system has already been discussed.[107a]

Mediation[108] is a method of conflict resolution whereby the parties to the dispute are made to realise that they themselves must find a way to solve the matter in dispute. The mediator cannot impose a solution. Rather he guides the parties into a willingness to accept their responsibility to seek a solution and points out alternatives that might have been overlooked.

In a crisis urban ghetto in the Bronx, a Neighbourhood Youth Diversion Program[109] was established geared toward intensive community participation in dispute resolution through informal mediation, using community residents trained as mediators. The mediation process sought to convince the disputants that they themselves had the responsibility to come to a mutually satisfactory resolution. The powerlessness of the forum was seen as its greatest asset, for its success was totally dependent on the genuine consent of everyone involved. In this voluntary environment, mediation effected resolutions where coercive court processing had previously failed. Hence, the project demonstrated to the community that it had the capacity to deal with its own youth problems.

Mediation-based child care conferences have also been proposed as a method of dealing with child protection cases.[110]

Conciliation is the label applied to mediation of domestic disputes. As in mediation, the conciliator has no power to impose a settlement. Rather he attempts to bring the parties to an awareness of their own responsibility to achieve a mutually satisfactory solution. A number of conciliation projects are underway across Canada.[111] In Toronto, for example, the Family Court Conciliation Project provides specialists trained in the socio-legal aspects of short-term crisis-oriented matrimonial counselling. The service is voluntary but the court's authority is used to encourage people to take advantage of it. A team aproach, utilising professionals of varying backgrounds, is employed to enhance the possibility of resolving the dispute outside the formal court structure. Of special interest is the project evaluation which exemplifies the type of empirical research seldom conducted but essential if meaningful conclusions are to be drawn from data collection. The investigators state that [112]

> The plans for evaluation ... include the use of experimental and control groups. Clients will be randomly assigned to the control group (the existing court intake service) and the experimental group (the conciliation project) for purposes of statistical comparisons.

Methodologically strong empirical research like that being undertaken at the Toronto Family Court will enable policymakers to base their decisions on solid, empirical data rather than mere surmise. In this type of multidisciplinary approach to family problems, however, there is often no clear demarcation between the social and legal services provided. In consequence, the professionals affiliated with such services may experience serious role conflict or confusion. Such conflicts can jeopardise the success of the progamme. It has been argued that lawyers should handle the strictly legal matters and leave the large social and personal matters of conciliation to the social workers.[113] One Canadian study observed that considerable friction among the various professionals working on a number of Canadian conciliation projects arose from their divergent views as to who should perform what duties along the social service-legal counselling continuum.[114] This problem merits consideration in the further assessment of such projects.

(b) Service hearings as a substitute for courts

In this second category, judicial hearings are eliminated and service hearings are held in their place. The most well-known example, which has been subject to some systematic research, is the Scottish lay panel system.

Children's panels were established in Scotland in 1971[115] to replace court proceedings in delinquency and protection matters with hearings before a panel of three lay persons. If the parents or child refuse to appear, deny the act in question or do not accept the panel's determination, then the matter may still be referred on to court. The nature of the offence is irrelevant at a panel hearing, its sole function being to apply training measures appropriate to the child's needs.[116] The process promotes a highly individualised approach to each case and relies heavily on persuasion in attempting to obtain the cooperation of the delinquent and his family.[117]

According to British criminologist Allison Morris, one cannot accurately talk about the "Scottish lay panel system". Her research indicates that a number of systems operate within the same statutory framework.[118] The children referred to panel hearings generally were found to be petty delinquents, more social nuisances than social problems.[119] Yet under this system, the number of children in residential treatment has increased even though the total number of cases being processed has not.[120] And while the panel system was designed to enhance community involvement, another criminologist, Nigel Bruce, maintains that it has had little impact in the general community.[121] Spencer, on the other hand, argues that it has indeed sharpened awareness of the real problems faced by children living in deprived circumstances.[122]

Sweden also had long held service hearings before their Child Welfare Boards. The Board has full authority to adjudicate both family and delinquency matters involving children under sixteen. The Board may, in delinquency matters, refer the child onto the courts.[123] Similarly, in 1974 British Columbia established a panel system, composed of two lay persons and a judge which, upon the application of a variety of persons including the child, may make a variety of dispositional decisions once the child is found in need of protection.[124] The effectiveness of these two systems has not, as yet, been subject to empirical assessment.

(c) Unified family courts

The move toward Unified Family Courts has developed in response to the inadequacies in the present system. The Ontario Law Reform Commission has summarised the deficiencies in the existing system as follows:[125]

> Four different branches in the judicial hierarchy ... administer family law in Ontario and this results in overlapping and competing jurisdiction ... and conflicts in philosophy and approach to the same problems among the different courts. The end result is inefficiency, ineffective treatment of family problems, and unnecessary confusion.
>
> ...
>
> [Moreover, t]he provision of such ancillary services as exist (and these are by no means sufficient) has been haphazard, marked by lack of uniformity of policy and of standards.

Despite the absence of empirical data to support their views, the Commissioners concluded that:[126]

> Only if a Family Court is given comprehensive jurisdiction in all family law matters, will it be capable of meeting the needs of the community.

There was no question, in the Commissioners' view that a strong, well-structured, well-equipped Family Court system, supported by adequate ancillary services, could be of inestimable value to the community.[127]

In response to such perceived deficiencies, the British Columbia Royal Commission on Family and Children's Law established a Unified Family Court pilot project in that province in 1974.[128] Their final assessment of the project is soon to be released. While the interim reports appear to be highly subjective, they indicate that the project was considered a success. Other provinces have established or are in the process of establishing their own Unified Family Courts, either experimentally or permanently. The problem of fragmented jurisdiction is usually overcome by giving this court power to administer all legislation relating to families and children.[129] Thus, the one court can handle any family law matter. Further, attempts are underway to streamline the ancillary services considered essential for the ultimate resolution of family problems. And before further government commitment is made to this reform programme, a full-time researcher is conducting an assessment of the effectiveness of this appoach.

Others, however, are not so optimistic about this trend. One Canadian researcher[130] has argued that the Unified Family Court movement is based upon the same rehabilitative philosophy which underlies the Juvenile Courts, in which, it is claimed, this philosophy has already failed. Similarly, Judge Herbert A. Allard of the Alberta Family and Juvenile Courts voiced this concern when he stated that:[131]

> Appraisals of American Family Courts are all to often marked by self-initiated statements of their own effectiveness and worthiness. Recent questionings of Juvenile Court practices will no doubt soon be extended to questioning of handling of domestic disputes as heard in the various courts.

An exhaustive review of Family Courts in the United States concluded that:[132]

> Family Courts, though little studied in depth, have garnered almost universal praise.
>
> . . .
>
> This uncritical consensus reflects a common practice in America, of looking to legal institutions for the correction of social ills. This tendency is dangerous; our experience is that Courts seldom contain the answers to problems arising *outside* the legal system. We delude ourselves if we think that delinquency and family disorganization can be cured simply by reforms in legal institutions.

Thus, in any of the above-described ways, children who come in contact with the legal system find themselves, and often their entire families, inextricably bound up in a social service network of, as yet, unproven worth. This service dimension cannot be ignored. Many view services as alternatives to legal processing rather than as mere adjuncts. Yet little data exist to endorse this approach. Even the utility of the present service component of the Family Court system remains undemonstrated. Service approaches which appear to enhance individual involvement and responsibility in decisionmaking, which save time and dollars or which increase the likelihood of lasting and satisfactory resolutions of family problems should be systematically evaluated to establish their efficacy. Then those programmes of proven value should be retained. In considering the service alternatives within the present legal system and services as alternatives to court, many questions remain unanswered. It is important to heed the warning that:[133]

> It is in the nature of services to develop like living organisms: to grow, to specialise, to seek more recognition and power.

Perhaps this alone accounts for the rapid proliferation of services. In terms of time, cost and the needs of children, the merit of these recent service innovations requires empirical validation based on hard data to provide answers about their effects and effectiveness.

CONCLUSION

This paper has sought to review a number of key issues relevant to the processing of children through the court system, asking firstly, "what do we know about what *actually happens* to children as they proceed through this system?", and secondly, "what do we know about how the decisions made actually affect children and their families?". When making decisions about the adequacy of present methods of processing children and in formulating future policy and legislation, it is imperative that those charged with the responsibility have some idea of the answers to these two questions. Yet to answer these two questions requires information gathered in a systematic and methodologically sound fashion. To this end the informed use of social science research techniques will allow the collection of reliable and valid data which can provide meaningful information on which to base such decisions and assess the effects of policy when translated into action.

Yet, as this review indicates, to date only scattered attempts have been made to undertake systematic empirical research on the effects and effectiveness of processing children through the courts. Without the information necessary to enlighten the choices made, policymakers are still in the Dark Ages of decisionmaking. Surely the "best interests" of children requires that the most informed decisions possible be made.

---

1 Statistics Canada: *Vital Statistics: Volume II — Marriages and Divorces* (Ottawa, 1974); see update of 17 November 1976, at 4.

2 (Ontario) Ministry of Community and Social Services, Children's Services Division: *Statistical Data Sheet* (Toronto, 1976).

3 These figures are estimates based on the statistics for December 1976, found in Statistics Canada: *Law Enforcement, Judicial and Correctional Statistics: Volume 5(2) — Judicial Division* (Ottawa, 7 May 1977); the last full report published by Statistics Canada was *Juvenile Delinquents* (Ottawa, 1973).

4 In the United States, the National Assessment of Juvenile Corrections at the University of Michigan has commenced data collection on the effectiveness of the Juvenile Courts in respect of the policies, standards and goals for which there is some societal consensus. See Rosemary Sarri and Yeheskel Hasenfeld, eds: *Brought to Justice? — Juveniles, the Courts and the Law* (Ann Arbor, Michigan, 1976).

5 Lawrence M. Friedman: *The Legal System — A Social Science Perspective* (New York, 1975) at 160.

6 *The King v. H.,* [1931] 2 W.W.R. 917 (Sask. Q.B.).

7 Robert H. Mnookin: "Foster-Care — In Whose Best Interests?" (1973), 43 Harv. Ed. Rev. 599; reprinted by Harvard Educational Review: *The Rights of Children — Reprint No. 9* (Cambridge, Mass., 1974) at 161.

8 *Idem,* at 177. See also Hillary Rodham: "Children under the Law" (1973), 43 Harv. Ed. Rev. 487 at 513.

9 Graham Parker: "Some Historical Observations on the Juvenile Court" (1966), 9 Crim. L.Q. 467 at 476.

10 Paul Lerman, ed.: *Delinquency and Social Policy* (New York), 1970) at 4.

11 Paul W. Tappan: *Juvenile Delinquency* (New York, 1949) at 32.

12 *The Queen v. X* (1958), 25 W.W.R. 97, 121 C.C.C. at 120, 28 C.R. 100 (Man. C.A.); reversed on other grounds, [1959] S.C.R. 638, 22 D.L.R. (2d) 129, 124 C.C.C. 71, 30 C.R. 230. See also the (Ontario) *Royal Commission Inquiry into Civil Rights* (Toronto, 1968) Report 1, Volume 2, at 554-555.

13 Paul Nejelski and Judith LaPook: "Monitoring the Juvenile Justice System — How Can You Tell Where You're Going, If You Don't Know Where You Are?" (1974), 12 Am. Crim L. Rev. 9 at 24. See also Graham Parker: "The Century of the Child" (1967), 45 Can. Bar Rev. 741 at 749.

14 Sanford Fox: "Juvenile Justice in America — Philosophical Reforms" (1975), 5 Human Rights 63 at 66.

15 *The Queen v. X, supra* fn. 12, at 119 (W.W.R.), 125 (C.C.C.), 121 (C.R.) *per* Coyne, J.A.

16 Diversion refers to the process by which certain types of delinquent behaviour are handled by means other than a Juvenile Court. It is characterised by the halting or deferring of the normal juvenile justice processing for children who are in immediate jeopardy of a court appearance.

17 Law Reform Commission of Canada: *Studies on Diversion* (Ottawa, 1975).

18 Charles W. Thomas and Christopher M. Sieverdes: "Juveniles Court Intake — An Analysis of Discretionary Decision-Making" (1975), 12 Criminology 413.

19 William Pink and Mervin White: "Delinquency Prevention — The State of the Art" in *The Juvenile Justice System,* Malcolm W. Klein, ed. (Beverley Hills, California, 1976) at 10.

20 Rosemary C. Sarri and Robert D. Vinter: "Justice for Whom? Varieties of Juvenile Correctional Approaches" in *The Juvenile Justice System, supra* fn. 19, at 164.

21 Larry C. Wilson: "Diversion — The Impact on Juvenile Justice" (1976), 18 Can. J. Criminol. & Correc. 161.

22 William Pink and Mervin White, *supra* fn. 19, at 10.

23 Note: "*Parens Patriae* and the Statutory Vagueness in the Juvenile Court" (1973), 82 Yale L.J. 745 at 747.

24 See section 38 of the *Juvenile Delinquents Act,* R.S.C. 1970, c. J-3.

25 Strictly speaking, the legislation allows very little discretion. Subsection 5(1) of the *Juvenile Delinquents Act* directs that the procedure of the Juvenile Courts must be that of a summary convictions Court. It is true that subsection 17(1) permits informality, but only so much as is "consistent with a due regard for a proper administration of justice." Subsection 3(2) and section 38 restrict the *parens patriae* philosophy only to the dispositional stage of a child's trial and never to the adjudicatory (or guilt-finding) stage. A child is entitled to all the defences open to an adult at a criminal trial, no matter how technical or marginal; see *The Queen v. Moore* (1975), 22 C.C.C. (2d) 189 (B.C. S.C.). In practice, however, Canadian Juvenile Courts frequently disregard due process rules.

26 *Royal Commission Inquiry into Civil Rights, supra* fn. 12, at 554.

27 *Idem,* at 555.

28 *Supra* fn. 7, at 626-627 (188-189 of the *Reprint*).

29 Hillary Rodham, *supra* fn. 8, at 514.

30 Alberta: ss. 30 and 35 of *The Child Welfare Act,* R.S.A. 1970, c. 45, as amended by 1973, c. 15; Manitoba: ss. 11, 13, 14 and 15 of *The Child Welfare Act,* 1974, c. 30; Nova Scotia: ss. 8, 9, 10 and 11 of the *Children's Services Act,* 1976, c. 8; Ontario: s. 23a of *The Child Welfare Act,* R.S.O. 1970, c. 64, as added by 1975, c. 1; Saskatchewan: ss. 7 through to 11 of *The Family Services Act,* 1973, c. 38. See also Newfoundland's Part III of *The Child Welfare Act,* 1972, No. 37.

31 Manitoba: s. 12 of *The Child Welfare Act,* 1974, c. 30; Ontario: s. 22a of *The Child Welfare Act,* R.S.O. 1970, c. 64, as added by 1975, c. 1.

32 Bernard M. Dickens: *Legal Issues in Child Abuse* (University of Toronto, 1976) at 11.

33 Michael Wald: "State Intervention on Behalf of "Neglected" Children — A Search for Realistic Standards" (1975), 27 Stanford L. Rev. 985 at 1000.

34 Michael H. Phillips, Ann W. Shyne, Edmund A. Sherman and Barbara L. Haring: *Factors Associated with Placement Decisions in Child Welfare* (Research Center, Child Welfare League of America, 1971) at 69-84.

35 *Supra* fn. 7, at 628.

36 Section 29 of *The Family Services Act,* Stat. Sask. 1973, c. 38. See fn. 50 of Bernard M. Dickens: "Legal Responses to Child Abuse" (1978), 1 Can. J. Fam. L. 85 at 110, for a discussion of the practice in other parts of the Dominion.

37 Robert H. Mnookin, *supra* fn. 7, at 612.

38 *Idem,* at 619.

39 Michael Wald, *supra* fn. 33, at 996.

40 *Idem,* at 998.

41 Bernard M. Dickens, *supra* fn. 32 at 24-25.

42 Robert H. Mnookin: "American Custody Law — A Framework for Analysis" in *Proceedings of the University of Wisconsin Conference on Child Advocacy* (Madison, Wisconsin, 1976) at 142.

43 John Eekelaar: "An Enquiry into Custody Disposition in Divorce Cases" in *The Child and the Courts,* Ian F.G. Baxter and Mary A. Eberts, eds (Toronto & London, 1978) at 1.

44 See Rules 30, 31 and 32 of *The Rules of the Provincial Courts (Family Division),* O. Reg. 210/78 and Rules 33, 34, and 36 of *The Rules of the Unified Family Court,* O. Reg. 450/77.

45 Abraham H. Lieff: "Pre-trial of Family Law in the Supreme Court of Ontario — Simplify and Expedite" (1976), 10 Law Society of Upper Canada Gazette 300.

46 Alberta: subs. 46(2) of *The Domestic Relations Act,* R.S.A. 1970, c. 113; subs. 10(1) of *The Family Court Act,* R.S.A. 1970, c. 133; British Columbia: s. 13 of the *Equal Guardianship of Infants Act,* R.S.B.C. 1960, c. 130, as amended by 1970, c. 2; para. 25(1)(*d*) of the *Family Relations Act,* 1972, c. 20, as amended by 1974, c. 99; Manitoba: no formal mention of the child's "best interests"; New Brunswick: subs. 6(1.1) of the *Deserted Wives and Children Act,* R.S.N.B. 1973, c. D-8, as added by 1977, c. 17; Newfoundland: no formal mention of the child's "best interests"; Northwest Teritories: subs. 34(2) of the *Domestic Relations Ordinance,* R.O.N.W.T. 1974, c. D-9; Nova Scotia: s. 2 of the *Infants' Custody Act,* R.S.N.S. 1967, c. 145; subs. 10A(2) of the *Wives' and Children's Maintenance Act,* R.S.N.S. 1967, c. 341, as added by 1970-71, c. 65; Ontario: subs. 1(1) of *The Infants Act,* R.S.O. 1970, c. 222; subs. 35(1) of *The Family Law Reform Act,* 1978, c. 2; Prince Edward Island: subs. 79(1) of the *Children's Act,* R.S.P.E.I. 1974, c. C-6; Quebec: article 245d of the *Civil Code,* as added by 1977, c. 72; Saskatchewan: subs. 2(1) of *The Infants Act,* R.S.S. 1965, c. 342; Yukon Territory: no formal mention of the child's "best interests".

47 A.H. Manchester: "Custody, the Child and the Legal Process" (1976), 6 Fam. Law 67.

48 Robert H. Mnookin: "Child-Custody Adjudication — Judicial Functions in the Face of Indeterminancy" (1975), 39(2) Law & Contemporary Problems 226.

49 *Idem,* at 253.

50 *Idem,* at 231.

51 *Idem,* at 260.

52 Sheila Rush Okpaku: "Psychology — Impediment or Aid in Child Custody Cases" (1976), 29 Rutgers L. Rev. 1117 at 1153.

53 Robert H. Mnookin, *supra* fn. 42, at 146.

54 Adrian Bradbook: "An Empirical Study of the Attitudes of the Judges of the Supreme

Court of Ontario Regarding the Workings of the Present Child Custody Adjudication Laws" (1971), 49 Can. Bar Rev. 557.

55 A.H. Manchester, *supra* fn. 47, at 67; see also Robert H. Mnookin, *supra* fn. 42, at 146.

56 Karen M. Weiler: "Re Moores and Feldstein — A Case Comment and Discussion of Custody Principles" (1974), 12 Osgoode Hall L.J. 207 at 219; Justice (British Section of the International Commission of Jurists): *A Report by JUSTICE — Parental Rights & Duties and Custody Suits* (London, 1975) at 35.

57 Sheila R. Okpaku, *supra* fn. 52, at 1141.

58 *Idem,* at 1139.

59 *Idem,* at 1141.

60 The child is, after all, the "accused" and must participate in order fully to defend himself. See (Ontario) Ministry of the Attorney General: *Report of the Committee on the Representation of Children in the Provincial Court (Family Division)*(Toronto, 1977) at 21.

61 Manitoba: subs. 25(7) of *The Child Welfare Act,* 1974, c. 30; Quebec: ss. 78 and 80 of the *Youth Protection Act,* 1977, c. 20. The Ontario Legislature has recently introduced Bill 114 (*The Child Welfare Act, 1978*), 2nd Sess., 31st Legislature, s. 31 of which would enable a child ten years of age or over to be present in court at the judge's discretion. Section 20 would grant to the judge the power to appoint a lawyer for the child if he or she is not already represented by counsel. Bill 114 was given second reading on 19 June 1978, when it was ordered to be studied by the Committee on Social Development before the Legislature resumes its sitting in the autumn.

62 *Re Helmes* (1976), 13 O.R. (2d) 4, 28 R.F.L. 380 (Ont. H.C.).

63 Subsection 25(3) of *The Child Welfare Act,* R.S.O. 1970, c. 64, as amended by 1972, c. 1.

64 Section 14 of *The Child Welfare Act,* Stat. Nfld. 1972, No. 37.

65 Section 42 of *The Domestic Relations Act,* R.S.A. 1970, c. 113 and para. 10(2)(*b*) of *The Family Court Act,* R.S.A. 1970, c. 133.
On 29 June 1978, Royal Assent was given in the British Columbia Legislature to the *Family Relations Act,* 1978, c. 20 (not yet proclaimed in force), in which s. 2 allows a "Family Advocate" to intervene at any stage of a custody proceeding "to act as counsel for the interests and welfare of the child".

66 See, for example, *Re Reid and Reid* (1975), 11 O.R. (2d) 622, 67 D.L.R. (3d) 46, 25 R.F.L. 209 (Div. Ct.).

67 Section 12 of the *Criminal Code,* R.S.C. 1970, c. C-34.

68 Olive M. Stone: "The Welfare of the Child" in *The Child and the Courts, supra* fn. 43, 229 at 242.

69 Michael Langley, Brenda Thomas and Ronald Parkison: "Youth's Expectations and Their Initial Juvenile Court Appearance" (1978), 20 Can. J. Criminol. 43 at 49.

70 Paul D. Lipsitt: "The Juvenile Offender's Percpetions" (1968), 14 Crime and Delinquency 49; Katherine Catton and Patricia Erickson: *The Juvenile's Perception of the Role of Defence Counsel in Juvenile Court — A Pilot Study* (Toronto, 1975).

71 Katherine Catton and Patricia Erickson, *supra* fn. 70, at 6.

72 National Assessment of Educational Progress: *Political Knowledge and Attitudes, 1971-2* (Washington, 1973); *Changes in Political Knowledge and Attitudes, 1969-1976* (Denver, 1977); and *Education for Citizenship — A Bicentennial Survey* (Denver, 1977).

73 Brendan Maher and Ellen Stein: "The Delinquent's Perception of the Law and the Community" in *Controlling Delinquents,* Stanton Wheeler, ed. (New York, 1968) at 187.

74 David Matza: *Delinquency and Drift* (New York, 1964).

75 Katherine Catton and Patricia Erickson, *supra* fn. 70.

76 Andrew Jay Kleinfeld: "The Balance of Power Among Infants, Their Parents and the State" (1970), 4 Fam. L.Q. 320 at 323.

77 *Supra* fn. 60.

78 In general, see Richard Gosse and Julien D. Payne: "Children of Divorcing Spouses —
Proposals for Reform" in *Studies on Divorce* by the Law Reform Commission of
Canada (Ottawa, 1975), at 186 *sqq.*

79 This would mean all of the Dominion except Manitoba and Quebec; see *supra* fn. 61.

80 *Re Helmes, supra* fn. 62. But see the possible solution provided by *Re Dadswell* (1976), 26
R.F.L. 214 (Ont. Prov. Ct. Fam. Div.).

81 Hillary Rodham, *supra* fn. 8, at 509.

82 Literally, "friend of the Court".

83 Inez Dootjes, Patricia Erickson and Richard G. Fox: "Defence Counsel in Juvenile
Court — A Variety of Roles" (1972), 14 Can. J. Criminol. & Correc. 132.

84 Patricia Erickson: "The Defence Lawyer's Role in Juvenile Court — An Investigation
into Judges' and Social Workers' Points of View" (1974), 24 U. Tor. L.J. 126; and
"Legalistic and Traditional Role Expectations for Defence Counsel in Juvenile Court"
(1975), 17 Can. J. Criminol. & Correc. 78.

85 W. Vaughn Stapleton and Lee E. Teitelbaum: *In Defence of Youth — A Study of
Counsel in American Juvenile Courts* (New York, 1972).

86 *Idem,* at 67-68 and 78-79. See also Katherine Catton: "Models of Procedure in Juvenile
Court" (1976), 18 Crim. L.Q. 181.

87 Robert H. Mnookin, *supra* fn. 7, at 627.

88 British Columbia: s. 8 of the *Unified Family Court Act,* 1974, c. 99, as amended by 1975,
c. 4; and the *Official Guardian Act,* R.S.B.C. 1960, c. 268; Manitoba: subs. 27(2) of *The
Queen's Bench Act,* R.S.M. 1970, c. C280, as amended by 1976, c. 13; Nova Scotia: s. 9 of
the *Infants' Custody Act,* R.S.N.S. 1967, c. 145, as amended by 1973, c. 39; Ontario:
s. 107 of *The Judicature Act,* R.S.O. 1970, c. 228; Prince Edward Island: sub-Rules
57.19(2) and 57.19(3) of the *Civil Procedure Rules,* 1977; Saskatchewan: s. 31 of *The
Infants Act,* R.S.S. 1965, c. 342.

89 Toronto *Globe and Mail,* 4 July 1977; see also the *Annual Report* of the Ontario Ministry
of the Attorney General for the fiscal year 1975-76 (Toronto, 1976).

90 Alberta: no legal aid statute or regulation in existence, but see Legal Aid Society of
Alberta: *Handbook and Tariff* (1976), para. C. 11, for the duty counsel system in effect in
the Juvenile and Family Courts 'in Calgary and Edmonton; British Columbia: *Legal
Services Commission Act,* 1975, c. 36; duty counsel service is provided by full-time staff
lawyers of legal aid offices; see Legal Aid Society of British Columbia: *Annual Report,
1977* (Vancouver), at 18; Manitoba: s. 20 of *The Legal Aid Services Society of Manitoba
Act,* 1971, c. 59 and s. 61 of Man. Reg. 106/72, as amended; New Brunswick: *Legal Aid
Act,* R.S.N.B. 1973, c. L-2; s. 59 of N.B. Reg. 71-114, as amended; Newfoundland: *The
Legal Aid Act,* 1975, No. 42; s. 123 of *The Legal Aid Regulations, 1976* in (1976), 51 Nfld.
Gaz. (Pt II) 15; Northwest Territories: no legal aid ordinance or regulation in existence,
but see paras. 5(*a*) and 51(*a*) of the *Legal Profession Ordinance,* 1976 (2d Sess.), c. 4; there
is no indication of a duty counsel system; Nova Scotia: no indication of a duty counsel
system in the *Legal Aid Act* 1977, c. 11 and N.S. Reg. 77/77; Ontario: *The Legal Aid Act,*
R.S.O. 1970, c. 239, as amended; s. 69 of R.R.O. 1970, Reg. 557, as amended; Prince
Edward Island: no legal aid statute or regulation in existence; there is a public defender
system, but only in criminal cases (presumedly covering delinquency); Quebec: no
indication of a duty counsel system in the *Legal Aid Act,* 1972, c. 14, as amended, and in
Que. Reg. 73-289, as amended; Saskatchewan: no indication of a duty counsel system in
The Community Legal Services (Saskatchewan) Act, 1973-74, c. 11, and in Sask. Reg.
236/74; Yukon Territory: *Legal Aid Ordinance,* 1975 (3d Sess.), c. 2; para. 5(*e*) of the
Legal Aid Regulations, C.O. 1976/286, as amended.

91 Katherine Catton and Patricia Erickson, *supra* fn. 70, at 20.

92 *Supra* fn. 60.

93 The Child in the City Programme, University of Toronto, is cooperating with the

(Ontario) Attorney General's Committee on the Representation of Children in designing the research component of these pilot projects.

94 In custody proceedings before a superior Court of record, it is possible that the inherent *parens patriae* powers might extend to the ordering of such reports, but the matter has never been in issue in any reported case. Justices of the Court appear to presume that they have this power. In the absence of special legislation, the position of inferior Courts is in some doubt, since these tribunals have no inherent *parens patriae* powers.

95 Nathaniel Gozansky: "Court-Ordered Investigations in Child-Custody Cases" (1976), 12 Williamette L.J. 511 at 552.

96 Sheila R. Okpaku, *supra* fn. 52, at 1132.

97 Bruce J. Ennis and Thomas R. Litwack: "Psychiatry and the Presumption of Expertise — Flipping Coins in the Courtroom" (1974), 62 Cal. L. Rev. 693.

98 (Ontario) Ministry of the Attorney General; *Annual Report, 1976-77* (Toronto, 1977) at 31.

99 *Ibid.*

100 Johnathan Kraus: "Decision Process in the Children's Court and the Social Background Report" (1975), 12(1) Journal of Research in Crime and Delinquency 17.

101 Sanford J. Fox: "Juvenile Justice Reform — Innovations in Scotland" (1974), 12 Am. Crim. L. Rev. 61.

102 Lucy Smith and Peter Lodrup: "The Child in the Divorce Situation" — Factors Determining the Custody Question and the Use of Experts in Custody Cases in Norway" in *The Child and the Courts, supra* fn. 43, at 25.

103 Adrien J. Bradbrook, *supra* fn. 54, at 561.

104 John C. Spencer: "Children's Hearings in Scotland" in *The Child and the Courts, supra* fn. 43, at 257.

105 Frederick W. Howlett: "Is the Youth Service Bureau All It's Cracked Up to Be?" (1973), 19 Crime & Delinquency 485.

106 Victor L. Streib: "The Informal Juvenile Justice System — A Need for Procedural Fairness and Reduced Discretion" (1976), 10 John Marshall Journal of Practice & Procedure 41 at 52.

107 J.A. Seymour: "Youth Service Bureaus" (1972), 7 Law & Society Rev. 247 at 251.

107a *Supra,* at 333-334.

108 Many arbitrators and mediators in family law problems possess training in marital and family counselling.

109 William P. Statsky: "The Training of Community Judges — Rehabilitative Adjudication" (1972), Columbia Human Rights L. Rev. 401; and "Community Courts — Decentralizing Juvenile Justice" (1974), 3 Cap. U.L. Rev. 1.

110 David A. Cruickshank: "Court Avoidance in Child Neglect Cases" in *The Child and the Courts, supra* fn. 43, at 203.

111 Richard Theuman: *An Assessment of Four Family Court Conciliation Projects Funded by the Department of National Health and Welfare,* unpublished paper in partial fulfillment of a Master's Degree in Social Work, Wilfred Lauier University, Waterloo, Ontario, 1977.

112 Howard H. Irving and John Gandy: "Family Court Conciliation Project — An Experiment in Support Services" (1977), 25 R.F.L. 47 at 52.

113 Meyer Elkin: "Conciliation Courts — The Re-integration of Disintegrating Families" (1973), 22 Fam. Coord. 63.

114 Richard Theuman, *supra* fn. 111.

115 Sections 33 *sqq.* of the *Social Work (Scotland Act,* 1968, c. 49 (U.K.); these provisions came into force on 15 April 1971. See S.I. 1971, No. 184 and S.I. 1969, No. 1274.

116 Allison Morris: "Scottish Juvenile System — A Critique" in *Crime, Criminology and Public Policy — Essays in Honour of Sir Leon Radzinowicz,* Roger G. Hood, ed. (New York, 1975) at 368.

117 Sanford J. Fox, *supra* fn. 101.
118 *Supra* fn. 116.
119 *Idem*, at 368.
120 *Idem*, at 371.
121 Nigel Bruce: "Children's Hearings — A Retrospect" (1975), 15 Brit. J. Criminol. 333 at 343.
122 John Spencer, *supra* fn. 104.
123 Tove Stang Dahl: "The Scandinavian System of Juvenile Justice — A Comparative Approach" in *Pursuing Justice for the Child*, Margaret K. Rosenheim, ed. (Chicago & London, 1976) at 327.
124 Sections 8A through to 81 of the *Protection of Children Act*, R.S.B.C. 1960, c. 303, as added by 1974, c. 69.
125 Ontario Law Reform Commission: *Report on Family Law: Part V — Family Courts* (Toronto, 1974) at 3-4.
126 *Idem*, at 3.
127 *Idem*, at 6.
128 See the *Unified Family Court Act*, S.B.C. 1974, c. 99. The British Columbia pilot project was quite different from the models implemented in other parts of Canada; *infra* fn. 129. The scheme consisted of placing a Provincial Court with its summary family law jurisdiction in the same building as a County Court presided over by a County Court Judge who was also a Local Justice of the Supreme Court and who could therefore deal in most of the matrimonial causes within the jurisdiction of the Supreme Court. There was no attempt to consolidate all family law powers within one tribunal. Since the scheme consisted only of a residential readjustment of two different Courts into one building, it has been criticised as not being a true Unified Family Court.
129 At present, three provinces have "true" functional Unified Family Courts;
Manitoba: *The Queen's Bench Act*, R.S.M. 1970, c. C280, as amended by 1976, c. 73; Ontario: *The Unified Family Court Act*, 1976, c. 85, as amended by 1977, c. 4; Prince Edward Island: subs. 16.1(3) of the *Judicature Act*, R.S.P.E.I. 1974, c. J-3, as added by 1975, c. 27.
The Manitoba scheme is a pilot project in St. Bonafice, forming the "St. Bonafice Family Law Division of the Manitoba Court of Queen's Bench". It has been given the jurisdiction to deal with virtually all family law matters handled by the Provincial Judges' Court (Family Division) in St. Bonafice with one appalling exception — that of juvenile delinquency. The Justices of the Queen's Bench felt themselves "unqualified" to preside over a Juvenile Court — an admission which can be construed in many ways, some rather unfavourable to the Justices.
Ontario's Court is also but a pilot project in the city of Hamilton, to expire in mid 1980. In the hierarchy of Courts, the Unified Family Court stands at the County Court level, but its Judges have been invested with the powers of a local Judge of the High Court and of a Provincial Judge presiding in a Provincial Court (Family Division).
The Prince Edward Island scheme is not a project at all but a fully operational, province-wide Family Division of the Supreme Court, which has been granted jurisdiction over the family law statutes formerly dealt with by the now-abolished Provincial and County Courts.
Two other provinces have already passed legislation to establish Unified Family Court projects, but as yet neither statute has been proclaimed in force. See:
Newfoundland: *The Unified Family Court Act*, 1977, No. 80;
Saskatchewan: *The Unified Family Court Act*, 1977-78, c. 41.
The Newfoundland tribunal, to be established at the Supreme Court level, has jurisdiction over all family law matters in the St. John's area. The Saskatchewan project appears to be set at the District Court level (somewhat similar to the Ontario Court) and

will likely begin operating in Saskatoon.

The province of New Brunswick is in the process of passing legislation for the creation of a Family Division of the Court of Queen's Bench. See Bill 94 (*An Act to Amend the Judicature Act, 1978*), 4th Sess., 48th N.B. Legislature.

130 Richard Theuman, *supra* fn. 111.

131 Herbert A. Allard: "Family Courts in Canada" in *Studies in Canadian Family Law,* Derek Mendes da Costa, ed. (Toronto, 1972) at 3.

132 Elizabeth Dyson and Richard Dyson: "Family Courts in the U.S." (1969), 9 J. Fam. L. 1 at 88-90.

133 P.D. Scott: "Children's hearings — A Commentary" (1975), 15 Brit. J. Criminol. 344 at 346.